Marxist Modern

Marxist Modern

An Ethnographic History
of the Ethiopian Revolution

Donald L. Donham

UNIVERSITY OF CALIFORNIA PRESS
Berkeley · *Los Angeles*
JAMES CURREY
Oxford

University of California Press
Berkeley and Los Angeles, California

James Currey, Ltd.
Oxford

© 1999 by
The Regents of the University of California

Library of Congress Cataloging-in-Publication Data

Donham, Donald L. (Donald Lewis)
    Marxist modern : an ethnographic history of
the Ethiopian Revolution / Donald L. Donham.
        p.   cm.
    Includes bibliographical references and index.
    ISBN 0-520-21328-9 (alk. paper). — ISBN
0-520-21329-7 (alk. paper)
        1. Gamo Gofa Kifle Håger (Ethiopia)—
Politics and government.   2. Communism—
Ethiopia—Gamo Gofa Kifle Håger—History—
20th century.   3. Christianity and politics—
Ethiopia—Gamo Gofa Kifle Håger—
Evangelicalism—History—20th century.
4. Gamo Gofa Kifle Håger (Ethiopia)—
Religion.   5. Maale (African people)—
Politics and government.   6. Maale (African
people)—Cultural assimilation.   7. Maale
(African people)—Religion.   8. Ethiopia—
Politics and government—1974–1991.
9. Communism—Ethiopia—History—20th
century.   I. Title.
DT390.G35D66   1999
963'.05—dc21   98-43144
                                            CIP

British Library Cataloguing in Publication Data

A catalogue record for this book is available from
the British Library.

ISBN 0-85255-269-6 (cloth)
ISBN 0-85255-264-5 (paper)

Printed in the United States of America

9   8   7   6   5   4   3   2   1

To the future and to my son, Ben

Contents

Illustrations

FIGURES

MAPS

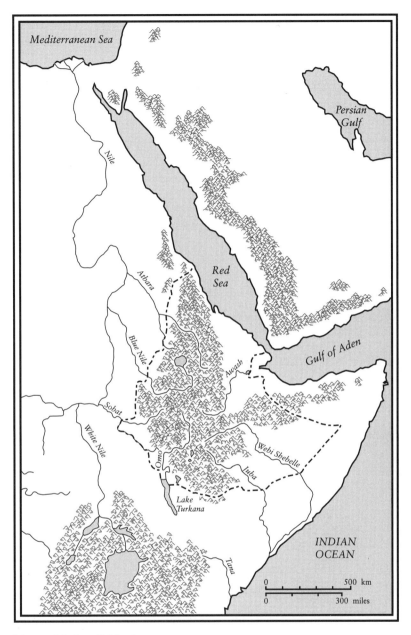

Map 1. Modern Ethiopia, c. 1974–1991

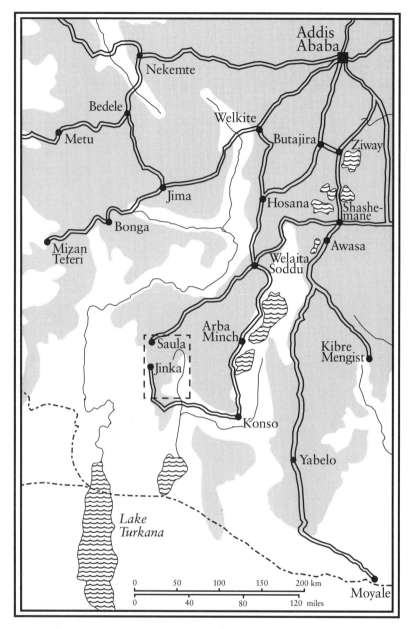

Map 2. Southern Ethiopia in the 1980s (showing the location of map 3)

Map 3. Maale

Orientations

*On Jazz, Modernity,
and Ethnographic History*

There is a mode of vital experience—experience of space and time, of the self and others, of life's possibilities and periods—that is shared by men and women all over the world today. I will call this body of experience "modernity." To be modern is to find ourselves in an environment that promises us adventure, power, joy, growth, transformation of ourselves and the world—and, at the same time, that threatens to destroy everything we have, everything we know, everything we are. Modern environments and experiences cut across all boundaries of geography and ethnicity, of class and nationality, of religion and ideology: in this sense, modernity can be said to unite all mankind. But it is a paradoxical unity, a unity of disunity: it pours us all into a maelstrom of perpetual disintegration and renewal, of struggle and contradiction, of ambiguity and anguish. To be modern is to be part of a universe in which, as Marx said, "all that is solid melts into air."

Marshall Berman,
All That Is Solid Melts into Air

However various the results of postmodernism have been, the post- has been revelatory in at least one aspect: It has made it far easier for us moderns to see the cultural peculiarity of a complex of interrelated ideas and feelings, namely, the tendency of social groups the world over—often influenced by stories about one another—to construct vernacular modernisms, local narratives of history that "separate the past from the present and reorient expectations toward the future."[1] Have anthropologists or historians yet appreciated the consequences that flow from the apparently simple fact that some actors view their societies as "behind" and therefore in need of a way to "catch up"?[2]

People's sense of living vis-à-vis, conscious of great gulfs of power and wealth, aware of making local history on a world stage, propelled by feelings of great possibility and great danger—these aspects of the experience of modernity—imply the necessity of new strategies for ethnography. For the local, long anthropology's focus, refuses to remain local.[3] Instead, events are surrounded by gatherings of ghosts, not only from the local past but from other pasts as well. Local narratives thus echo with local appropriations of world narratives, and it is precisely these echoes that ground the chord of local meanings.

And meanwhile, what of the slaves? They had heard of the revolution and had construed it in their own image: the white slaves in France had risen, and killed their masters, and were now enjoying the fruits of the earth. It was gravely inaccurate in fact, but they had caught the spirit of the thing. Liberty, Equality, Fraternity. Before the end of 1789 there were risings in Guadeloupe and Martinique. As early as October, in Fort Dauphin, one of the future centres of the San Domingo insurrection, the slaves were stirring and holding mass meetings in the forests at night.[4]

In the face of the challenge presented by the global-in-the-local, I seek to develop in this book a new way of doing ethnographic history.[5] To begin, my goal is prosaic enough: to stay close to people's lives, concentrating on small facts piled on top of small facts. It is impossible, however, to remain within the confines of any one "cultural system." Michael Walzer argued that revolutions are typically made by the interaction of two broad social groups—a vanguard and a class: "analysis cannot begin, then, with either vanguards or classes considered alone, for what is crucial is the relation between a particular vanguard and a particular class at a particular moment in time."[6]

I have found this methodological advice useful for understanding the Ethiopian revolution. An educated vanguard in Addis Ababa eventually instigated a revolution by fomenting revolt among Ethiopian peasants—particularly those in the south. In the following chapters, I oscillate between Addis Ababa and Maale, an area of the south in which I was doing fieldwork in 1974–75 as the revolution commenced.

For each of these groups—and for the principal divisions within them—I seek to convey Ethiopians' own narratives of history and how they understood the revolution as it developed about them. The stories that people told themselves hardly remained constant, of course, and accounts by various social groups, both within and across vanguards and peasants, interacted, clashed, and sometimes metamorphosed. For vanguards in particular, it is important to understand the ways in which Ethiopian actors continually called upon narratives of other revolutions to make their own meaningful; thus it sometimes seems that the an-

cestral spirits of other great upheavals—from Marx to Lenin to Mao—
presided over Ethiopian events like Greek gods.

What I have found critical to accomplish, then, is precisely an understanding of the layering of meaning that motivates social action. In the
case at hand, each of these layers was situated in chains of reference that
depended upon events far beyond Ethiopia: for the student vanguard,
narratives of the Chinese and Russian revolutions, both of which had
been carried out under the banner of Marxism—Marx himself having
been profoundly affected by the French revolution; for the peasant vanguard in places like Maale, stories of a previous conversion to evangelical Christianity, missionaries from Canada, the United States, and New
Zealand, anti-modernists in the religious sense, who by the 1970s had
inspired the formation of small communities of believers in the south—
hyper-modernists in the social sense.

I have used the metaphor of a chord; if this be apt, I should perhaps
ask the reader to think of a musical phrase by, say, jazz pianist Art
Tatum: "Impossible runs . . . cushioned by shifting, pastel chords that
split the thinnest of harmonic hairs into filaments leading into corners
no one knew existed before."[7]

*Some of the habits of the mzungu [Europeans] were little understood in Liganua,
and were not copied or borrowed, but were admired all the same, like his lying
in state fully dressed before burial. In terms of superlative reference, the mzungu
became the man of culture par excellence, the one to whom all deferred, the subject of so much conversation at the places of employment and back in Liganua.
You dressed well like a mzungu, or you spoke English well like a mzungu, or
even if you spoke Dholuo particularly distinctively, you were said to speak like a
mzungu. . . . Another element that came into Liganua in the same period was the
idea of playing tennis. The servants of the mzungu saw him dress in white, wear
a scarf and "turkeys" (tennis shoes), take his racquet and tennis balls, and go to
the tennis court. By the time the idea of tennis reached Liganua, the sequence had
been revised a bit. Wilson Oluoch Oton, who was employed on a European farm
as a cook, bought tennis clothes and a tennis racquet, came home on holidays
and would take an afternoon walk through Liganua in this uniform, not playing
the game, just exercising his hands and arms swinging the racquet. The idea
caught on, and others in Liganua did the same. Similarly, in the 1940s, men like
Okech Oraro Kobambo would dress in full coat and tails, and then go to Siaya
Market and play golf in the mid-day sun on market day.[8]*

In 1990, I published a book, *History, Power, Ideology: Central Issues in
Marxism and Anthropology*, that laid out and argued for a Marxist approach to anthropology. As I worked on issues of Marxist theory within

anthropology, Ethiopia, the place I had done fieldwork, adopted its own Marxism. But it quickly became apparent to me that Marxism meant something quite different to its Ethiopian adherents than to me. This disparity was the initial irritation that led me to write this book: How does one understand Ethiopian Marxism in its own context?

Since the present analysis may strike the reader as quite different from my earlier work, let me say at the outset that I believe that the "modernity" that I have alluded to above has essential material underpinnings. Without uneven development, without increasing capitalist competition and commodification across world markets, without the unidirectional and universally present pressures created by technological advance, and perhaps most of all, without capitalist media, it would be impossible to understand why intellectual vanguards the world over have posed the problem of "backwardness."

But the effects of the world capitalist system are hardly exhausted by its obvious material consequences. Ethiopia, after all, was about as remote from those consequences as it is possible to be in the late twentieth century. And in Maale, no Western colonial power had had much impact, no labor migration existed, no introduced cash crops. Maale was and continues to be a subsistence economy, probably as "pure" as any that has existed. And yet, interaction and cultural flows across the globe have had their effects in areas far beyond those most obviously affected by capitalist economic transformation. In a phrase, what has been altered are peoples' imaginations—their sense of their place in the world and the shape of their pasts and their futures.

Vernacular modernisms—attempts to reorder local society by the application of strategies that have produced wealth, power, or knowledge elsewhere in the world—develop in this conceptual space.[9] And resistances, rejections, and reactions develop alongside them. Such currents rarely run in stable or cleanly distinguished lines, however, so that modernist movements often incorporate rejections and refusals at other levels. If the shape of these constantly negotiated local struggles are hardly given by the structure of world capitalism, what is needed to follow them is, then, an ethnography of local historical imaginations.[10]

If Ethiopians' own narratives of history are one foci of this book, I have my own narrative in what follows, one like the stories told by Ethiopian revolutionaries that appropriates and reworks another, Alexis de Tocqueville's classic *L'Ancien régime et la révolution:*[11] Mine is an account of an unexpected slippage between discourse and a developing, long-term continuity. Most Ethiopian actors saw the revolution as a break, a new beginning, a revolt against everything that Haile Selassie stood for, but in an (important) sense the revolutionary outcome only furthered what the Emperor had in fact begun: a modernization of the state. By the 1980s, the revolutionary state extended its writ across local society, digging its heels into peasant communities in an altogether unprecedented way.

This is not the story that any revolutionary faction told itself about the revolution. (Indeed, as I shall describe, it is a result that the newly empowered elite did much to disguise or to deflect attention from or to try to legitimate.) But if not, a central conundrum of this book is posed: If an expanded and more centralized state was not the primary intention of revolutionary actors, how did such a result nevertheless occur?

Why, at the outset, did a small educated vanguard in Ethiopia become so enamored of the notion of revolution? And why, in a matter of only months, did virtually *all* Ethiopian political actors at the center take up Marxism? Once a section of the armed forces with the help of students had begun to export the revolution to the countryside, why, of all groups, did evangelical Christians become the principal local revolutionaries in the south? And, irony of ironies, after the great majority of peasants had been totally alienated from the new order, how was the revolutionary state nonetheless able to strengthen itself, to penetrate local society to new depths?

Across these events, at least three stances—modernist, anti-modernist, and traditionalist—appear to have constituted an unstable triangle.[12] Both Marxist modernism and evangelical anti-modernism looked to the future: to a communist utopia or to a Christian millennium, respectively. Traditionalism, on the other hand, looked backward: to the first king of Maale who had brought "fire." At any moment in time, each of these stances entailed a particular way of constituting the future, and each, in fact, depended upon the others, in the semantic sense that each used the others to differentiate itself, but also in the more historically active sense that each used the others to "produce" itself. In the dialectic that developed, it was not unusual for one side of this triangle to transmute itself into its supposed opposite.

We French cannot really think about politics or philosophy or literature without remembering all this—politics, philosophy, literature—began, in the modern world, under the sign of a crime. A crime was committed in France in 1793. They killed a good and entirely likable king who was the incarnation of legitimacy. We cannot not remember that this crime was horrible. This means that when we try to think about politics, we know that the question of legitimacy is

*always at issue. We can say the same for literature. The difficulty that Ameri-
cans, and also English and Germans have in understanding what we ourselves
call writing [écriture] is linked to the memory of this crime. When we speak
about writing, the accent is on that which is necessarily criminal in writing.*[13]

Ethnography, in its classic sense, rests upon "being there." I arrived in
Maaleland five months before Haile Selassie was deposed, and I stayed
for a little over a year more, a total of twenty months, witnessing the in-
augural events of the revolution in Maale. A little less than ten years
later, I was able to return in 1983–84 for another eighteen months of
work, after the revolutionary state had consolidated itself. These periods of research, plus a number of later and shorter trips, the last during
the summer of 1997, total about three years spaced over twenty-five.

How Maale understood the revolution also structured the way they
saw me. I began fieldwork in the only way possible: I was given a letter
from the university, then Haile Sellassie I University, to the provincial
governor in Arba Minch. From his office, I took a letter to the governor
of Hamer Bako *awraja* in Jinka. And from there, I received a letter to
the *woreda* governor and from him, finally, a letter to the Maale *balabbat* and king-to-be, Dulbo (these titles will be defined below). In the beginning, I pitched my tent (literally) in Dulbo's compound in Bala, later
to build a house in a vicinity near the sacred grove of Dufa that contained the bones of Dulbo's father. I was, thus, identified by most Maale
with "tradition"—both because of the way I entered the field and because of my evident interest in Maale culture. On the other hand, like
Christian missionaries, I was incredibly wealthy by local standards,
even though I lived in a Maale house just like everyone else's. Only one
of the icons of my wealth were plastic water buckets. One old Maale
man opined that white people did everything with plastic: They even
have sex with it (he had heard about condoms but had never seen one
and assumed that they must make sex better). My wealth made me fas-
cinating to local modernists, and I had little difficulty in collecting their
stories—even though I was intimately associated with their enemies. I
was, then, a liminal figure in more than one sense, a representative of
the modern who was interested in Maale tradition.

Initially, of course, I did not go to Ethiopia in order to study a revolution. Having set out to study the political economy of labor in Maale,
I was overtaken by events. What took place alternately seduced and re-
volted me. During the first years of the revolution, I, like many Ethiopians, was swept up by the allure and promise of the future. It seemed

Figure 1. The ethnographer's tent, Maale house, and plastic jerrycan, Irbo, 1975. Photograph taken by the author.

that everything was up for grabs. The country had been turned into a virtual seminar. I remember my surprise traveling from Maale to the capital, Addis Ababa, to discover that the local newspaper, freed from imperial censors, had begun to sell for *more* than its printed price.

But this mood of expansiveness did not last. By the time I was back in Maale during 1983–84, agents of the newly consolidated state had begun to peer into every corner of Ethiopian society in order, as they said, to identify anti-revolutionaries. Toward the end of my stay, I came close to being expelled as an American spy. Around July 1984, my Maale assistant was detained and for about a week placed under arrest.

I cannot detail the full series of events that led up to this arrest. The context included the developing drought in 1984, the impending formation of the Ethiopian Workers' Party, and plans for the tenth anniversary of the revolution. During the celebration, local Marxists intended to display their own master-narrative of the Ethiopian revolution, one that justified their new power to the world. Any organized dissent in the months leading up to and during the celebration was especially threatening, and the security forces went on the alert.

I came athwart this situation through a mixture of my own foolishness and perhaps my excessive knowledge of local conditions. Early in

1984, the drought was beginning to affect the Maale. Local peasant association leaders had repeatedly asked the government for relief. One day an official showed up in Bala and identified himself as a member of the Ethiopian Relief and Rehabilitation Commission. He called for a meeting with my neighbors. Those who attended would be signed up for relief, he said; those who did not would get nothing.

Very few people attended the first planned meeting. Before a second gathering was organized, this official visited me in my grass-thatched Maale house, and we talked about local affairs. Educated to some degree and English-speaking, he explained that he had been an assistant to a French anthropologist who had worked among a neighboring people to the Maale. Assuming that I could trust another anthropologist's assistant, I explained that there had been some tension locally between peasant association leaders and local supporters of the Maale kingship. Although the first identified the second as "anti-revolutionaries," I opined that the situation might be more complex. If one understood local culture and history, then support for the Maale kingship might not necessarily be antithetical to support for the revolution. After all, Maale kings had been as much religious as political leaders. And Orthodox Christians were still allowed to have their priests.

My attempt at cultural translation was ill advised. This "official" of the Relief and Rehabilitation Commission turned out to be a secret security agent. He called the second meeting, which was well attended. After haranguing the assembled with revolutionary rhetoric, and after asking me to photograph all those present so that there would be a record for the future, he proceeded, with machine gun in hand, to arrest a number of my friends and neighbors. These men—accused of working against the revolution—were asked to step forward one by one from the crowd, and they were taken off to Jinka to jail. In a matter of months they would be released, but this piece of revolutionary theater had its intended effect: The power of the revolutionary state was etched in everyone's mind, most particularly mine.

In each country, some equivalent of the KGB was instrumental in maintaining surveillance, with varying degrees of intensity and success. Particularly effective were the Secret Police in the Soviet Union, East Germany, and Romania, but networks of informers and collaborators operated to some extent in all. These formed a highly elaborate "production" system parallel to the system of producing goods—a system producing paper, which contained real and falsified histories of the people over whom the Party ruled. Let us call the immediate products "dossiers," or "files," though the ultimate product was political sub-

jects and subject dispositions useful to the regime. This parallel production sys-
tem was at least as important as the system for producing goods, for producers
of files were much better paid than producers of goods.[14]

Several months later I unwisely refused to give a "bribe" to a chairman of a peasant association adjacent to the one in which I was living. After the chairman had allied with the security agent in Jinka, already suspicious of me, one thing led to another. With the local governor away, my Maale assistant was jailed, and I was told not to leave Jinka. When the governor returned, he immediately freed my assistant and upon hearing my story gave me some useful (anthropological) advice: "Know the culture of the people you're living among." With the expansion of state power after the revolution, giving gifts to revolutionary officials had extended on a scale unknown under Haile Selassie. Such gifts were something more than an illicit economic transaction: They constituted obedience and obeisance to the revolution.

My own experience of the revolution was, then, fairly direct. Documents convey indispensable kinds of information about societies and cultures (and I shall be using documents particularly to reconstruct the history of an evangelical Christian mission in southern Ethiopia), but documents rarely rise up and hit one over the head. Fieldwork—or what is the same thing, a kind of disciplined attempt to learn from one's mistakes in interacting with people—does.

In the quote above, Jean-François Lyotard points out the necessarily "criminal" or transgressive in writing. I would suggest that fieldwork contains its own necessary transgressions, which can be richly productive. My own ethnographic sense of both revolutionary hope and betrayal lies beneath the writing that follows, and though my ordeals pale in comparison to those of millions of Ethiopians, I have written this book in part in order to come to terms with my own experiences.

By the 1920s their [American missionary] successors were scattered across
China and totaled some 5,000 persons if one includes the missionary wives,
who often served as teachers or nurses. Together with a similar number of
British and European missionaries, they had built up an impressive establish-
ment of Christian churches, schools, colleges, hospitals, and other institutions,
which were inherited in 1949 by the Chinese People's Republic. By that time it
had also become evident that few of the Chinese people were likely to become
Christians and that the missionaries' long-continued effort, if measured in num-
bers of converts, had failed. Curiously, however, the Chinese Communist revo-
lution of recent decades has stressed the spread of literacy to ordinary people,
the publication of journals and pamphlets in the vernacular, education and

equality for women, the abolition of arranged child-marriages, the supremacy of public duty over filial obedience and family obligations, increased agricultural productivity through the sinking of wells and improved tools, crops, and breeds, dike and road building for protection against flood and famine, public health clinics to treat common ailments and prevent disease, discussion groups to foster better conduct, student organizations to promote healthy recreation and moral guidance, and the acquisition and Sinification of Western knowledge for use in remaking Chinese life. Missionaries of the nineteenth century pioneered in all of these activities. Little wonder that the revolutionaries of China since 1949 have resented them in retrospect. The missionaries came as spiritual reformers, soon found that material improvements were equally necessary, and in the end helped to formed the great revolution. Yet as foreigners, they could take no part in it, much less bring it to a finish. Instead, it finished them. But in the Maoist message of today, "serve the people," one can hear an echo of the missionary's wish to serve his fellow man.[15]

Acknowledgments

For research support, I would like to thank the National Science Foundation for three grants: for 1987–90, Grant BNS 87–18823: "Religion and Revolution in Maale, Ethiopia"; for 1982–84, Grant BNS 81–21547: "A Comparison of Peasant Production Systems in Southwest Ethiopia"; and for 1974–76, Dissertation Grant GS-41672.

I began writing this book while I was a Fellow at the Center for Advanced Study in the Behavioral Sciences in 1989–90. I would like to thank other Fellows at the Center that year, especially Reggie Zelnik and Shelly Errington. Afterward, more people than I can remember made important contributions to my work. I would like to thank the anthropological audiences to which I presented parts of this work at a number of institutions: Boston University, The Graduate Center of City University of New York, Johns Hopkins University, Yale University, Duke University, and the University of California at Santa Cruz. The Agrarian Studies Program at Yale, under Jim Scott's direction, provided the setting for an especially stimulating discussion of religion and revolution.

I would like to thank the SIM, Society for International Ministries (formerly the Sudan Interior Mission), for access to their archives and library in Charlotte, North Carolina. In Charlotte, Gary Corwin, Jo-Ann Brandt, and Sarah Ely provided me with indispensable help. Former SIM missionary to Ethiopia Brian Fargher was especially helpful in telephone interviews. In Ethiopia, SIM missionaries Lila and Paul Balisky

generously read and commented on two chapters, as well as sharing unpublished work with me.

Terrence Lyons and Marina Ottaway read and commented on parts
of the book. Fredrik Barth, Michael M. J. Fischer, Alexander Naty,
Donald Levine, Dessalegn Rahmato, Bahru Zewde, Eric Wolf, and Ahkil
Gupta provided help and advice. And Don Crummey, Jim Ferguson,
Bruce Knauft, Don Moore, Charlie Piot, and Ben Orlove read the entire
typescript and gave me the considerable benefit of their criticism.
Joanna Davidson helped me with the proofs. I am more grateful than I
can say for all these forms of support.

Part of Chapter 3 covers materials I have previously published in
Work and Power in Maale, Ethiopia, 2nd ed. (New York: Columbia
University Press, 1994), pp. 40–52. Here I elaborate the analysis, using
the actual names of Maale kings (something I felt I could not do while
the revolutionary state survived in Ethiopia). Unlike in previous publications, I do not disguise place names in what follows, or identities, except for members of the party in Maale. Parts of the following analysis
have been previously published in three articles: "The Increasing Penetration of the Revolutionary State in Maale Life, 1977–1987," *in* Katsuyoshi Fukui, Eisei Kurimoto, and Masayoshi Shigeta, ed., *Ethiopia in
Broader Perspective,* Papers of the 13th International Conference of
Ethiopian Studies (Kyoto: Shokado Book Sellers, 1997); "A Note on
Space in the Ethiopian Revolution," *Africa* 63 (1993): 583–590; and
"Revolution and Modernity in Maale: Ethiopia from 1974 to 1987,"
Comparative Studies in Society and History 34 (1992): 28–57.

Since one goal of this book is to deconstruct a simple (Marxist) view
of the future, I would like to dedicate this book to the hope for better
days in Ethiopia and, most specifically, to my son, Benjamin.

Introduction

*Genealogies of the Modern
and the Anti-Modern*

The secret of Elvis' art lay not in an act of substantive creation but
in a recasting of one traditional style in terms of another. To make
such a transposition, you have to be stylistically sophisticated. You
have to see all the familiar styles lying before you like so many spots
of colour on a painter's palette. Such sophistication would have taken
many years to develop in the premedia world of popular music. Once,
however, every American child started growing up with unlimited
access to every kind of music provided by radio, any boy with a
good ear and the necessary talent could get hip fast.

Albert Goldman, *Elvis*,
quoted in Dick Hebdige, *Cut 'n' Mix*

There is perhaps no concept more central to modernism than revolution. Indeed, for us moderns, it is difficult to see the idea of revolution
as culturally constructed. We live within a set of concepts and a series of
material practices that make revolution—the promise or threat of it—
appear almost a natural feature of politics. But such was not always the
case. It was only after 1789, in fact, that the contemporary concept of
revolution crystallized in Europe, the notion of revolution, that is, as an
attempt rationally to design a *new* political order. "The modern concept
of revolution, inextricably bound up with the notion that the course of
history suddenly begins anew, that an entirely new story, a story never
known or told before is about to unfold, was unknown prior to . . . the
eighteenth century."[1]

In the sixteenth century, the meaning of revolution applied to political affairs was no different from that relating to the movement of plan-
ets; indeed, the second was often seen as influencing the first. Embedded
in a circular view of time, revolution meant, not the creation of a new
order, but a return to a previous state of affairs. Thus, when the French
king, Henry IV, converted to Catholicism and thereby won over his op-

ponents, the political change was widely described as a revolution—a reversion to the status quo ante, a coming back that occurred, it seemed, "as irresistibly as a planet rotates."[2]

Gradually in the modern era—incompletely in the English revolution, further in the American, but most dramatically in the French—the contemporary concept of revolution emerged (and, along with it, the idea of the *ancien régime*). According to Keith Baker, the new notion of revolution reflected a new reckoning of historical time; time was linearized as the past was separated from the present, and expectations reoriented toward the future.[3]

From the standpoint of this linear, secular time, revolution became *the* way to jump "ahead." And as the shape of time changed, so did the identity of social units embedded in history. By the early eighteenth century, nations—horizontal communities held together by putative cultural commonalities—began to emerge from the debris of old (vertical and mostly multicultural) empires.[4] Nations thus conceived were seen as in "front" or "behind" one another, all on a straight line defined by relative wealth, power, and knowledge.[5] With the partition of Africa toward the end of the nineteenth century, virtually the whole world was caught up in this—what I shall call—metanarrative of modernity. By the twentieth century, local elites everywhere had to react to it, in one way or another, in order to define who they were.

In the *Eighteenth Brumaire*, Marx pointed out that revolutionaries have continually accomplished their ends in historical blackface:

> Just when [people] appear to be engaged in the revolutionary transformation of themselves and their material surroundings, in the creation of something which does not yet exist, precisely in such epochs of revolutionary crisis they timidly conjure up the spirits of the past to help them; they borrow their names, slogans and costumes so as to stage the new world-historical scene in this venerable disguise and borrowed language. Luther put on the mask of the apostle Paul; the Revolution of 1789–1814 draped itself alternately as the Roman republic and the Roman empire.[6]

While Marx looked forward to a socialist revolution that would dispense with this (in his terms) timidity, in fact such a day has not arrived. Modern historical actors across the globe have always been involved in crosstalk[7] —French revolutionaries with Roman republicans, Russian with French revolutionaries, Chinese with Russian revolutionaries. Indeed, actors' consciousness—condescending or painful—of their place in an unequal world is one of the distinctive features of modernity compared to previous eras. For China, Joseph Levenson pointed out:

[Imperial] Peking neglected to send George III an English version of the Confucian classics. But [Communist] Peking thoughtfully broadcasts far and
wide, in English, Spanish, Arabic and everything else, the thought of Mao
Tse-tung. . . . Mao, quite unequivocally, represents himself not as a Chinese
sage prescribing for the world, but as a world sage in a line of sages (Marx,
Lenin, Stalin . . .), bringing China—agreeably, to the nationalist spirit—to
the forefront of history, everybody's history. To the culturalistic Confucian
spirit (Ch'ien-lung's), Chinese history was the only history that mattered. To
the nationalistic Communist (Mao), the satisfaction comes in having Chinese
history matter to the world.[8]

This consciousness of producing *a* history in relation to other histories
was initiated in part, as Benedict Anderson has argued, by the reception
of the French revolution into a world conversation of print:

Once it [the French revolution] had occurred, it entered the accumulating
memory of print. The overwhelming and bewildering concatenation of
events experienced by its makers and its victims became a "thing"—and with
its own Name: The French Revolution. Like a vast shapeless rock worn to a
rounded boulder by countless drops of water, the experience was shaped by
millions of printed words into a "concept" on the printed page, and in due
course, into a model.[9]

Lately, the means by which political actors connect themselves with
others—including the ghosts of past revolutionaries—has expanded
beyond print. Whatever the political effects of this change in the over-
developed world core (and they seem to have been conservatizing), the
consequences for places like Ethiopia have been destabilizing. The relative detachment of political actors from local contexts, the quickness
with which social groups can be mobilized, and the resulting power of
very small groups to effect fundamental historical changes: all these aspects of modern times have introduced new processes, new rhythms,
and new juxtapositions.

In the new and interactive universe that has developed—one charac-
terized, in Arjun Appadurai's apt phrase, by a "new condition of neigh-
borliness"[10]—cultural and social differences themselves have become
objects for self-conscious manipulation and commentary. Viewing cultural styles and political ideologies not so much arranged in a natural
hierarchy but as a simple horizontal array of possibilities—so many
spots of color on a painter's palette—people have begun to pick and
choose, juxtapose and combine, to create complex socio-semantic fields
in which boundaries are blurred and shifting, sometimes intentionally
so. In short, everyone, not just southern white boys like Elvis, has begun

to "get hip fast." As I shall show in succeeding chapters, Mengistu Haile Mariam became revolutionary Ethiopia's preeminent Elvis—an Elvis with a gun.

ANTI-MODERNISM

The modern notion of revolution is one necessary backdrop for the Ethiopian events I shall describe. But another, equally necessary, is anti-modern Christianity—specifically, a "faith" mission, the Sudan Interior Mission, that came to inspire the development of probably the largest Protestant denomination in Ethiopia. Since Max Weber, cultural theorists have been hypnotized by the Enlightenment's self-representation. Secularization and the disenchantment of the world have proceeded for some groups, during some periods of time, in some places. But the larger outline of what might be called cultural "modernization" is arguably better captured as a set of continuing, if intermittent, cultural wars than a supersession of one cultural regime by another. According to Susan Harding, anti-modernist Christianity represents "a willfully 'mad rhetoric,' and speaking it (being spoken by it) is a political act, a constant dissent, disruption, and critique of modern thought."[11]

Daniel 7:23. Thus he said, The fourth beast shall be the fourth kingdom upon earth, which shall be diverse from all kingdoms, and shall devour the whole earth, and shall tread it down, and break it in pieces.

24. And the ten horns out of this kingdom are ten kings that shall arise; and another shall rise after them; and he shall be diverse from the first, and he shall subdue three kings.

25. And he shall speak great words against the most High, and shall wear out the saints of the most High, and think to change times and laws; and they shall be given into his hand until a time and times and the dividing of time.

26. But the judgment shall sit, and they shall take away his dominion, to consume and to destroy it unto the end.

27. And the kingdom and dominion, and the greatness of the kingdom under the whole heaven, shall be given to the people of the saints of the most High, whose kingdom is an everlasting kingdom, and all dominions shall serve and obey him.

28. Hitherto is the end of the matter. As for me Daniel, my cogitations much troubled me, and my countenance changed in me; but I kept the matter in my heart.

How did anti-modernist Christianity—which was eventually to furnish Maale's principal revolutionaries—originate? As it turns out, the reception of the French revolution not only let loose a worldwide discourse on modernism—how to reshape and improve human society by the application of human reason—it also provided the occasion for the birth of a significant anti-modernism. In an important sense, the second shadowed the first. It was "part" of the first. In Britain, this reaction crystallized in a tradition with a much longer history—namely, millenarian strands of Christianity:

> The violent uprooting of European political and social institutions forced many to the conclusion that the end of the world was near. . . . [Believers] became convinced (in a rare display of unanimity) that they were witnessing the fulfillment of the prophecies of Daniel 7 and Revelation 13. The Revolution brought the cheering sight of the destruction of papal power in France, the confiscation of church property, and eventually the establishment of a religion of reason; the final act occurred in 1798 when French troops under Berthier marched on Rome, established a republic, and sent the Pope into banishment. Commentators were quick to point out that this "deadly wound"' received by the papacy had been explicitly described and dated in Revelation 13.[12]

Across the Atlantic, the effects of revolution on religious outlook—in this case, the American revolution—were generally the opposite. The view of a progressive and improving social project was strengthened. The future of both the state and of Christianity, these two increasingly identified in what became known as the American civil religion, looked bright. In the eighteenth century and well into the nineteenth, the dominant view among North American Christians (called postmillennialism) was that the church would progressively expand to include the whole world, that human society would be steadily improved until—history acting on its own—a millennium of peace and harmony would be reached. *Then* Christ would return.

> The millennium seemed easily within reach through the dual agencies of revival and social reform. Evangelists prodded sinners to be born again, and evangelical do-gooders founded societies for the abolition of slavery, for temperance, for alleviation of the miseries of the poor, and the like, in order to make the country as Christian as possible. So successful were their efforts that by the mid-1830s evangelical leaders were declaring that "the millennium is at the door" and "if the church will do her duty, the millennium may come in this country in three years."[13]

Meanwhile in a Britain considerably more affected by the dislocations of industrialization—with the example of the darker French revolution much nearer at hand—a different Christian worldview was beginning to form, one dramatically more pessimistic and therefore urgent, one destined to influence North Americans by the end of the century. So-called premillennialists in Britain gave up faith in secular progress and even in the church's ability to stem the tide of evil. As the situation irreversibly deteriorated, Christ would return—any day now, according to the signs of the times—*before* the millennium, not after. Christ's sudden intervention in history would mean salvation for the blessed few but damnation for the sinful many.

This new conviction not only transformed the shape of history as it was experienced by believers—times were getting worse and worse, not better and better—but far from the modernist disenchantment of the world, it emphasized the role of the supernatural in the mundane aspects of everyday life. Premillennial anti-modernism made "room for angels, demons, lakes of fire which burned forever, and a personal Son of Man who was coming soon on the clouds of heaven to put an end to evil and establish the perfect order."[14] Human history was produced, then, not as a series of secular cause-and-effect relationships, but as the outcome—set out by prophecies in the Bible decipherable by any believer—of an all-encompassing struggle between the forces of good and evil: "The great conflict preceding the millennium would be a terrible confrontation between the hosts of Christ and the minions of Satan. This coming conflict, moreover, would mark the culmination of a fierce struggle that dominated all of history. Accordingly, Christians must view themselves as caught between two powers, Christ and Satan."[15]

Perforce, the leaders of premillennialism did not believe that they could do anything to change the overall shape of history. Yet, their view of a foreordained future hardly led to a quietism, indeed, if anything to the reverse—an increased anxiety and urgency, an escalating commitment to oppose apostasy wherever it occurred, and most particularly for the events I shall describe, an enlarged emphasis on evangelicalism and foreign missions.[16] "Although apparently paradoxical it is possible to show that the [pre]millenarians were at the same time convinced of the irreversible downgrade tendencies at work in human society and the utter futility of attempts to ameliorate the effects of sin, while working for the success of their own movement when that success was defined as awakening Christians to their peril."[17] In 1827 in Britain, one Henry Drummond went so far as to state that the "first fifteen chapters of Revelation had already been fulfilled and that . . . European history was hovering somewhere between the twelfth and seventeenth verses of Revelation 16."[18] And across the Atlantic in upper New York State, William

Miller announced the actual date of the second coming: 22 October 1844.[19] When that day came and went as any other, premillennialism was discredited for a generation within North American Christianity.

By the 1870s, however, a new kind of premillennialism called "dispensationalism" was beginning to attract many adherents in the United States and Canada. Unlike the discredited Millerites, dispensationalists "denied that prophecies were intended for the church age as a whole, [hence] they were for the most part relieved of the dangerous and often embarrassing task of matching biblical predictions with current events."[20] By the end of the nineteenth century, premillennialism in its dispensational form maintained:

> The belief that acceptance of the divine authority of Scripture required that the believer expect a literal rather than spiritual fulfillment of the prophecies; the belief that the gospel was not intended nor was it going to accomplish the salvation of the world, but that, instead, the world was growing increasingly corrupt and rushing toward imminent judgement; the belief that Christ would literally return to this earth and the Jews be restored to Palestine before the commencement of the millennial age; and the belief that this whole panorama of coming glory and judgement was explicitly foretold in the prophecies where one could, if taught by the Spirit, discover the truth and be ready for the coming of the bridegroom.[21]

If premillennialists were still a minority in North America in the 1870s, they were by no means seen as cultural deviants. They fitted easily within a wider group of evangelical, revivalistic Christians who, in fact, enjoyed cultural preeminence. "In 1870 almost all American Protestants thought of America as a Christian nation. Although many Roman Catholics, sectarians, skeptics, and non-Christians had other views of the matter, Protestant evangelicals considered their faith to be the normative American creed."[22]

A mere fifty years later, matters would be altogether different: "Christendom," remarked H. L. Mencken in 1924, "may be defined briefly as that part of the world in which, if any man stands up in public and solemnly swears that he is a Christian, all his auditors will laugh."[23] Impressed by the discoveries of natural science, its social life transformed by urbanization and the industrial revolution, its world power confirmed by the results of World War I, parts of public culture in the United States had been rapidly and dramatically secularized.

It was in reaction to these changes—and to what became known as modernism[24] within Protestant denominations themselves—that a militantly anti-modernist Christianity formed, one that built itself on the revivalism and premillennialism of the nineteenth century and that by the 1920s termed itself "fundamentalist."[25] It was out of these streams of North American cultural development that an interdenominational "faith" mission was established in Canada at the end of the last century. The Sudan Interior Mission (SIM) would bring Christ's "good news" to southern Ethiopia by the 1930s.

ON NARRATIVE

A tour of Israel with Jerry Falwell's Old-Time Gospel Hour Tours seems not unlike a tour of Greece with a secular tourist agency. Familiar landscapes and events and actors from history "come alive," and what was a two-dimensional story about the past, about the "the origin of civilization," pops vividly into three dimensions. One feels and sees oneself walking within history; history, somatized, becomes somehow "more real." But the two tours are also absolutely unlike each other, for Jerry Falwell's Holy Land tourists also find themselves in the future, walking its landscape, knowing its actors, foreseeing its events. They walk within the scenes of Christ's First Coming two thousand years ago and of his Second Coming, which they know will be soon. They know they will be with him, among his troops, as he returns to rule on earth for the Kingdom Age. So real, immediate, specific, and unarguable is the future they foresee that the Old-Time Gospel Hour tour guide and teacher Harold Willmington buried a Protestant Bible wrapped in plastic in one of the caves in the Valley of Petra for the Jews who will hide there after the "destruction of the Jews" begins during the Tribulation. . . . In the Bible he inscribed this note: "Attention to all of Hebrew background: This Bible has been placed here on October 14, 1974, by the students and Dean of the Thomas Road Bible Institute in Lynchburg, VA., U.S.A. We respectfully urge its finder to prayerfully and publicly read the following Bible chapters. They are: Daniel 7 and 11; Matthew 24; II Thessalonians 2; Revelation 12 and 13."[26]

Narrative figures in at least two ways in the following analysis. The first and most obvious is in the overall arrangement of the book itself—what I have called *my* narrative, a story that is meant to highlight a certain recurrent dialectic among modernist, anti-modernist, and traditionalist stances, a kind of ratcheting interaction that led, in the end, to the modernization of the Ethiopian state.

To paraphrase Louis Mink, narrative converts congeries of events into storied concatenations—a task whose object is not so much to isolate social laws as to develop an understanding of contingent connections. Stories have a unique ability to convey this kind of knowledge:

Narrative is a primary cognitive instrument—an instrument rivaled, in fact, only by theory and by metaphor as irreducible ways of making the flux of experience comprehensible. . . . Theory makes possible the explanation of an occurrence only by describing it in such a way that the description is logically related to a systematic set of generalizations or laws. One understands the operations of a spring-powered watch, for example, only insofar as one understands the principles of mechanics, and this requires describing the mechanism of the watch in terms, and *only* in terms, appropriate to those principles. . . . But a particular watch also has a historical career: it is produced, shipped, stored, displayed, purchased, used; it may be given and received, lost and found, pawned and redeemed, admired and cursed, responsible for a timely arrival or a missed appointment. At each moment of its career, that is, it is or may be part of a connected series of events which intersects its own history, and at each such moment it may be subject to a particular description, which is appropriate only because of that intersection. . . . This is what narrative form uniquely represents, and why we require it as an irreducible form of understanding.[27]

Renato Rosaldo was the first anthropologist to emphasize the central role of narrative in ethnographic history. Americanizing W. B. Gallie's discussion of cricket, Rosaldo used baseball as an example to convey the analytical work that narrative accomplishes:

Perhaps the most economical way to convey a sense of how narratives can embody the historical understanding is through the example of a game of chance and skill. Consider for a moment the game of baseball, an often used example of what is involved in telling about and following a complex event through time. As the action starts, the perceptive fan begins to think strategically by considering who is at bat (an often-dangerous pull hitter now in a slump), who is pitching (a fresh reliefer whose knuckleball is as often erratic as it is effective), who is on base (an able base runner, on first), how the fielders are playing (at double-play depth), and what the score is (one out, bottom of the ninth, the tying run on first). Clearly there is a vast difference between merely knowing the rules of the game and having the knowledge required to follow the game in the manner of an experienced fan of fine judgment. . . . A storyteller wishing to achieve a proper sense of proportion and possibility would require a peculiar double vision, focused at once on each unfolding moment and on the totality of the long-term course of action. On the one hand, a sense of proportion would come from seeing the particular game in the context of the entire season. How important, after all was said and done, did this single game happen to be? Was it a turning point? On the other hand, a sense of open-ended possibilities would emerge from the forward-looking vantage point of each significant instant of play. Like the avid fan, the storyteller might plot strategies several moves ahead as she or he thinks about who is in the bullpen, possible pinch hitters, how to play the infield if the batter is walked, and so on.[28]

But issues of narrative occur at another level as well. As philosopher David Carr has argued, social actors themselves experience time in terms of culturally specific stories. Modernists, anti-modernists, or traditionalists in Maale only became so *through narrative*, through contrasting temporalizations of history. If this be so, then the anthropologist's or historian's analysis does not arbitrarily impose narrative conventions on a nonnarrative reality (as some postmodernists such as Hayden White have suggested).[29] Rather, social actors themselves experience time through particular patterns of beginnings, middles, and ends. Carr, expanding upon Husserl, offers the example of "following a melody":

> What is remarkable about hearing the melody is the manner in which consciousness spans past and future to encompass the melody as a whole and construes the note sounding as a part within this whole. When I experience a melody, I do not experience my hearing as an object; but the temporal phases of my hearing stand in the same part-whole relation to each other as do the notes of the melody I hear.[30]

In other words, one's experience of a note at any moment in time exists only in relation both to past notes and to expected future ones. When the future surprises us, "then in an important sense the past is changed. That is, earlier, now-retained phases have become parts of a different whole and thus change their significance for us altogether."[31]

Marshall Sahlins, Sherry Ortner, and J. D. Y. Peel[32] have all emphasized related points within ethnographic history: How historical actors apprehend events about them and therefore what they do in any particular situation depends, in part, upon their expectations for the future, expectations shaped by local narrative conventions.

Let me illustrate this contention with examples that will appear in succeeding chapters. For anti-modernist evangelical Christians, the future is mapped out in the prophecies of the Bible; today and tomorrow are determined by an epic struggle between Christ and Satan—one that Satan will win again and again until Christ reverses the slide of time by returning to bring world history to an end. The shape of this future is so real for believers that any number of consequences follows: an Old-Time Gospel Hour tour guide buries a Bible in Israel for the use of Jews who, in the last days, will either convert or be lost. The same sense of God's plan takes missionaries to southern Ethiopia, there to endure hardship after hardship (setbacks that are, after all, only the Devil's apparent victories). By spreading the word of God, missionaries bring the end of time nearer by completing Christ's Great Commission to take the gospel to the ends of the earth.

Modernist conceptions of the future are dramatically different from evangelical Christians ones. But they are—particularly during revolutionary times—no less self-assured. An eyewitness of the Russian revolution described the exhilaration of one of his friends, Nadya, who had given her life to the revolution. Nadya worked as a cadre to collectivize peasant villages:

> Impassioned revolutionary that she was, she could not and would not be concerned with the hurt of the individual. Not that it had passed her unobserved, but it failed to stir her sympathy. She seemed no more concerned with the peasant's perplexity than is a surgeon with the pain of the patient over whose body he is wielding a scalpel. Her mind and heart were fixed on the glories of tomorrow as she visualized them, not on the sorrows of today. The agony of the process was lost to her in the triumph of achievement.[33]

The modernist future that anesthetized Nadya to the agonies of the present is one evacuated of gods and spirits, one that is now unknown and open—indeterminate and therefore accessible to human intervention and human rationality. At any one point in time, progress depends only upon a willingness to take up the scalpel of history. But in a larger sense, the shape of the future is also determined, for human rationality, in the end, cannot be repressed and has to lead to gain and advancement. Thus the past is experienced as "behind" and the future as necessarily "ahead" of the present. Because of the arrow of progress, particularly of technological progress, the future continually arrives ever more quickly. Time speeds up.[34]

Finally, the distinctive Maale conception of the future, anchored in the notion of divine kingship, is different yet again. The first king of Maale brought "fire"—knowledge, custom, culture. The struggle of the present is, then, a struggle to maintain that fire (this is not my imagery but that of a number of Maale rites and myths). Because Maale believe that people inevitably make mistakes—for one reason or another, they stray from tradition—the future continually threatens to fall apart. "Our country is destroyed. The rains are not coming. Our women are not having children. Our cows don't calve. Our goats don't kid." It took me some time to understand these statements, which I heard over and over again, not just in their literal senses (sometimes droughts *did* occur) but in their wider symbolic connections. Even during what an outsider might interpret as "good times," Maale traditionalists did not expect that the future would match the past.

As a threatening space in which tradition would have to be protected, as a definitely better place to be reached through science and rationality, or as an imminent millennium that makes meaningful any amount of current hardship—differently constructed futures affected how variously situated groups interpreted events of the Ethiopian revolution. And people did what they did, in part, because of these understandings. This is the second sense in which narrative figures in what follows—in this case, actors' own (past) narrative outlines of the future, what Reinhart Koselleck called "futures past."

What is the relationship between these two levels of narrative—actors' own narratives and those of the analyst? The first does not issue in any simple or direct way to the second.[35] Yet, it is the first, in a particular context, that conditions the events that become the subject of the second.

In summarizing, it is difficult to write about revolution without suggesting a sense of inevitability. What happened in Ethiopia beginning in 1974 was hardly inevitable. It depended upon the contingent coupling of a series of conditions, all the way from the constitution of peasant societies like Maale to the international system of states and the Cold War. What I have sought to accomplish in this book is to construct a narrative of narratives that illuminates these contingencies, that tells its story through the stories of Ethiopian actors themselves. It's stories all the way down—stories of stories of stories.

CHAPTER I

The Metanarrative of Modernity in Ethiopia: 1974

For a long time now, people have pondered the ambiguity, at least in English, of "history": the records men make, the records men write. In modern Chinese history, these are beginning to correspond. Revolutionary spirits like the famous writer Lu Hsün (1881–1936) felt that the old high culture was dead, and they resented being instructed, as it seemed, to rest quietly, uttering platitudes in silk-fan attitudes. They wanted to create (and destroy): to make their own history, not to be politically stricken by forces from abroad, or culturally sterile at home, their past frozen solid in the present. The revolution they helped to foster in a cosmopolitan spirit—against the world to join the world, against their past to keep it theirs, but past—may be interpreted, in cultural terms, as a long striving to make their museums themselves.

Joseph Levenson,
Revolution and Cosmopolitanism

The tenth anniversary of the Ethiopian revolution came on 12 September 1984—ten years to the day when Haile Selassie, Emperor of Ethiopia, Elect of God, and the Conquering Lion of the Tribe of Judah,[1] was taken off to prison in the back seat of a Volkswagen.[2]

After ten years, much in Ethiopia had changed—the people in power, the rhetoric of rule, the system of social stratification, the pattern of international alliances. The new head of state, Mengistu Haile Mariam, was now Chairman of the Provisional Military Administrative Council, Commander of the Revolutionary Armed Forces, and Chairman of the Commission to Organize the Party of the Working People.

Preparations for September 1984 were extraordinary. According to one estimate, the government spent a minimum of U.S. $50 million on the celebrations, this at a time of developing famine in the country.[3] Plans included a flurry of building in Addis Ababa. Concrete was in such short supply in the countryside that it was difficult to repair bridges during the preceding year. To mark the occasion, the Soviet

Figure 2. The tenth anniversary celebration of the Ethiopian revolution, Addis Ababa, 1984. Press photograph, Archives, Institute of Ethiopian Studies, Addis Ababa University.

Union gave Ethiopia a larger-than-life-size statue of Lenin, and the East Germans, with Erich Honecker present, a bust of Marx. Finally, the North Koreans sent advisers to teach Ethiopians how to march and to perform those massive card shows, such as North Americans sometimes see at football games.

Clearly, to those in power, the tenth anniversary celebrations were a serious matter. They *were* serious because their fundamental goal was to narrate, and thus to define, the revolution. The story that revolutionaries told themselves that day becomes clearest in a museum exhibit organized for the occasion. The exhibit was placed along a wall, in front of which a red carpet led viewers from one installation to the next.

The first stop was the bones that American paleontologist Donald Johanson had found in Hadar, Ethiopia, of an individual he named Lucy (after the Beatles' song), supposedly the earliest evidence of our hominid ancestors.[4] Ethiopians had renamed Lucy, Dinḵenesh, which means in Amharic "You [feminine] are something spectacular." After Dinḵenesh came photographs of stelae from the earliest civilization in Ethiopia, Axum. After Axum, came the famous rock churches of Lalibela from the twelfth century.[5] The exhibit continued to the Battle of Adwa in 1896, in which Ethiopia defeated Italy and thereafter, alone in

Africa, managed to remain politically independent during most of the twentieth century. Finally came the overthrow of Haile Selassie in 1974. At that point, let us join a local reporter writing for the government English-language newspaper:

> Walking leisurely and comfortably on the red carpet, one starts enjoying the melodious music and the continuous eruptions of the revolution till he reaches the terrifyingly concerted campaigns launched against the revolution [the so-called white terror of 1977–78]. Devastated factories, bridges, buses, and blasted airplanes, massacres of revolutionaries and the attempt to assassinate Comrade Chairman Mengistu makes the visitor hold his breath. But the masses are soon armed, the plot was foiled, and the Committee to Organize the Party formed. Then emerges a tranquil environment when the Committee evolves into the Workers' Party of Ethiopia. The Ethiopian revolution embraced by the progressive world, the visitor finally feels like dancing and the red carpet ends there.[6]

In other words, a story of progress from the very beginning of humanity itself (in Ethiopia as it happens) to the creation and preservation of the nation we call Ethiopia, to, finally, the communist redemption of that culture by the party.

How this story became the master narrative of the revolutionary state involves a complex history—one that contrasts, dramatically, with the linearity of the events depicted above. Even though Ethiopian intellectuals had begun developing a left critique of their society in the 1960s, no communist party existed in the country by the mid-1970s—unlike the case of neighboring Sudan, for example.[7] It was the revolution itself that "made" organized radical groups in Ethiopia, rather than the reverse.[8] This chapter will examine the first steps of this process—what at the time was called the "creeping coup."

THE COLLAPSE OF THE *ANCIEN RÉGIME*

Some time ago, George Petee wrote, "Revolutionists enter the light, not like men on horseback, as victorious conspirators appearing in the forum, but like fearful children, exploring an empty house, not sure that it is empty."[9] In Ethiopia, the discovery that the palace was empty began in an out-of-the-way military garrison in the far south:

> The revolution began in a most unexpected manner. On January 12, rank-and-file soldiers of a small garrison in Neghelle Borana, a semi-arid region in southern Ethiopia, mutinied against their commanding officers. It was not political grievances that motivated the revolt, but vile food and a shortage of drinking water. The soldiers' pump was out of order, and the officers

refused to allow them to use their own. After first detaining their superiors, the soldiers had the audacity to seize the Emperor's personal envoy, Commander of the Ground Forces Lt. Gen. Deresse Dubale, and force him to eat and drink as they did. In this dramatic fashion the ordinary Ethiopian soldiers, the NCOs, and low ranking officers entered upon the stage of Ethiopian history.[10]

When Haile Selassie did not punish the rebels and when the mutineers transmitted news of what had happened to other military installations, events began to snowball out of control. On 10 February 1974 at Debre Zeit, the major Air Force base in the country, technicians and NCOs rebelled; holding their officers hostage, they demanded better pay and working conditions. On 25 February, another group of soldiers led by sergeants and corporals in the Second Division mutinied in the strategic north of the country, took over the country's second largest city, Asmara, and began "broadcasting their demands over the radio station for the entire world to hear."[11] One of their points was the return of a private's body to his home village in case of death—as was routinely done for officers. "The 'centurions' of the Empire, the despised non-commissioned officers, poorly treated, recruited from the colonized nations [Ethiopian ethnic groups different from the dominant Amhara and Tigreans], bogged down in distant wars where they bore all the suffering and endured all the horrors while the senior officers, the warlords, cavorted in the provincial capitals, they refused to carry on being cannon fodder."[12] Rising in support of the Asmara soldiers, a group in the strategically located Fourth Division in the capital went so far as to begin to arrest most of Haile Selassie's cabinet.[13]

As the Emperor gave in to military demand after demand, civilian unrest in Addis Ababa added to a developing sense of crisis. On 14 February, students demonstrated against a proposed educational reform that would restrict educational opportunity at the secondary and university levels; four days later, teachers went on strike for higher pay and against the reform. And the same day, taxicab drivers poured into the streets in response to the government's 50 percent increase in fuel prices—a move required by the increase in world prices brought about by the Organization of Petroleum Exporting Countries, OPEC:

> There were riotous demonstrations, the stoning of buses and luxury cars in an attempt to bring public transport to a halt and the robbing and destroying of property. On 24 February, it was reported that the taxi drivers, students and the lumpenproletariat had caused the death of three and the wounding of twenty-two individuals in and around Addis Ababa and had

damaged seventy-five buses, sixty-nine cars, two trains, and a motor-bike, and thirty-eight houses.[14]

Retreating again, the Emperor announced a partial cut in the price of gasoline and a postponement of any changes in the educational system. By 28 February —after the beginning of the Asmara mutiny—he accepted the resignation of his prime minister, Aklilu Habte-Wolde, in office since the early 1960s: "Whether this move was wise or even warranted was debated long afterwards, for none of the demonstrating groups had specifically called for Aklilu's resignation. Moreover, it hinted at panic and weakness in the palace which soldiers and civilians would fully exploit in coming months."[15] Demonstrations by labor unions followed, and from early March to late May, urban Ethiopia, particularly the capital, Addis Ababa, was plagued by a series of strikes. The call for work stoppages focused almost entirely on economic demands. During the previous decade, consumer prices in Ethiopia had outstripped wage increases, and during the first quarter of 1974 alone—after the drought of the previous year—inflation rose at a rate of 80 percent.[16]

> For the first time in the empire's history, the normally mild-mannered Labor Confederation managed to organize a general strike that paralyzed all economic activity from March 7 to 9. The success of this action unleashed a wave of wildcat strikes that left the government running from factory to factory and from one semi-state company to another to deal with the explosion of labor demands. Practically every group from prostitutes to lay priests went out on strike for better wages and working conditions.[17]

None of these actions, including those carried out by the soldiers, were the result of an organized political opposition. Rather, particular urban groups—lower-ranking military, students and teachers, labor unions—expressed local grievances in their own, sometimes contradictory, ways.[18] Each step emboldened oppositional actors further, and it slowly dawned upon the city that the power of the imperial center might not hold.

> Addis Ababa became a permanent seminar. Everything was discussed, everything examined closely, nothing escaped the rolling fire of criticism. But what had been intended only as a safety valve [lifting press censorship] became a catalyst. Drunk with their freshly acquired liberty, all the social forces began to raise the horizon of their demands. Addis Ababa took to the streets again. On 18 April, 150,000 Muslims marched, thus demonstrating the strength of Islam which had for centuries been stifled by the state religion [Orthodox Christianity].[19]

The new prime minister, Endalkachew Makonnen, an Oxford-educated aristocrat, promised liberal reforms: an investigation of the corrupt practices of the past government, a constitutional monarchy, an economic recovery, and land reform. But to succeed, Endalkachew required the means to enforce his decisions; this meant the support of the Army and, in particular, that of the Fourth Division located in Addis Ababa.

In this context, the armed forces were inevitably drawn into the vortex of the political struggle. What had been particularist, mostly economic, issues quickly escalated into the broadest and most political questions. Ordinary soldiers began to see themselves as political actors with a certain script: "Pay increases and improvements in the conditions of the other ranks were derisory ambitions for those who felt that they had a rendezvous with History. It was at this time [May 1974] that the first terms of Marxist vocabulary made their appearances, alongside references to the great revolutions of the past: 1789, 1917, China, the Paris Commune."[20]

Then the Talk, beside which Carlyle's "flood of French speech" was a mere trickle. Lectures, debates, speeches—in theatres, circuses, school-houses, clubs, Soviet meeting-rooms. Union headquarters, barracks. . . . Meetings in the trenches at the front, in village squares, factories. . . . What a marvelous sight to see Putilovsky Zavod (the Putilov factory) pour out its forty thousand to listen to Social Democrats, Socialist Revolutionaries, Anarchists, anybody, whatever they had to say, as long as they would talk! For months in Petrograd, and all over Russia, every street-corner was a public tribune. In railway trains, streetcars, always the spurting up of impromptu debate, everywhere.[21]

After an abortive attempt at a coup was put down in late March,[22] April witnessed some of the most violent demonstrations and strikes of the uprising. Moreover, unrest moved out of Addis Ababa into the provincial cities, especially in the south: "The demand for the dismissal of government officials was spearheaded by residents of provincial and sub-provincial capitals. Between 29 March and 6 April, it was reported that there had been strikes and demonstrations in all of the provincial capitals with police actions against the demonstrators being at their severest in four of them: Jimma (Kefa), Metu (Illubabor), Asela (Arusi) and Arba Minch (Gemu Gofa)."[23]

By May, the armed forces had divided into three factions riven by one great cleavage: at the top was the high command, dominated by the old Ethiopian elite, who retained real control of little more than the Imperial Bodyguard.[24] Posed against them were virtually all of the middle-level officers and NCOs. This latter group, particularly the NCOs, contained many soldiers from nonelite ethnic groups. They began to divide into two overlapping groups: reformists who felt that a change in the cabinet was probably enough, and radicals—not yet Marxists—who distrusted any quick return to civilian rule and who began to dream of using their power to transform the system of privileges in Ethiopian society.[25] According to Andargachew Tiruneh, the first group was dominated by officers like Colonel Alem Zewd, while the second was composed predominately of NCOs.[26]

The key question, then, was whether the military would hold together or split and allow itself to be used against itself (as had in fact occurred during an attempted coup against Haile Selassie in 1960): "In the event, surprisingly, a common front was attained, through a device unique in the long history of military regimes. This was the Derg—a little used Amharic word for committee—formed as a parliament of the armed forces, with representatives from each of the main units of the army, air force, navy and police, and total membership of one hundred and eight."[27]

When it appeared that an effort was under way to free those already arrested, the "Coordinating Committee of the Armed Forces, Police, and Territorial Army," was hastily organized. Middle-ranking officers (none were above the rank of major) and NCOs seized effective power, as the old generals were shoved aside. The cleavage between top and bottom no longer existed; the top had been lopped off. Reminiscing more than a decade later about the first three days of meetings, Major Mengistu Haile Mariam recalled the emotions of the moment:

> It seemed as though "fire" was coming out of the mouths of the speakers when they were making speeches about the backwardness of Ethiopia, the history, the suffering of its people and the progress made in other countries. The small, round room in the Fourth Division where they met, he said, was gradually becoming charged with emotion until finally it reached a climax and exploded with scenes of war songs and declarations of readiness to die "not the death of a dog but that of a lion" in the course of liberating the Ethiopian people from oppression. On the third day (30 June) they took an oath never to see the suffering and humiliation of the Ethiopian people again and to remain united to the point of death. According to a Derg report of September 1975 they actually swore an oath, "In the name of the living God" not to betray the secrets of the Derg.[28]

Even though the Derg did not, at the time, seize official state power, and even though at first it pledged allegiance to Haile Selassie, it was clear that a major transformation had occurred. Western newspapers

reported the change as a coup. In the first two weeks, sixty-one ministers, vice ministers, provincial governors, top-ranking police officers,
and army generals were taken into custody. Apart from reasons of se-
nility—the Emperor was over eighty years of age at the time—it is difficult to understand why Haile Selassie allowed these arrests. Had he ordered the still loyal eight-thousand-man Imperial Bodyguard against the
badly organized, mutinous Derg in June, he would, in all likelihood,
have been successful.[29]

> The most extraordinary aspect of the arrests was the way in which those
> wanted, whose names were made public in the press and over the radio, vol-
> untarily gave themselves up, simply appearing at the gates of the Fourth Di-
> vision headquarters in Addis Ababa for incarceration. The paradoxical pa-
> rade of the Ethiopian aristocracy to the revolutionary gallows is difficult to
> account for fully. It was due partly to the superior attitude of the aristocrats,
> who thought that no sergeant or major would dare touch a *ras* or *dejazmach*;
> there was also the conviction that the new military committee was a passing
> phenomenon and would collapse shortly.[30]

*Rabochi Put blossomed out as Pravda, Lenin's newspaper which had been sup-
pressed in July. It crowed, bristling: "Workers, soldiers, peasants! In March you
struck down the tyranny of the clique of nobles. Yesterday you struck down the
tyranny of the bourgeois gang . . . " . . . What few Cadet organs appeared, and
the bourgeoisie, generally, adopted a detached, ironical attitude towards the
whole business. . . . the bourgeoisie laid low, abiding its hour—which could not
be far off. That the Bolsheviki would remain in power longer than three days
never occurred to anybody—except perhaps to Lenin, Trotsky, the Petrograd
workers, and the simpler soldiers.[31]*

When Haile Selassie did not react, the Derg cautiously began to consolidate its hold on power. In retrospect, its actions from June to September—its initial refusal to claim state power, its secrecy about its own
composition, its slowly building campaign to demythologize Haile Selassie—can be seen as a brilliant deployment of a Machiavellian plan.[32]
In fact, no such scheme probably existed, for once the generals were
neutralized, the Derg had to face its own profound internal differences.
Radicals, those who wanted to use military power to stay in power,
came into opposition with reformists, who were prepared to see a civilian government resume power. From June to November this struggle
was played out until, finally, the radicals were to win a decisive victory.
But in mid-June, the political landscape was different: at that point,
most of the Derg appeared only to have wanted to help Prime Minister
Endalkachew carry out "much-needed reforms."[33]

A month later, Endalkachew was forced to resign and was arrested, and in his place, the Derg choose *Lij* Michael Imru—another aristocrat but a man with many fewer ties to the old order. Work continued on the new constitution, and the Derg forced Parliament to stay in session during its summer vacation in order to complete the draft. By the time this was accomplished in mid-August, however, a majority of the military committee moved to block steps to return to civilian government. Instead, a graduated campaign against the Emperor was begun. The institutions that financially supported the crown were dissolved on 15 August, and the records uncovered were used in the media to paint a picture of the Emperor as uncaring and wealth-crazed:

> The capital was covered with posters, naive didactic paintings which took up all the images of popular iconography. On the right side, a cadaverous child would be weeping; on the left the Emperor would be throwing meat to his dogs. Or the court shedding tears at the grave of Lulu, the Emperor's favourite dog, would be contrasted with the court jubilant and laughing over the grave where the victims of starvation in Wollo had been buried.[34]

At last, during a four-day meeting 6–9 September, the Derg voted to depose the Emperor. From the length of time that it took to reach a consensus, it would seem that the action was painfully controversial.[35]

> It is said that the police officer's hands shook uncontrollably while he read the proclamation and that some of the soldiers in the room wept so profusely that they had to leave. The Emperor refused at first to leave the palace. But then Ras Imru walked up to him, kissed him on the cheek, and said, "Go." The Emperor, dazed and apparently still uncomprehending, walked with the Ras to the palace steps looking for one of his six different-colored Mercedes limousines. Instead, he was driven in a small blue Volkswagen the short distance to the Fourth Division Headquarters and imprisoned in a small wattle-and-mud building.[36]

THE DERG STEALS ITS OPPONENTS' IDEOLOGY

Once the Emperor was out of the way—with no public outcry and with no bloodshed—the Derg formally took state power as the Provisional Military Administrative Council (PMAC). Even though the radicals on the Council clearly had gained the upper hand, the struggle with reformists continued. The two principal issues revolved around how to deal with secessionist movements in Eritrea and calls for a return to civilian government.[37] Radicals rejected any compromise to national unity, and they opposed a transition to a civilian government.

[handwritten margin note: information management]

Outside the armed forces, however, the call for a "people's government" immediately went up from the students and the labor unions:

> On September 16, four days after the Emperor's removal, two thousand students staged a demonstration outside the main Addis Ababa university campus, chanting "down with the military government" and "we want a people's government." That day, the Confederation of Ethiopian Labor Unions issued a communiqué containing similar demands. When its three top leaders were arrested on September 24, it threatened a new general strike [never to be carried out].[38]

This time, open resistance was quickly put down, and the PMAC went on to choose an outsider, General Aman Andom, as the new head of government. General Aman was a popular figure among soldiers, a war hero who had been dismissed by Haile Selassie for insubordination. Aman—who supported more moderate positions, some degree of autonomy for Eritrea, and an Ethiopian republic set up after a referendum—quickly came into collision with the radical-dominated Derg. As tensions rose, high-ranking members of the Derg made themselves known publicly for the first time: among others, Major Mengistu Haile Mariam. On 22 November, the line between the Derg and Aman had been clearly drawn:

> During the night, Aman Andom's house was surrounded and then destroyed by tank guns, and the "Desert Lion"' was buried beneath the ruins. Mengistu, alone or possibly with Atnafu, had given the order for it. The following night he stampeded a terrified and horror-stricken Derg into agreeing to the execution of 57 notables deemed to be anti-revolutionaries. They were transferred from the cellars of the Old Guebbi Palace where the Fourth Division was installed, to the Akaki Prison and executed a few hours after, as were two members of the Derg who had supported Andom. According to common rumor, Mengistu killed Aklilu [Haile Selassie's prime minister, who had been forced to resign at the end of February] with his own hands.[39]

Now, there was no turning back. The Derg had, in effect, signed a "blood pact."[40] Sixty corpses—bodies of the most influential men in Ethiopia—separated the lowly NCOs and officers from the imperial past.[41] Whether Mengistu and others like him calculated this action as an attempt to ratchet the revolution to a higher level or whether in fact they acted in desperation in the face of anticipated failure—if they failed, at least a major part of the old order would be destroyed with them—all this is not clear.

In any case, when possible retaliation by Aman's base of support, the Second and Third Divisions, failed to materialize, a turning point had

Figure 3. Mengistu Haile Mariam. Press photograph, Archives, Institute of
Ethiopian Studies, Addis Ababa University.

been reached. The Derg emerged with a vindicated and newly articu-
lated resolve to grasp Ethiopian history: to implement a "revolution."
In doing so, the soldiers had come to see themselves in a fundamentally
new way. With ghosts of Mao, Lenin, and Robespierre in the wings,
they had became revolutionaries acting on a world stage—dreamers of
"progress," rational designers of a new Ethiopia.

*The [Ethiopian] uprising of 1974 was based on the "urban" residents who
numbered about 3 million out of a total population of almost 32 million. Of
these, it was only the civil servants, industrial workers, the army and the students who took an active part in the protest movement. The total number of
civil servants was 100,000, about a third of whom were employed in the state-
owned or dominated enterprises; the employees of some of the state-owned or
dominated enterprises like the Ethiopian Air Lines were allowed to form trade
unions but most were not. The Confederation of Ethiopian Trade Unions,
which included the employees of the state-owned enterprises which could form
unions, had a total membership of about 80,000. The Ethiopian Teachers' Association, whose members were civil servants, was 18,000 strong. In addition
to the civil servants, there was the army of 55,000 including the 10,000 territorial army in active force and a police force of about 30,000. The number of en-*

rolled school students was about 70,000 and that of the university 6,000. Thus out of the total urban population of 3 million, the politically active group made up of civil servants, workers, the soldiers and students was less than 300,000.[42]

The question became: Who would lead this revolution? Who would design Ethiopia Modern. A group of lowly soldiers? Or educated Ethiopians? One of the most remarkable aspects of the events that followed—events that would place the Derg in direct opposition to the leftist intelligentsia—is the extent to which the military "stole" its ideology from its enemies:

> Time and again the Derg announced radical reforms even while arresting leftists. . . . For all its confusing contradictions, the conflict between the military and civilians led to much more radical policies than either would have implemented on its own. Each side vied with the other to establish itself as the real revolutionary force in the country. Civilians radicalized the military and the military radicalized civilians.[43]

The Derg's appropriation of left rhetoric not only undercut the claims of its civilian opponents, but—in the bipolar world of the Cold War— eventually opened channels for massive amounts of military aid from the Soviet Union.

The defeat and expulsion of the united opposition at the party congress of December 1927 removed the last formidable obstacle in the way of Stalin's progress towards absolute power. . . . Trotsky had confidently predicted that the victory of Stalin and Bukharin would presage a sharp reaction to the Right. What happened was exactly the contrary. . . . Stalin scarcely waited to expel Trotsky from the party and from Moscow before embarking on a policy of forced industrialization at a pace, and at a cost for other sectors of the economy, far beyond anything hitherto contemplated by Trotsky or by anyone else. The exiles languishing in Siberia could now persuade themselves that Stalin had adopted the policies of the opposition.[44]

The passage of ideas from civilian opponents to the Derg—from the university to the barracks, as it were—was conditioned by the particular history of the military in Ethiopia. Most armies are composed of officers, recruited on a voluntary basis, presiding over lower ranks, usually conscripted. In Ethiopia, this pattern was reversed. The lowest ranks were composed mostly of poor volunteers, while many educated officers, junior ones at least, had been conscripted:

> During the period of the army's rapid expansion in the 1950s and early 1960s, the best secondary-school students were often compelled to join the army, and nursed a lasting resentment against a government which sent them

to serve in distant and inhospitable areas . . . while their contemporaries gained professional or civil-service jobs in Addis Ababa. Army officers in the capital frequently attended evening classes at the university, and were affected by the prevailing climate of ideas; quite a number of these officers, indeed, later held high office in the revolutionary regime.[45]

The university—then named Haile Selassie I University—was perhaps the most significant modernist institution in all of Ethiopia.[46] The grand scheme of modernization—the march of advanced nations, followed by backward ones, along a continuum defined by different groups' success in applying science and knowledge—had come to define reality for many of the new Ethiopian educated elite. And as such ideas diffused to the cities and towns of the country, yetamarē, educated persons—those who would lead Ethiopia out of backwardness—enjoyed unquestioned prestige.

On the eve of the revolution in Ethiopia, there were two great world models of modernization, two mutually exclusive paths to wealth and power for underdeveloped countries, namely, capitalism and socialism. In the stories told by apologists for each, the same factors—the market on the one hand, and planning on the other—were alternately the very secret of progress or the most basic explanation of backwardness. The very idea of a revolution in Ethiopia demanded a rejection of Haile Selassie's government as an ancien régime—as, in fact, the cause of past backwardness. In the context of the time, a rejection of Haile Selassie meant also automatic pressure to reject capitalism and the United States —for the latter were intimately identified with Haile Selassie's rule.[47] One step further in the syllogism of modernist discourse in the 1970s, a rejection of capitalism meant ipso facto a spontaneous pressure to embrace socialism. It was this set of modernist discursive pressures that had affected the dreams of many of Ethiopia's educated elite, and it was these dreams that the Derg stole.

Having rejected traditional Chinese intellectual and political values, the intellectuals still looked to the West for guidance, but they now began to look more to Western socialist theories, which were themselves critical of the West as it was. . . . It was from this new political and intellectual environment created in the wake of the May Fourth incident that a portion of the Chinese intelligentsia began to turn to the example of the Russian Revolution and the Marxist promise of worldwide revolutionary transformation. . . . Marxism was seen as the most advanced intellectual product of the modern West, but one that rejected the Western world in its capitalist form and its imperialist relationship with China.[48]

There were, of course, many Ethiopians who favored some midpoint between unrestrained capitalism and Soviet socialism, but in the heat of revolutionary struggle, modernist discourse quickly lost contact with qualifying reality, and its binary logic took on an unhindered life of its own. All grays became shades of black or white. When the ventriloquist Derg began to appropriate the voice of its opponents, that voice came to speak in increasingly rigid Marxist phrases. A whole new vocabulary was created; the Amharic language itself was changed, along with the stories and patterns of meaning that motivated revolutionary action. According to the *Teramaj mezgebe-ḳalat* (Progressive Dictionary) published in Amharic in 1976—the second year of the Ethiopian revolution—words were "like guns and ammunition" for the masses.[49]

Every revolution creates new words. The Chinese Revolution created a whole new vocabulary. A most important word in this vocabulary was fanshen. Literally, it means "to turn the body," or "to turn over." To China's hundreds of millions of landless and land-poor peasants it meant to stand up, to throw off the landlord yoke, to gain land, stock, implements, and houses. But it meant much more than this. It meant to throw off superstition and study science, to abolish "word blindness" and learn to read, to cease considering women as chattels and establish equality between the sexes, to do away with appointed village magistrates and replace them with elected councils. It meant to enter a new world.[50]

With blood on its hands from the executions of November 1974, the Derg could not embrace liberal values that would call their murders into question. They had, in some way, to reach out to their opponents on the left. The first statement of its policy came in December. "Ethiopia First!" (*Ityopia tikdim*) had been a slogan of the revolution since June. On 20 December, the Derg published a ten-point program explaining the "philosophy" of Ethiopia First. Its statement emphasized themes of equality, self-reliance, the indivisibility of the nation, state control of the economy, and the elimination of landlordism.[51]

A homespun socialism allied with nationalism, or perhaps more accurately, a kind of Ethiopian communalism, not unlike the so-called African socialism of Tanzania in the 1970s, this political program was hardly Marxist-Leninist. But in the context of the time, it struck distinctly new themes for Ethiopian society, and it placed the Derg to the left of most civilian groups at the time: that is, in the position required to be seen as leading the nation in the modernist socialist narrative.

The notion of equality was as revolutionary in deeply class- and status-conscious Ethiopia as it had been in 18th and 19th century revolutionary Europe. Self-reliance was also a singular innovation in a society where begging is pervasive and carries little stigma, and where the patron-client relation is central is social relations. . . . But perhaps the most important new idea of Ethiopian socialism was that the common good was to take precedence over individual, ethnic, or regional interest.[52]

On 1 January 1975, the government nationalized all financial institutions, and on 3 February, took over seventy-two private enterprises, including all the major foreign-owned companies. According to Andargachew, it was not economic motives but "the desire to be seen to be progressive in the eyes of the leftists and win them over to its side" that propelled the Derg's nationalizations.[53] In any case, because the capitalist sector of the economy was minuscule, these changes had little impact on wider class relations. To this point, a change in political regime had taken place in Ethiopia, but little had occurred to transform the basic structures of power and privilege.

THE DERG INITIATES A REVOLUTION

In Proclamation 31 on 4 March 1975, the Derg amazed even the most radical of Ethiopian leftists by decreeing a sweeping land reform. All rural land was nationalized. Previous owners would receive no compensation. Every peasant family was to be given access to a plot of no more than ten hectares—but only if they themselves farmed the land. Rural wage labor was made illegal, and peasant associations, with locally elected officials, were to be organized to oversee the distribution of land and to undertake local administration and development. The prologue to the reform carefully spelled out the revolutionary implications of the act in terms that reverberated with the French revolution's *Liberté, Egalité, Fraternité:* "It is essential to fundamentally alter the agrarian relations so that the Ethiopian peasant masses which have paid so much in sweat as in blood to maintain an extravagant feudal class may be liberated from age-old feudal oppression, injustice, poverty, and disease, and in order to lay the basis upon which all Ethiopians may henceforth live in equality, freedom, and fraternity."[54]

In analyzing the Ethiopian revolution, it is essential to understand just how little the land proclamation responded to peasants' own agitations and how much it owed to Ethiopian modernism—that is, to the intelligentsia's image of their society as "feudal," as a type of society that Europe and the developed West had left behind centuries ago:[55]

> The conviction that the major constraint on development in Ethiopia lay in its "feudal" land tenure system was deeply rooted among college students by the late 1950s. From there it was spread by a generation of college graduates to all circles in Ethiopia's nascent educated elite. The students' slogan, "land to the tiller," was echoed in the reform program announced by the leaders of the abortive military coup of 1960. [Haile Selassie's] government responded to the growing demand for land reform by appointing a Land Reform Committee, which was later transformed into a Land Reform and Development Authority and finally, in 1966, into the Ministry of Land Reform and Administration (MLRA).[56]

It was functionaries in Haile Selassie's old Ministry who drew up the Derg's land reform in late 1974. Educated—often in the West, many at the USAID-funded University of Wisconsin Land Tenure Center— young radicals in the Ministry did what Ethiopian intellectuals had dreamed about for decades. They designed Ethiopia Modern.[57]

The measures that the Derg eventually adopted went well beyond what most Ethiopians—even the most radical—hoped for at the time. Apparently, the advice that the committee had received with respect to land reform had been considerably more moderate, even that from the Chinese and Soviet embassies.[58] The announcement of the reform set off rumblings within the military itself, for many soldiers owned land, this having been one of the principal ways that the Emperor had rewarded followers. It took several days of meetings before the radical faction of the Derg prevailed and, finally, the proclamation could be printed in the government's official journal.[59]

In many respects, the design of the reform made brilliant sense in the Ethiopian context. Anything less sweeping would have been administratively impossible to carry out. The state did not possess the resources or the personnel to measure and redistribute land according to some agreed-upon formula. In the past, Haile Selassie's government had depended upon landowners for local administration; indeed, at the community level, landlords *were* the state. Without a cadre of new state agents, these lords could hardly be expected to carry out a reform that undermined their own interests. In this context, to abolish the very concept of private land ownership and to make redistribution a matter for the new peasant associations was a radical stroke.

Besides making administrative sense, the reform also had a strong political rationale, for it immediately won over at least part of the intellectual left to the Derg. Through their support, students in particular would provide the means for organizing the peasant associations that would be required for the land reform to be put into effect. Shortly after the February days, students themselves had proposed that the university be closed and that they be allowed to go out into the countryside to assist in famine relief and to teach peasants how to read and write. In September, just before it deposed Haile Selassie, the Derg seized upon this idea and made it mandatory for all students and teachers in the last two years of high school and in all levels of the university. In doing so, the military committee apparently hoped to remove the intelligentsia from the capital and hence from the center of Ethiopian politics.

Grandly titled (in English) the Development through Cooperation, Enlightenment, and Work Campaign,[60] the operation was conceived with a potent mix of military and modernist metaphors. The Amharic word for campaign, *zemecha,* perhaps even more than its counterpart in English, retained strong military associations. In the nineteenth century, "zemecha" was the word used to designate military crusades into the south to conquer new peoples and to expand the borders of the Ethiopian empire. The students, dressed in khaki uniforms and caps with zemecha insignia, would be sent, like an army, to reconquer the countryside. But they would do so, this time, not with force, but with knowledge, *eukat.* According to an official statement of the campaign, "For centuries the people in general and the rulers in particular have lived with out-moded beliefs. . . . These dividing ideas worked against progress and enlightenment."[61] It would be the students who would bring progress and enlightenment to the countryside. They would "teach reading, writing, hygiene, and basic agriculture; instill the principle of self-reliance; rid Ethiopians of the spirit of individualism and teach them to strive for the common good; conduct research and gather data."[62]

Backed by threats that no student or teacher who refused to participate in the zemecha would be allowed to work in the new Ethiopia, the government managed to inaugurate the campaign on 21 December 1974, a day after the announcement of the philosophy of Ethiopia First. At first reluctant, many of the students became enthusiastic supporters of the Derg after the announcement of the land reform in March:

Many of those who, a few weeks earlier, had been shouting "Down with the fascist Derg!" enrolled sincerely, even enthusiastically; students broke through the security marshals controlling the march [in celebration of the

Figure 4. Zemecha students marching in Addis Ababa, 1975. Press photograph, Archives, Institute of Ethiopian Studies, Addis Ababa University.

land reform] to go and embrace Mengistu. In the months that followed, thousands of zemachs were to leave their parents in tears to climb into the buses which would take them to carry the revolution into the depths of the countryside.[63]

In the event, approximately fifty thousand students and teachers were sent to almost four hundred stations around the country.[64] The presence of the zemecha created a distinctly new space for peasant insurrection. Until the announcement of land reform, the revolution had been an entirely urban affair—one concentrated in the capital Addis Ababa. After the fall of Haile Selassie, peasants in some areas had refused to pay rents, expelled landlords, and, in a few cases, destroyed farm machinery.[65] But such incidents had been few and had been, in fact, suppressed by the Derg.[66]

The announcement of the land reform and, more important, the organization of the student campaign effectively extended the revolution to the countryside. According to Christopher Clapham, "It is this extension, more than events in Addis Ababa no matter how violent or spectacular, which places Ethiopia firmly in the category of revolutionary states."[67]

THE REVOLUTION ARRIVES IN THE COUNTRYSIDE

The reaction of the rural population varied from region to region and from class to class. In general, peasants in the northern highlands from the Semitic-speaking heart of the old Abyssinian empire saw little to be gained from the reform. In those areas, the great majority of peasants already had customary rights to land, and tenancy was limited. Moreover, there was no ethnic difference between peasants and lords, and indeed there had been a fair degree of mobility across strata so that peasants had some basis on which to identify with local rural elites. According to one Amhara elder interviewed at the time:

> When I heard about land reform, I thought, "that will be good for the southern provinces, but here we don't need it—we already have our own land." Then the students came and called a meeting. No one went. They came again, by appointment, on another day. They told us that we would have to plow our land together and share the crops. They read out a list of names . . . and told us we would have to tell them how many oxen each of us had. They went away and never came back.[68]

If northern peasants were at most neutral toward the rural revolution, northern lords stood to lose everything.[69] Some of the great ones, like *ras* Mengesha Seyoum of Tigray, had already gone into rebellion after the November 1974 killings. With the March 1975 reform, this opposition crystallized into the Ethiopian Democratic Union (EDU). Led by noblemen like Mengesha, the EDU was not able, finally, to mobilize peasant support, and after 1977, it no longer posed any real threat to the Derg.[70] "In many parts of the country, and especially the north, noblemen and landlords simply took to the hills with bands of retainers, in unorganized resistance to the new order. Newspapers of the period regularly report the 'liquidation' of reactionaries or bandits, sometimes up to several hundred of them at a time. . . . Most of this round of killings was over by 1978."[71]

If the response of northern peasants was tepid, that of southern ones secured the revolution. In the late nineteenth century, the Ethiopian empire, under Emperor Menelik, had expanded its territory southward by more than half. In the conquered territories, an exploitative system of land tenure had been instituted, in which many northern soldiers, *neftenya*, literally, "gun men," had been made local lords. Some conquered chiefs were also given land, but peasants in the south had far fewer reasons than their northern counterparts to identify with rural elites—who, more often than not, were from different ethnic, as well as religious backgrounds. Given the coincidence of class with ethnic cleavages, the south became a revolutionary tinderbox. Indeed, the support given to the Derg by southern peasants was one of the secrets of its survival over the first years:

> For three months, the zemachs from the urban centres, beginning with all those who had come from the capital, had been chafing at the bit. When the Land Reform Proclamation of 4 March threw them into the fray, their ardour was multiplied tenfold. Coming out of their encampments, they discovered the incredible misery of the Ethiopian countryside. . . . The local administration had no idea what to do, or locked itself up in glacial hostility. The capital was far away, very far away. The shock of the zemachs confronted with this misery, their giddiness at the immensity of their power and their rather missionary militancy came together with the impatience of the tenants. The alliance between peasants and zemachs came about in the first place to hunt out landlords. The few months following the Land Reform Proclamation were to be the most chaotic and the bloodiest of the revolution in the south.[72]

After a second proclamation that nationalized urban land and rental houses in July 1975, the alliance between the Derg, parts of the intelligentsia, southern peasants, and the urban poor had accomplished a sweeping change: Landlords had been removed from the Ethiopian political economy. Ownership of land, urban and rural, could no longer underpin the stratification of persons into classes.

If a combination of political actors had emerged that would carry out a revolution in Ethiopia, it was by no means an unconflicted group. In a few areas of the south such as Welaita, the land reform was interpreted by local peoples as a chance to reestablish local autonomy and to expel all "northerners":

> A dispute between a tenant coffee farmer—Amhara—and a zemach gave Solomon Wada [the leader of the zemecha in Welaita and a Welaita himself] the opportunity to seize the arms from these "strangers" who were for the most part rich Amhara traders. Incidents occurred. Alerted, 60,000 peasants, it is said, came crowding into the town [Soddo]. The temperature rose. They attacked and looted the houses of the city-dwellers [most of whom were "Amhara"]. It was a night of disturbances and revelry. In the midst of all this, two lorries crammed with soldiers arrived: they set up a regular house-to-house search to take back all the weapons and confined the zemachs to their camp. Solomon Wada, arrested a few weeks later, was executed at Addis Ababa for "attempting to disturb the Ethiopian revolution."[73]

Any attempt to politicize ethnicity quickly fractured the coalition between the Derg and southern peasants, and it was invariably met with force. After all, the redemption of the nation and national unity were the first principles that guided the radical wing of the Derg.

Despite the military's commitment to unity, the very logic of the revolution, its attack on a system of class relations—that were inextricably bound up with ethnic identifications in the south—encouraged the opposite. "Paradoxically, the military exacerbated ethnic feelings by seeking to put all ethnic and religious groups on an equal footing. Ethnic consciousness blossomed, and the government was soon talking about the 'nationalities problem' and discussing means to solve it."[74]

The events in Welaita provided one scenario. In other places in the south, the zemecha students found not support but fierce opposition from peasants. Most of the students came to the south not only with a superiority born of modern education but with the traditional contempt of Orthodox Christian believers for so-called pagans. The mixture of these sentiments made southern chiefs, who typically occupied religious as well as political roles, appear to the zemachs as especially egregious figures who oppressed their followers through superstitious beliefs. In Kefa, such attitudes led to a bloody confrontation between students and peasants:

> The student campaigners, encountering little serious opposition from the northern landlords in Keffa, turned their attacks on the traditional unofficial Keffa authorities. In an act of calculated effrontery the semi-divine and normally secluded *geramanja* was unceremoniously paraded in the streets of a provincial town. Later a group of students visited his compound, where they were feasted by his followers. Just what happened is not clear, but several accounts agree that the students deliberately desecrated the *geramanja*'s sacred eating utensils and, after dinner, seated a low-caste *manjo* on his special horse. The outraged followers of the *geramanja* waited until the students had assembled in a school building in the neighborhood. The building was surrounded and put to the torch. According to reports, which could not be cross-checked, all the students died in the blaze or were shot as they fled.[75]

Finally, in a great many other areas, it was not ethnic identifications that split revolutionary actors so much as political visions of the revolution itself. Above all else, the Derg wanted a process of land reform that it controlled from above, even if it meant continuing the support of local state agents, especially policemen. In contrast, zemecha students often attempted to arrest and disarm policemen who had been allied with local landlords. Such actions were required, many in the campaign believed, for a true revolution to take place, one organized by people from below, from the grass roots:

Student revolutionaries had their own vision of the new rural order, which included immediate implementation of collective farming, equality of the sexes, elimination of traditional authorities, and suppression of the rich and moderately wealthy peasant class. Their vision, of course, blithely disregarded the fact that even China had taken decades—and numerous carefully planned campaigns—to organize rural society. Nevertheless, students, carrying Mao's Little Red Book, would lecture peasants on class struggle and the necessity for collective farming, while peasant association leaders kept asking where they would get the oxen urgently needed for plowing and when fertilizer would be delivered.[76]

By the summer of 1975, the Derg once again found itself in opposition with radical intellectuals, particularly those in the zemecha campaign. By the fall, many student campaigners had been arrested by the Derg and confined for periods to their quarters. In response, many zemachs had grown bitterly disillusioned with the military government, had deserted and returned illegally to Addis Ababa. By the end of the year, only an estimated eighteen thousand of the original fifty thousand campaigners remained at their posts.[77]

> The whole zemecha project had in part rebounded against those who had promoted it. The plan for dissolving the student opposition by spreading it around the countryside and removing it from the capital had failed. The shared experiences, the discovery of a world that most of them were quite unaware of, their clashes with the new regime, had united the zemachs in their opposition to the Derg, strengthened and confirmed their conviction that they embodied the salvation of the revolution, and brought them to agree on their language and their analysis. . . . the zemecha, far from signalling the decline of the student opposition, gave it the opportunity to reappear much more determined, war-hardened and coordinated.[78]

Toward the end of 1975, many of these war-hardened students poured into the Marxist-Leninist political parties being organized in Addis Ababa, the first such parties in Ethiopian history. But as they did so, they left behind a revolution in the countryside. Nearly everywhere, landlords had been eliminated and peasant cooperatives organized.

According to Theda Skocpol, the defining feature of social revolutions, what makes revolutions, is the coincidence of two basic changes: in the way the state is organized, on the one hand, and in the means by which social inequality is structured and legitimated, on the other.[79] In revolutions, these two transformations take place coincidentally and interactively through political upheaval and class conflict. "A revolution marks a fundamental and irreversible change in the organisation of a society;

the destruction, often rapid and violent, of a previous form of social and political organisation, together with the myths which sustained it and the ruling groups which it sustained, and their replacement by a new institutional order, sustained by new myths and sustaining new rulers."[80] By September 1975, the first anniversary of Haile Selassie's fall, it was clear that a genuine revolution had commenced. The Derg had captured the state. The previous system of class relations based on land ownership had been upturned. And old myths and founding charters no longer made much sense.

But it is, perhaps, altogether too easy and ultimately misleading to speak in such summary, abstract phrases. What the Ethiopian revolution actually entailed was a countlessly repeated uprooting of social relations, in thousands of local communities, in millions of lives. These micro-processes—for some people unthinkably dreadful, for others millennially hopeful, for still others (probably by far the majority) their emotions determined by distinctly local concerns and parochial issues—all this means that the Ethiopian revolution is hardly a unitary entity. In order to convey more of its essential heterogeneity, the following chapter turns from the political center of Addis Ababa to a locale in the far south, Maale.

CHAPTER 2

Revolution within a Revolution

Divine Kings and
Zemecha Students in Maale

Despite all their claims to represent "the people," revolutionaries—those self-consciously committed to the creation of a new social order—are minority actors in any social revolution. As Samuel Huntington pointed out some time ago, successful revolutions couple the actions of a revolutionary intelligentsia—usually drawn from an alienated urban middle class—with the rebellion of other actors—typically peasants. "By themselves . . . opposition groups within the city can unseat governments but they cannot create a revolution. That requires the active participation of rural groups."[1]

The difficulty is that rural people typically live in different cultural worlds than urban revolutionaries, and, as James Scott argued, they consequently rebel for different reasons:

> The radical intelligentsia, at least initially, is often as culturally distant, if not more distant, from the peasantry than the dominant elites whom they wish to replace. In structural terms as well, their place in the "hierarchy" of revolution, embodying as it does a national and formal ideological perspective as opposed to the local and more concrete perspective of a peasantry, is bound to create systematic differences in interest. The result is likely to be a kind of stratification of issues: some of which are almost exclusively the concern of the radical elites, some of which are shared, and some of which are almost exclusively peasant concerns.[2]

The coupling, then, of the actions of an urban intelligentsia with the deeds of a rebellious peasantry makes the phenomenon we call "revolution" a complexly layered affair—more often than not dependent on unexpected and ironic couplings.

For the analyst, it is difficult to retrieve this heterogeneity, since most successful revolutionary groups immediately act to repress its memory. This occurs, as the beginning of the previous chapter suggested, when newly powerful actors create the stories that legitimize their position, that give meaning to new social arrangements, and that justify the bloodshed of the revolutionary struggle. If not actively suppressed, the memory of heterodox elements (such as the peasant who rebels for the "wrong" reasons) is given no official way of preserving itself. As the new order consolidates, the revolution inevitably tends toward one story.

In this chapter and the next, I attempt to undercut this tendency by turning from the events in Addis Ababa to those in Maale. There, actors were less concerned with nationalism or with Ethiopia's place in an international world of power and wealth, still less with abstract social theories such as Marxism. As Eric Wolf noted some time ago, "Transcendental ideological issues appear only in very prosaic guise in the villages."[3] This is not to say, of course, that the Maale or other peasants like them were unaffected by revolutionary events; as I shall show, they certainly were. Given their own context, some Maale enthusiastically participated in the revolution as it occurred locally, and none—at least initially—actively opposed it. What factors account for this "revolution within the revolution"?[4]

THE *ANCIEN RÉGIME* IN MAALE

To begin, let me sketch the outlines of prerevolutionary Maale political history. The Maale are a small ethnic group, probably about 25,000 at the time of the revolution, who live at the southern edge of the Ethiopian high plateau. In the nineteenth century Maale, and indeed all of what is now southern Ethiopia, was independent of the north and consisted of a mosaic of chiefdoms and kingdoms. As Map 3 shows, the rugged mountains in the center of the country and the river Woito that curled around Maale territory were critical geographical features.

Given this topography, most Maale lived their lives within one of four regions. At the center there was a highland valley core, region 2 (wetter and therefore favored horticulturally), surrounded by three lower and dryer peripheral valley systems, 1, 3, and 4 (split between Maale on one side and surrounding ethnic groups on the other). Most Maale found their most significant social relationships, married and interacted with kinsmen, contracted bond friendships and so forth, within the boundaries of the region (sometimes across ethnic boundaries).

This last assertion about social space does not rest on Maale cultural categories. That is, people in region 2 did not share a common identity vis-à-vis others; each region was instead divided into a number of different chiefdoms—the culturally appropriate units for local Maale. What *was* culturally encoded was the hierarchical relation among chiefdoms (and by implication, what I am calling regions). One, namely the chiefdom of Bala, dominated the others—it was higher.[5]

It was in Bala that the ritual king of Maale lived. A figure not unlike Sir James Frazer's divine king, the *kati* maintained the fertility and prosperity of the country in all its aspects—the ripening of crops, the fecundity of women, the reproduction of cattle and goats—through sacrifices and invocations to his ancestors, the past kings.[6]

In the nineteenth century, then, Maale life, fragmented and compartmentalized as it was, focused on region 2. It was there that all Maale traveled at times to present labor tribute to the king, there that chiefs and important elders carried out rituals for the whole country. It was there also that people from drier areas regularly exchanged cattle for grain, there that Maale sometimes retreated when relations with surrounding ethnic groups turned to fighting.

At the end of the nineteenth century, this organization of space began to change as Maale and all of what is now southern Ethiopia were conquered and incorporated into the expanding Ethiopian empire, dominated by the Amhara of Shewa. Because imperial Ethiopia had few resources with which to penetrate and control local society in the south, it had to depend upon a policy of indirect rule in many areas. Consequently, over the early twentieth century, Maale kings and chiefs were maintained in their positions and made local representatives of the imperial state. As long as a minimal degree of order was maintained and a modest amount in taxes exacted, the empire was content to leave local affairs in local hands. By mid-century, Haile Selassie, Emperor of Ethiopia, was seen by most Maale as a kind of distant divine king, in the image of their own kingship.

On the eve of the revolution, then, Maale continued to be presided over by twelve chiefs and a ritual king. In fact, the king had recently died, and his body was preserved in a sacred grove until a successor could be installed. His teenaged son functioned politically as the head of Maale, but during the interregnum, the dead king was said still to be king. His

Figure 5. Dulbo Tolba, heir apparent to the Maale kingship, on his mule, Bala, 1974. Photograph taken by the author.

bones protected Maale and ensured the rains and the fertility of the country.

As the revolution began to unfold in Addis Ababa during early 1974, many Maale were aware of the upset conditions in their country. The event that signaled to the Maale the possible beginning of a new era, however, was the arrest of Haile Selassie in September. Who could imagine arresting a kati? Radios were not plentiful in Maaleland (a few educated, Christian Maale possessed radios, a higher portion of northern settlers and market villagers), but news of the Emperor's arrest immediately spread throughout the country, diffusing a note of uncertainty to local political relationships.

In less than two months, an unusual coalition of the locally disaffected had formed, including evangelical Christian converts mostly from Koibe (who, of course, rejected Maale religion) and traditionalists from southern Maaleland (tired of increasing demands for tribute from a northern landlord, Danyi, and from their own Maale chief, Artamu).[7] Timidly, as if testing the revolutionary waters, this group brought a court case against the heir apparent to the kingship, Dulbo, the richest Maale chief, Artamu, and various northern landlords living in Maaleland. This group of influential men were accused of "oppression." The Amharic word for oppressor, *aķorķwaj* (literally, a person or object that presses down, like the load on a donkey's back), had been adopted into the Maale vocabulary only a few months before from radio broadcasts from Addis Ababa.[8] Many Maale did not know quite what the word meant or how to pronounce it, but the leaders of the accusers had quickly realized its value as a weapon in the developing atmosphere of late 1974.

Among the instigators of the opposition was, ironically, a son of chief Artamu himself. When asked to explain why he participated in the accusation of his own father, the son replied:

> The reason that I thought to bring the accusation was that my father was richer than anybody in Maale. When an Amhara came, he would give him a hundred and twenty cows. But he gave us [me and my full brothers] none. He purchased guns. But he gave all of them to the children of Gwiye's mother [his half-brothers]. He refused to let us drink milk. Even though my father had many things, he didn't feed us. . . . The cattle we as boys had herded he took away. The gun that we used in herding he took away. After all this, when the Derg's law had really come, we wrote to the meeting [in Koibe].[9]

The formal accusation by this unusual coalition (otherwise, Maale traditionalists had little good to say about Maale Christians) was signed by forty-four men:

> Our accusation is as follows: During the time Haile Selassie was Emperor of Ethiopia, there were great and rich people who lived everywhere. These were the *balabbat, çhiķashum,* and *grazmach* appointed by Haile Selassie. Most of these people did us much damage: (1) A balabbat who lives in Maale and name is Dulbo Tolba has done many bad deeds at market and elsewhere. When we bring our things to market to sell them, he forces us to sell to him at very low prices. Because we are poor people, we sell in the market in order to earn money. But he disturbs the market and makes the country poor by buying something worth five dollars for two, something worth ten dollars for five. If someone protests about the price, he is sent away from the market, and the thing is simply taken from him.
>
> In addition, there were Maale who had been paying land taxes since 1950. He took those fields for himself and his relatives and some Amhara living in Maale. He talked with the çhiķashum, Artamu Shinke, and the two of them together instigated quarrels among the people about these lands.
>
> Since Dulbo and Artamu hold the positions of balabbat and çhiķashum, they force the people to elect members of their own families to government committees. The people would like to elect someone else but they cannot.
>
> (2) Amhara in Maale and their misdeed: Mr. Manakule Sime took land from six Maale landowners who had been paying their taxes since 1950. As a result the people whose land had been taken away went repeatedly to court, shouting and waving their deeds in their hands. But Mr. Manakule divided each of the plots into two parts. He took half for himself and sold the

other to rich Amhara living in Maale. Because of this, everyone quarrels with everyone else.

In addition, Mr. Manakule disturbed the land by telling a lie. He said, "There is a new kind of deed which the government has given to landlords." If that were true, it should have come to all Ethiopian landlords. Since it has not, we are protesting to the court so that the previous Maale landowners can get their land back.

Besides Manakule Sime, there are other Amhara who are doing the same things. They are: (1) Mr. Danyi Dubale, (2) Mr. Taddesse Teferra, and (3) Mr. Dubaiye Danye.

(3) Finally, our balabbat, Mr. Dulbo Tolba, and our chikashum, Mr. Artamu Shinke talked with the new committee members in Maale and decided to collect money from everyone in Maaleland. They said that they would bring a new and special law for us. So they gathered about 8,000 Ethiopian dollars, but they did not do anything useful for us. They only bought things for themselves.

We also built two big grass-roofed houses in Maale so that our children, brothers, and sisters could go to school. But unknown persons burned the buildings at night. We went to our balabbat and chikashum and protested so they could look into the matter and find the culprits. But they refused to do anything, so we still do not have schools.

For all of these reasons, we are protesting to the court and requesting that these men be removed from the offices of balabbat, chikashum, and committee person.[10]

Written several months before the land reform was announced, this document reveals fundamental cleavages in Maale society. Not all of the Maale chiefs were accused of "oppression," only the two richest who had most forcefully used their positions to extract monies from their tenants. And of the northern settlers in Maaleland, only those who owned land were accused.

Judged by the standards of the urban intelligentsia at the time, the viewpoint of the Maale dissidents was no doubt parochial. They did not ask for the abolition of chiefship and kingship or indeed for the elimination of land ownership; they did not look forward to the creation of a "new" society but petitioned instead for the restoration of what they conceived was a previous moral order.

Nonetheless, what the court accusation requested—the replacement of local officials—was a significant departure from traditionalist Maale ideology. For traditionalists, kings and chiefs could not be removed (or installed) at will; they occupied their positions because, in a line of perfect connecting links from first sons of first sons, they and they alone had inherited the power to bless the land from the very first leaders in Maale—those who had brought fire and civilization.

From late November 1974, the case dragged on. At that point, judicial functionaries serving the state were almost all left over from Haile Selassie's government. To them, such a vague accusation must have looked suspect indeed. After all, by previous rights, landowners were entitled to "oppress." At first, the subprovincial court was reluctant to accept the accusation as a proper case, but a local representative of the Derg posted to Jinka intervened, and the case began. The district governor then asked the accusers themselves not to give testimony; only people not on the list but who had personally been harmed should be called. Again, it was only the Derg's representative who saved the case by insisting that the accusers themselves be allowed to give testimony. The result, finally, was that the court ordered the accused arrested and brought to Jinka.

In early December, Dulbo, the king's son, sent five large gourds of butter from Bala to Jinka; Bala people said that these would be used for bribes for court officials. By that time, Dulbo had moved from Bala, the traditional residence of Maale kings, to near Bushkoro, the police town in the west. There, he had apparently won the police to his side. According to Taddesse, one of the Christians leading the accusation:

> After we had given our testimony, the woreda [subdistrict] court ordered them arrested. But by the time we arrived back in Bushkoro, all of the police had taken Dulbo's side. They all refused to act. Perhaps he had given them bribes. How could we have seen? The police said, "Don't you people have anything better to do? Why don't you farm like everyone else? The Derg has encouraged everyone to farm. They haven't said that you should just bring court cases." [11]

In late December, two of the accusers, representing the group, pleaded to the Jinka court:

> Since we forty-four have accused them, everywhere we live and work and also where we sleep, they try to beat us. Sometimes we hear from others that they insult us. And sometimes they even insult us in person. We are afraid because they threaten us again and again. Therefore, the people whom we have accused should be caught and our affairs should be settled. In the meantime, our rights should be protected. [12]

Again, on 20 January 1975:

> Some of the people we have accused have said that if we do not deny the accusation and sign a letter to that effect, they will throw us out of our homes. Now they have forced many people to sign such a document, and some of the signers did not even understand what they were signing. In this way, they are trying to prevent the case from being heard. We are protesting so that the

court may guard our rights and these men will not damage us or our property. Ethiopia First![13]

As the case dragged on, additional witnesses were called and testimony taken, but the Maale lords were not brought to Jinka. Finally, Taddesse, exasperated, accused the Bushkoro police of not carrying out government orders, and a representative of the police station was recalled to Jinka. The *ancien régime* in Maale was coming under increasing pressure, but far from Jinka and far from the coercive power of the new government, the old elite still commanded formidable resources and influence in early 1975. By April, the stalemate in the local revolution was thoroughly destabilized by the announcement of the land reform—the abolition, without compensation, of all ownership of rural land. Government officials based in Jinka rarely came to Maale, but on 21 April, a new district governor came to Maale (Bushkoro) to explain the land reform. His speech, as it was translated from Amharic into Maale (and hence by me into English), began as follows:

> The reason that I am standing before you is that I want you to know a few things about the previous time, how the previous kati, the previous fathers of the country ruined your way of life. As you know, this land belonged to your fathers and your mothers. But the previous kati sold the land and you with it to wealthy people. The present government, because it realizes this is your land, is giving it back to you. For the previous landlords, you were working on Mondays and Tuesdays. You were collecting firewood. You were carrying water. Going beyond her own work, your wife was grinding corn for the landowner, making bread. You were cutting grass for his cattle. These were the ways that he made life difficult for you. In addition, if he saw a good cow or a good [castrated] goat or a good sheep at your house, he said, "Bring it to me." If you didn't let him have it, he evicted you from your house. But now, because you control this little land, there is no one who can evict you. A few landlords say that they will go to Addis Ababa and get this proclamation overturned. Unless the new government falls, they will not be able to change things. But if you do not unite as before, if you do not unite in strength, the previous landlords can still cause you trouble. If you really unite, like the gathering here, then the landlords will not be able to hurt you. If we become one, landlords will not be able to hurt us in the future.[14]

The governor went on to explain that all Maale families were now entitled to at least ten hectares of land, that the fertility of the land should be taken into account in the distribution (so that plots in areas of lower fertility would be larger), that wage labor was illegal, that renting out land was illegal (except for the elderly and the sick, widows and orphans), and that selling land was illegal. Finally, he added: "There are

Figure 6. The new awraja governor addressing the crowd through
a translator with a loudspeaker, Bushkoro, April 1975. Photograph taken by the author.

other things that we must do if Ethiopia is to mature. In the past, women
have had a disproportionate share of the work. Now men must help
them. In addition, men must stop wasting their money on drink. And
superstitious practices like praying to trees and stones, going to sooth-
sayers, and looking at intestines have been prevented under the law."[15]

Each new announcement by the revolutionary government created
new space for the dissatisfied in Maale. But even after the announcement of the land reform, Dulbo, Artamu, and the northern landlords

remained free. Like lords in other parts of the country, they began to congregate in the towns and at police posts—since their tenants were growing increasingly rebellious and the police generally remained sympathetic to the old ways of doing things.

Top-level squires and rural bullies fled for safety to Peking, Tientsin, Muken, Shanghai and even New York. Second-ranking gentlemen ran to such provincial towns as Taiyuan, Tsinan, Paoting, and Kaifeng. Those of third rank took refuge behind the thick fortress walls of county seats such as Anyang, Yungnien, Kalgan, and Tatung. Lesser fry, lacking the means to get away, threw themselves on the mercy of the newly-empowered Peasants' Associations and Village Congresses, and lived for the day when the Home Return Corps, organized in the cities by their fleeing brethren, would sally forth to wreak vengeance.[16]

THE ARRIVAL OF THE ZEMECHA STUDENTS IN MAALE

The arrival of the zemecha students in Maale in July 1975 decisively transformed the local balance of power. Without the appearance of the urban revolutionary intelligentsia, it is unlikely that there would have been a revolution in Maaleland at all. Once on the scene, however, the students created an atmosphere in which some Maale became willing to take matters into their own hands.

By April 1975, a large encampment of several hundred student campaigners had arrived in Jinka, and a month or so afterward, a contingent of approximately thirty had been posted to far western Maale, to Ashekere and Bushkoro. By early July, four of these campaigners arrived in Bala. The following account comes from my field notes of 8 July 1975:

Today, market day, for the first time, four zemecha students came to Bala. . . . The leader of the group—a smiling, self-assured, almost arrogant young man of about twenty—"lectured the people" as he said. But before doing so, he accosted me, smiling, moving close to my face, and accused me of being an American imperialist. He said that he knew that I was against the revolution and that I was opposed to Marxism. When it seemed that all he wanted to do was to denounce me, I became angry and walked away. But after I had gathered my wits, I went back and invited him to talk with me about my work. They evidently suspected me of being a CIA agent.

With Mao's red book in his hand, this handsome young man addressed the crowd at the market [in Amharic] in great oratorical style, with his voice raised and arms moving about. The students' principal mission he said was to organize farmers' cooperatives. The people should tell them, for instance, whether the chiefdoms of Bala and Irbo should become one association or two. The students would come again Saturday after next to hear the people's views and to establish the cooperative. . . . The lackeys of the kati and the

godas would not be admitted to the associations he said (at this murmurs of
approval from the Christians in the crowd). He also made the point that low-
castes such as potters and blacksmiths should not be discriminated against.
. . . And then he came to the climax: "Your real enemies are the kati and the
goda [these were the Maale words that the local Christian translator used for
the zemecha students' Amharic reference to balabbat and chikashum]. If
they try to take money from you, you catch them and bring them to the police. If they resist, then kill them!"

Incendiary words indeed, words that ignited, finally, a revolution in
Maale.

According to Eric Wolf's study of peasant revolutions, the principal
predictor of peasant rebelliousness is the local system of economic stratification.[17] Poor peasants and landless laborers are so dependent upon
local elites that typically they do not have the tactical space to rebel.
Similarly, rich peasants are often in alliance with external power holders, so they too are unlikely to act. In contrast, middle-level peasants
stand out. At once the most conservative culturally and the freest to ma-
neuver, middle peasants provide the impetus for uprising—in Barrington Moore's memorable phrase, the dynamite that blows apart the old
order. Any factor that increases tactical mobility reinforces peasants'
revolutionary potential, and, according to Wolf, one of the most important is peripheral location with regard to the state's coercive apparatus.

To preview what happened in Maale, let me summarize by saying
that it was exactly the opposite of the cases that Wolf examined. Not
simply class categories—poor, middle, and rich—but religious and ethnic ones—evangelical Christian, traditional Maale, and Orthodox Christian Amhara—correlated with the structure of local rebellion.[18] And it
was not those farthest from centers of state power that took up the revolutionary cause but, in fact, those nearest.

In order to explain why this was the case let me return to prerevolutionary Maale history and to two of its principal transformations during the twentieth century: first, the settlement of ethnically different,
"Amhara" landlords after the Ethiopian conquest, and, second, missionization by evangelical Christians that began in the 1960s. Each of
these processes was patterned across space, and each was involved in
structuring Maale rebellion.

After the incorporation of the south into Ethiopia in the 1890s, a military administrative center was established at a mountaintop garrison
called Bako, just to the west of Maale territory. As a consequence, the
spatial organization of local affairs began to change. In the nineteenth

century all Maale had, as it were, stood facing the center of the country (region 2), those farther away occupying more and more peripheral positions. By the twentieth century the political center on which Maale life focused had moved from the highlands of Maale to Bako. Now all Maale faced, as it were, westward. Region 1 formed the new core—foreign landlords settled there and replaced Maale chiefs as local notables. Separated only by the escarpment, region 1 enjoyed the easiest access to Bako. Region 2, the old core, sank to the role of new semi-periphery; there, the kati remained in power but subordinate to the imperial state. People in region 2 crossed the mountain pass into region 1 in order to reach Bako. Finally, regions 3 and 4 remained peripheries, with Maale chiefs still in charge. To reach Bako, inhabitants traveled through both regions 2 and 1 before they climbed the escarpment.

Gradually, over the twentieth century, an uneasy alliance between local Maale chiefs and Amhara landlords evolved, an alliance in which the Maale elite took on more and more of Amhara culture. Among Maale commoners, though, Amhara landlords—as compared with Maale chiefs and the king—were never seen as legitimate, and resentment against outsiders who demanded tribute and taxes accumulated in various ways. This accumulation was spatially defined; as we have seen, the settlement of Amhara landlords was itself mostly confined to region 1, the area nearest the military garrison at Bako. This patterning meant that ethnicity, a feeling of aggrieved Maaleness, was most available to be tapped by any revolutionary intelligentsia in precisely those areas nearest state power.[19]

Let me turn briefly to the process of missionization (Chapters 4 and 5 will take up this topic more fully). If the evangelization of Maale began "late"—the Sudan Interior Mission built a station in Bako in 1954—Christianity nevertheless played a key role in the Maale revolution. By the early 1960s, the mission station at Bako, sponsored by fundamentalist Protestants mainly in North America, worked with native evangelists from Welaita (a neighboring ethnic group in which the Church was already strong) to convert the Maale. Welaita evangelists taught a certain contempt for traditional ways—particularly for smoking, drinking, and Maale ritual—along with the value of working hard and getting ahead. They offered access to modern medicine at the mission station in Bako at a time when the imperial government provided none. And they offered access to schooling in Amharic, the national language, when there were no government schools in Maale.

Gradually, over the years, Christianity attracted converts in Maale.

And because the conversion process was supported from Bako, it too was played out over Maale space in a distinctive way. By 1974, knots of Christian converts were concentrated in region 1, the new core area nearest Bako, thinned out in region 2 (where conversion was actively and forcefully suppressed by the kati), and were almost nonexistent in peripheral regions 3 and 4.

As a group, Maale Christians were more educated and entrepreneurial than others. They were beginning to identify themselves as Ethiopians, rather than simply as Maale. They had come into collision with the Maale chiefs and king not only over religion—none of the Maale elite had converted—but also over land ownership.

Chafing against their economically and spiritually "backward" neighbors, Christians were primed to support almost any forward-looking social change in 1975. And that is exactly what they did. Maale Christians were the principal supporters of the zemecha students, and Christians overwhelmingly dominated the leadership of the new peasant cooperatives set up in region 1 and 2.

It is striking that the structure of the new cooperatives organized by the zemecha students was an almost exact replica of existing evangelical church organization in southern Ethiopia—down to the same Amharic names for offices. Churches in Maale already had youth associations and women's associations, as the new peasant associations would soon have. Church organization was presided over by elected chairmen, who represented local congregations to the next highest organizational level—again, the same pattern that peasant associations would adopt. Maale Christians already had experience in running these types of social arrangements. They were pre-adapted, as it were, to the revolutionary order.

The patterning across space of Christian communities in tandem with the configuration of ethnic resentments—and the concentration of zemecha students in region 1—gave the Maale rebellion its shape. In core region 1, Maale were the most revolutionary. By July, the kati's son and most of the northern landlords had placed themselves under the protection of the Bushkoro police. When the students demanded the arrest of the lords, the police refused: Who were young students to order about the duly constituted representatives of the government? But the students quickly organized the Maale around Bushkoro (many of whom owned rifles) to surround the police station. A gun battle ensued in which one Maale man died. The police finally had to surrender. Dulbo, Manakule, and Dubaiye were all arrested and put under armed guard. Hours later, the other principal northern landlord in Maale,

Danyi, was apprehended at his home by a female campaigner. The story of how a mere girl arrested the most powerful and feared northerner in Maale—one who kept known murderers for henchmen in his household—spread throughout the land, retold with much amazement and not a little laughter and celebration. Meanwhile, the Maale began to slaughter the landlord's cattle and to feast on the meat.

The gun battle and the arrests, apparently, did not immediately change the attitudes of the local elite. Dulbo, on seeing Taddesse sometime after his arrest, defiantly called out, "Taddesse, why don't you just use my skin for a belt? Why do you use cow leather?"

Taddesse answered, "Is a person's skin something to wear?"

"Don't you have the gun that you stole from the Baana?" Dulbo asked. "Why don't you sling it across your shoulder? Why are you coming with just a walking stick?"

"Should I have done so?"

When Taddesse sat down beside Dulbo, the latter stood up and walked away saying, "A balabbat cannot sit beside a tenant."[20]

Maale in region 2, as I shall describe in more detail below, peacefully supported the arrests of northerners but protested that of the Maale elite. After the zemecha students refused to listen to this protest, the office of the Maale kingship was abolished and replaced by a peasant cooperative presided over by a Christian. Finally, the transformation in peripheral regions 3 and 4 was quieter still. In the cooperatives set up there, elements of the old Maale chiefly elite, not Christians, managed to retain leadership roles.

THE CULTURAL REVOLUTION IN MAALE

If the local revolution was most violent in core region 1, it was most culturally significant in the old seat of Maale kings, region 2, where I resided. There, the effects of the arrests in Bushkoro—along with the arrival of the zemecha students in Bala—was electric.

Immediately after their first speech in the marketplace, the students were surrounded by Maale seeking redress for one grievance after another. First, a man from Gongode accused Ali, a merchant living in Bala market village, of not paying him the four dollars he had been promised for driving a cow from Gongode. After the students asked Ali about the matter, he paid up.

Another man accused Dore of embezzling six dollars that he was supposed to given to Alimaiyu. Alimaiyu had been cut above his eye at a funeral, and on the appointed day for hearing the case, Alimaiyu had sent Dore to escort the accused perpetrator to court. Instead of contesting the case, the accused had given Dore a goat and six dollars to give to Alimaiyu to beg forgiveness. Dore had given only the goat to Alimaiyu, keeping the six dollars for himself. Later, the man found out from Alimaiyu that his money had never been passed along. The students made Dore pay (after he had borrowed the six dollars from me).

Then Dore accused Silsa of taking his goat in order to become bond friends, *belli,* but Silsa had never returned anything. The students refused to hear this case since Dore had freely given the goat in the first place.

Then Dore was accused of preventing low-caste people from passing through his fields. When he refused to acknowledge any wrongdoing in a matter on which the students had just lectured—How, Dore asked, could he let a "crooked" person walk through his field?—he was arrested. Belief in caste, to the students, was not just a backward superstition, it was anti-revolutionary.

Dore's arrest encouraged yet another accusation against him. The previous year, Maja's fields had produced good crops while most of the surrounding ones had not. Dore went around saying that Maja had "speared" the rains (certain people are believed to have magical knowledge of how to prevent the rains from coming); finally, Dore went to Maja's house and took a sack of millet by force. When Maja recounted this story to the students, Dore's fate was sealed. He was taken off to Bushkoro (and allegedly later beaten).

This outpouring of long-suppressed grudges, the spectacle of nineteen-year-old students earnestly listening and judging the legitimacy of pent-up resentments of peasants twice their age, the retelling of wrongs in a cultural idiom that was entirely unfamiliar to the students—these scenes ushered in "the new beginning." Later, the new regime would remember this time in epic terms: the broad masses rose up and threw off the chains of feudal oppression. The reality in Maale, for all of its admitted drama and intensity, was considerably more mundane, shot through with parochial passions and local cultural concerns.

After the first appearance of the zemecha in Bala, the following Saturday, 12 July 1975, people from the chiefdoms of Bala and Irbo gathered on the their own to discuss the formation of the new peasant associations. Without the zemecha students present and without much discussion of whether there should be one or two cooperatives, the people divided into two groups and proceeded to select six nominees for the new offices. The Bala group immediately broke into factions over whether

Maja should be chosen; unable to come to any decision, one faction simply wrote up a list including Maja's name. The Irbo group, less fractious, selected six men, including Taddesse, the young Christian, who had taken the lead in the accusation against the king's son.

A week later, on Saturday, 19 July, six zemecha students returned on the appointed day in order to hold elections for the new peasant association. By that point, the students had realized that no self-respecting American spy would be living in such an out-of-the-way place, and one had even come to my house early in the day to interview *me* about Maale culture—the students were expected to make reports about local culture.

As the meeting got under way, Bala and Irbo people sat in two separate groups. After long speeches to each group ("Your women are exploited; you should help them with their work. Women are eligible to hold association offices. Previous officeholders and landlords should *not* be chosen as association leaders."), the students assembled the two groups and asked whether Bala and Irbo should be one or two cooperatives. "We think," they said, "they should be one." Largely because of the students' stand, the meeting acquiesced. Then, the campaigners asked for nominations for the six positions of the new association. According to my field notes:

> By that time, the crowd had grown restless from the long speeches, everyone began talking at once, and the whole thing broke up. Then the leader of the students got the papers with the names of nominees drawn up last week, read out the names, and asked people to raise their hands for the candidates they wanted. First, he called out Nuru's name, and when only a few people raised their hands, he said that Nuru had been defeated [before any of the other names had been called out]. Then Maja —he was elected. Then Taddesse—he was elected. . . . Then Lami Feta (a middle-aged Christian from Dukusho who had been involved in a long court case with [the dead king] Arbu and had won)—he was elected. Then the procedure changed. Dore Sulunge [freed by that point] stood up and nominated Nukuso Donse—and the group elected him (in his absence).[21]

At that point, the students advised the meeting that there should be some women chosen. Taddesse suggested the names of a Christian woman, Dirke, and a low-caste woman, Gufa. After a perfunctory showing of hands—not unlike Nuru's case in the beginning—the students announced that the women had been elected. There was a certain amount of laughter, jokes, and uneasiness about this result. The fact that not just a woman but a low-caste woman had been placed in a position of leadership upset all previous sense of local proportion.

In conclusion, the students themselves chose Taddesse as the chairman of the new association. Undoubtedly, his lead in the November accusation of the king's son made Taddesse seem the logical candidate to the students, plus Taddesse's fluency in Amharic.

The first act of the new peasant association, on the next day, Sunday, 20 July, sent shock waves through Maaleland. Dulbo had never been installed as kati. Preparations for the series of required rituals had, in fact, been started during mid-1974, but the events of the revolution had interrupted local planning. According to Maale tradition, Dulbo's dead father, Arbu, was still kati; his body lay above ground in a sacred grove called Dufa until his successor was installed. It was to Arbu that traditionalist Maale still brought tribute, through him that they still prayed to the royal ancestors for rain and fertility.

Christian converts, Taddesse and Lami, newly elected leaders of the cooperative, apparently told the zemecha students about these customs and about the fact that "Maale still brought cattle and goats to Dufa to feed the king." As the students later said, they decided "to sweep the house clean." After calling the *gojo*, the Maale official who presided over Dufa, and a local traditionalist elder to guide them, the students, along with a group of local Christians, entered the sacred grove and tore down the fence and gate around the house that contained Arbu's body. It was taboo for any foreigner or any Maale woman to enter Dufa. Previously, I myself had asked to attend sacrifices in Dufa and had been gently told that this was against Maale custom.

The week before, afraid of such an attempt, local elders had quickly gathered Arbu's bones from the bed on which they were laid and buried them inside the house. The campaigners discovered the freshly dug grave and exhumed the hollowed-out log that contained the kati's bones. After considering burning the bones, the students decided that the best ideological effect would be produced by requiring local elders to bury the bones the next day.

From Dufa, they proceeded to Dibo, where the sacred heirlooms of the past Maale kings were kept. In Maale custom, these valuables could only be displayed to the public (and then they were very dangerous for women) on the occasion of a kati's funeral and the simultaneous installation of his successor. Otherwise, for the rains to come, the king's heirlooms had to be kept hidden. Amazed, the students found ancient spears, six very heavy and large metal blades called *melmaite*, beads, a large number of cow bells, two iron walking sticks, a horn, knife, and fragments of an ancient and thickly walled pot. The students and the

Christians broke the shafts of the spears, loaded all of the royal treasury into gunny sacks and sent it to the marketplace.

Finally, the students and peasant association officials entered the most sacred place of all, the *tsozo*. There, a small structure housed a quiver that contained, according to the Maale elders, the tongues, penises, fingernails, and teeth of all past Maale kings. After taking the quiver out of its house and examining its contents, the students burned it in that most profane of places, the marketplace.

Most Sundays I tried to do something besides fieldwork, but toward the end of the day, I heard that the student campaigners had entered Dufa. When I arrived late on Sunday in the marketplace, one of the students pointed out a tooth taken from the quiver in Dibo on the ground that had not burned. It was in the marketplace also that I discovered the king's treasury—none of which I knew about before. The zemecha students excitedly talked about taking the melmaite to the local blacksmith to turn them into tools for the working people. This, they said, would make a wonderful symbol for the revolution. Ever the anthropologist, I suggested that knowledge of the past was also useful and that these items might be deposited in the museum in Addis Ababa rather than being destroyed. This course of action finally appealed to the students and association officials, and gunny sacks full of spears, cow bells, melmaite, and pot shards were later deposited in my house.[22]

On Monday, I witnessed the student campaigners preside over the unceremonial burial of the king's bones beside the path leading downward from Dufa. According to custom, the king's bones should have been buried on the highest mountain of the land, beside the graves of all the past kings of Maale, only on the day that one of his sons was installed as the new kati. Burying the king's bones "down," as in the case of an ordinary Maale person, instead of "up"—with no successor as kati—was the quintessential revolutionary act in Maale. As such, this event functioned semiotically as Maale's equivalent of the beheading of Louis XVI.[23]

It is doubtful that the students understood the full significance, in local cultural terms, of what they had done in those extraordinary three days. They were fighting against the "backward" superstitions of peasants only in a very general sense. But this was assuredly not the case with the Maale Christians who had guided and urged on the campaigners. Christians understood exactly what they were doing. As iconoclastic as revolutionaries anywhere, they saw their actions as the beginning of a new dispensation, when darkness would finally be pierced by a new light and people would no longer be oppressed by Maale kings and chiefs.

Figure 7a. Two of the
six *melmaite*

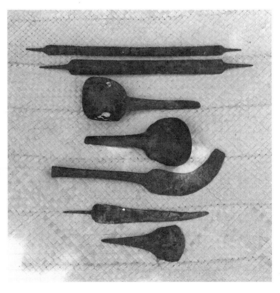

Figure 7b. Various
instruments

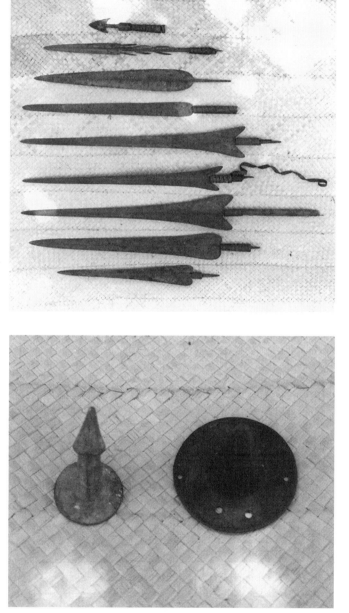

Figure 7c.
Spears

Figure 7d.
Phallic
ornaments

The execution was a solemn and extraordinary event. Under leaden January skies, a procession of sixty drummers and hundreds of guards, soldiers, and cavalry escorted Louis from the Temple prison across Paris to the Place de la Révolution. Guards brandishing bayonets and lances lined the way, forming walls of steel. Behind them, silent crowds watched. The king prayed with his priest as his carriage slowly made its way through the subdued streets. The silence that shrouded the city was broken only by the noise of horses and drums and by a few lone calls for mercy. Awaiting them at the Place de la Révolution (formerly Place Louis XV, today Place de la Concorde) stood the guillotine.

Since the dawn, an immense crowd had been gathering around the hideous machine. People were crammed everywhere: on the bridges, along the riverbanks, even hanging from the branches of trees. A sea of a hundred thousand heads was waiting to witness one head of state fall.

When the king arrived at the scaffold, three executioners attempted to undress him, but he angrily pushed them away, insisting on taking off his own jacket. Indignant that the executioners demanded to bind his hands, he vigorously protested. A struggle was about to ensue when Louis's priest advised him to submit to this last humiliation, which, he said, would draw him closer to Christ. Leaning on the priest for support, Louis arduously mounted the steep steps of the scaffold. At the top, he suddenly broke free, ran to the other side of the platform, and, making a gesture to silence the steady beat of the drums, cried out to the crowd:

"People! I die innocent! I forgive my enemies, and I pray God that the blood you spill will never fall on France . . ."

He wanted to continue, but General Santerre ordered a roll of the drums, and the king's speech was cut off, seconds before his head. His body was strapped to a board and then thrust horizontally into the inexorable apparatus. The board tipped down, the blade fell. Moments later, one of the executioners held the dripping head aloft for the crowd to behold. Many people shouted, "Vive la république!" A few drowned themselves or cut their own throats; for these people, a once finely ordered universe had been destroyed.[24]

On the following Saturday, 26 July, the campaigners returned to Bala for what would be a final time. In imperial Ethiopian custom, persons who were unable to obtain justice would sometimes lie prostrate before some great lord, placing dirt on their head, and crying out, "Abet. Abet. Abet." Hopefully moved by this display of abjectness, the lord would give justice. Deeply offended by the zemacha's desecration and adopting this decidedly nonrevolutionary stratagem, about forty traditionalist elders in Bala, along with two Muslim market villagers, lay before the students and begged that the kati's treasury and the kingship itself be given back to the people. According to my field notes:

Their spokesman was a dynamic, middle-aged man, Zirane, one of the leaders of the [newly organized] cooperative in [neighboring] Makana. Zirane began: "When you first came, we were happy, but now we are sad. We have just died. Our cows will not calve; our goats will not kid; our women will not have children; our fields will not ripen." After a minute of confusion, the students understood what the men were saying, and they asked everyone to sit down, and they proceeded to lecture the people: "Who are your enemies? I want you to think carefully. Before you assumed that [low-caste] blacksmiths and potters were your enemies—they are your relatives. Their work allows your living. Your real enemies are the tribute-takers, the landlords. And it is not just Amhara who have exploited you in this way. Now your kati's son, Dulbo, and your goda, Artamu, are in prison in Jinka. Know your enemies! Before you believed that your godas and kati brought rain. But that was just a trick. People are all the same; no one can cause it to rain; the rain comes when it comes. When you protest to us like this, you are saying in effect that you refuse the new law we bring, the new law that will free you from past oppression. And now you are asking us to restore the old oppressive system. We say sweep the whole house clean. This is what we want to teach you. We want to teach you about two classes of people—one the oppressor class, people like Danyi and Dulbo, the other class, people like you. The only way you can free yourselves of oppression is to unite, to become one. The government will not give you anything; you have to do this for yourselves. You say that your cattle will die. Then you need a veterinarian. With the proceeds from your cooperative field, you can support one. You say that you will be sick. Then you need a doctor. You say that it will not rain. Today, this day, it rained. We want you to think very carefully. How can you beg us to bring back your old and oppressive customs? Some of your traditions are good—the ways you work together in the fields. Those are the traditions you should cultivate." When the students finished, Zirane stood up again and almost as if he had not heard what the students said, he repeated, "We're finished. . . . But if this is what you say, then all right." At the end of the meeting, the Christians who were present clapped and seemed pleased. The protesters, meek, making no further objection, accepted the decision.[25]

By late August, Dulbo, Artamu, and all of the northern landlords in Maale had been imprisoned in Jinka. Only one relatively minor northerner would be allowed to return and live in Maaleland during the following decade and a half. When Danyi attempted to do so in the early 1980s, he was arrested by the local peasant association and expelled once again. Most of the evicted northerners settled in Jinka, where many already owned houses.

As far as the indigenous Maale elite was concerned, Artamu, already an elderly man, was soon to die. And Dulbo, a young man with an eighth-grade education, was lucky enough to obtain employment as a veterinary assistant in the next administrative region. He would not visit Maaleland again for the length of the revolutionary period. The other chiefs were not arrested but simply turned out of their administrative positions by the new cooperatives.

By August 1975, the zemecha students themselves were under arrest and confined to camp in Jinka. Reacting to "excesses" by campaigners in the south, the Derg quickly reasserted its control and re-empowered the local police. Over the next decades, new campaigners would come to Maale during school vacations to teach literacy and hygiene, but never again would they be allowed to politicize the peasants—to encourage them to take revolutionary destiny into their own hands.

Despite the brevity of the original zemecha campaign in Maale, it left behind a sweeping revolution. The power of the Maale elite, rooted not only in ritual cult but also in land ownership and local administration, was crushed. In its place, new peasant associations were organized. Viewed retrospectively, the July days were a crucial local turning point in Maale, a new beginning in which sixteen- and seventeen-year-old students from the north—sometimes clumsily, often with no small amount of condescension, and always with an enormous confidence in their mission—shoved Maale peasants onto the stage of Ethiopian history.

CHAPTER 3

Revolution as a Return to Tradition in Maale

The notion of modernity is inevitably shadowed by its opposite: tradition. Indeed, these two serve mutually to construct one another; the very notion of tradition takes its semantic weight from the contrast with modernity. So why was there no assertion of "tradition" in Maale as the revolution commenced? Why was there no counterrevolutionary impulse in 1975?

As I have already pointed out, peasants *did* fight back in a few parts of southern Ethiopia. Indeed, in Kefa they burned student campaigners alive. Why did Maale actors whom we might otherwise label as "traditionalists" acquiesce to the new order—at least initially?

To answer these questions requires a deeper archeology of the Maale past and, in particular, an examination of Maale notions of hierarchy among persons. Hierarchy, after all, was *the* concept targeted by revolutionaries. It was various sorts of hierarchy that Ethiopian intellectuals interpreted as "feudal." And it was the revolution that would replace feudal hierarchy by social equality.

By 1975, the Maale idea that certain persons, by birth, possessed the inherent power to bless and to curse others was by no means dead.[1] When Zirane pleaded with the zemecha students, "Without a king, our wives will not have children, our cattle will not calve, our goats not kid," such a concept lay behind his words. Only the kati could ensure fertility for Maaleland. And when an elder complained to me after the meeting, "What will we do without a king? Bees have a king. Cattle

59

have a leader. Without a king, we will kill each other off," the idea of a naturally given social hierarchy was even clearer.

It would be wrong, however, to assume that tradition was simply reproduced over the twentieth century in Maale. Tradition, like revolution, was always actively "made." Maale's placement within imperial Ethiopia at the end of the nineteenth century both preserved and challenged local concepts of hierarchy. These contradictory processes become especially clear in struggles over succession to the Maale kingship. After incorporation into Ethiopia, Maale kings not only acted as ritual figures internally, they served, as well, as functionaries in the imperial state.

In this chapter, I shall consider competing definitions of hierarchy in twentieth-century Maale, particularly as they are evidenced in the record of royal succession. This history conditioned how Maale initially understood the revolution. Given the interconnected events that I shall describe, many traditionalists in 1975 interpreted the arrest of the heir apparent as, in fact, a vindication of tradition, "real" tradition, which would prepare the way for a return to proper Maale custom.

ANCESTRAL HIERARCHIES IN MAALE

To understand nineteenth-century Maale notions of hierarchy, it is perhaps best to begin with kinship rather than kingship. The power that Maale kings were said to have, both to bless and to curse their people, was no different in kind, only in scope, from that of ordinary fathers and eldest brothers. Given this grounding, Maale ideas of hierarchy were reproduced (and transformed) not just in wider political processes but in the very bosom of families, where people lived much of their day-to-day lives.

According to Maale traditionalists in 1975, fathers and mothers, having contributed the very blood and bones of their offspring, had the power to affect the fate of their children. This power over well-being, which in the Maale scheme of things was synonymous with a power over fertility—the fertility of women, animals, and fields—was called *baliti,* literally, "forehead." When a father or a mother died, forehead, or fate, luck, power over wealth and good fortune, was transferred to the eldest son. In the climax of the funeral ceremony, the eldest son touched his forehead to that of his dead father three times, to that of his dead mother four times (the numbers three and four recur in Maale rituals with male and female associations, respectively).

This process of inheritance (only the eldest son was said to "inherit," *dakalane,* even if younger sons received some material wealth from their father) set up a recurrent inequality within male sibling sets. After the death of his father, the eldest son acted as a ritual father to his younger brothers. Only he could present first fruits to the ancestors; no one could partake of new crops or new honey or new milk until, first, the ancestors had been made to eat and drink of them, and, second, the eldest brother himself had done so. In other words, it was only through the eldest brother that dependents had access to the ancestors. And ancestors, like living fathers and mothers, retained the power to bless and curse their descendants. Their power over fertility, over forehead or fortune, was continuously (and unevenly) channeled to their sons—as long as proper hierarchies were maintained, as long as those who had gone before ate and drank before those who came afterward.

Expanded over time, this hierarchizing process within the family created internally ranked lineages. Eventually, the eldest brother made his younger brothers "go out." Younger brothers, with all of their material possessions, passed out of their father's cattle corral (in many Maale lineages, male ancestors were buried in the cattle corral), while the eldest brother stood by the gate with his right arm extended over the top. From that time forward, each younger brother presented first fruits to the ancestors—but only after the eldest had done so. Over time, a so-called conical clan was produced, in which each lineage member was either higher or lower in status depending upon his proximity to the trunk line of eldest sons of eldest sons. According to Maale, ancestral blessing, forehead or fortune, was channeled principally through the trunk line. As side branches of the lineage were created, their status and destiny declined.[2]

Of course, such ideas of proper hierarchy were rarely perfectly realized. As far back as can be traced, some Maale younger brothers resisted control by their eldest brothers. Indeed, the founders of many clans in Maale were described as younger brothers who came to Maaleland from surrounding ethnic groups in order to escape unjust exploitation by their eldest brother. In fact, the very first kati of Maale, Maaleka, was a youngest brother from neighboring Bussa.[3]

The actual creation (and recreation) of hierarchy was, then, never easy or automatic. It took social work. Be that as it may, the notion that *some* inherent hierarchy divided persons was an idea that was apparently difficult for Maale to escape. In order to resist the claims of a superior, a person had either to invert his opponent's definition of inequality or escape altogether to a foreign ritual field. The notion that

Figure 8. Constructing the entrance to Dulbo's lion house in preparation for installing him as king, Bala, late 1974. The revolution put an end to these preparations. Photograph taken by the author.

one could fight back as a "free and equal" individual became available in Maaleland only with the coming of evangelical Christianity in the early 1960s (see Chapter 4).

In any case, the hegemony of hierarchy—grounded in the power of ancestors to bless and curse—provides the background against which nineteenth-century Maale kingship can be understood. The kati occupied the still point that anchored the entire hierarchy.[4] Descended from the trunk line of all trunk lines, the kati, it seemed, was the person against whom every other male in Maaleland could be counted as a younger brother.

In actual fact, descent relations did not group Maale clans into one grand conical structure. Nonetheless, because royal ancestors were believed to possess the power to bless the whole land (not just their descendants), everyone was dependent upon the kati. When new crops ripened, no one in Maaleland could partake of them until the king had presented first fruits to his ancestors and eaten of them himself. Then, each of the thirteen chiefs in Maaleland did the same, followed by the subchiefs. Only then could local lineages commence their first-fruits rites—in the order specified by the ranking within lineages described above.

In the nineteenth century, then, politics and ritual were virtually the same thing. The quintessential way to proclaim social precedence was to perform the first-fruits rite before someone else; by doing so, a person claimed a closer position to the principal channel of fortune and forehead that descended from the ancestors. From local lineages to chiefdoms to the very center of politics at the kingship, ritual intensified, and the kati was required to carry out a Wagnerian cycle of rites that continued for most of his lifetime. (If he died before all rites were completed, the outstanding rituals were carried out before his bones were buried.) These included building a new "lion house" (an elaborate compound with a cattle corral to contain the *tsozo,* the quiver with the tongues and penises of all past kati), mock cattle raids against neighbors, the king's killing of a man purchased from afar so that the king became a *zia,* a "bull," the "bringing" of his wife, the cultivation of fields that only he could farm, and finally, the king's circumcision. All of these rites made the kati king and in doing so instituted and celebrated the Maale definition of precedence and hierarchy.

AMHARA CONCEPTS OVERLAID ON MAALE NOTIONS OF HIERARCHY

After the south was incorporated into the Ethiopian empire at the end of the nineteenth century, the Maale definition of hierarchy did not fit altogether easily with that held by the newly dominant Orthodox Christian northerners. When *ras* Wolde Giorgis's army reached the south in the mid-1890s, the Maale had recently been defeated and part of their territory occupied by the neighboring Baaka. In that context, the Maale did not oppose the northern army; instead, they allied themselves with the invaders—against the Baaka, who chose to resist. In the ensuing battle of spears against guns, the Baaka were cruelly defeated. A military garrison called Bako was established in Baaka territory. From that point on, the kings of Maale were subject to northern governors resident at Bako and at Bulki, another garrison farther north in Gofa territory.[5]

Shortly after the incorporation of Maale and its surroundings into imperial Ethiopia, the kati Girpe died in a smallpox epidemic. According to Maale tradition, Girpe succumbed because a northern soldier, Dembal, had made him transgress a royal taboo and look, face to face, at the Chief of Makana.[6] A period of unrest and general upset ensued. According to the incumbent of the chiefship of Makana in 1975:

After Girpe died, stealing and looting gripped the country. People climbed up *shabo* trees [especially tall] to hunt and kill others. After the country had been finished, after Kanti [the Makana chief at the time] had died, then Irbano began to cooperate with the Amhara, my father [Deozumbe] and Irbano together. Then gradually things got better. The few cattle that were still here calved. Goats kidded. Then people built houses and stayed in one place. Before, everybody had lived like baboons in the forest. Abandoning their granaries, their grinding stones inside houses, some people went with northern soldiers looking for buried pots of grain, tracking people's footprints. When they found a pot, they scrapped up the contents into a gourd and went back to the Amhara's place [Goddo] covering their tracks.[7]

With the country stricken by famine, disease, and looting, it is not clear from whence came the initiative for installing a new kati. Was it from the imperial administration? Or from the Maale themselves? In any case, because Girpe had no sons or brothers, the only way to maintain the royal succession as a series of perfect connecting links back to the first kati was to install the bones of Girpe's dead uncle, Maki—after which Maki's living son, Irbano, could be installed.

Irbano was installed as kati sometime in the first decade of the 1900s, but already the character of the Maale kingship had begun to change. In the nineteenth century, the kati had been a reclusive, primarily ritual figure who rarely left his lion house. By the time he was installed, Irbano was a well-traveled soldier; after obtaining a gun, he had joined northern armies and gone to conquer areas to the south of Maale. After he was installed, he made trips, apparently more than once, to the capital of the empire, Addis Ababa.

There were other ways in which Irbano was an innovative figure. Traditionally, a kati-to-be would have had no children before he was installed (if children had been born, they would have been smothered); in addition, he would have eaten no grain (the permitted starch for a kati-to-be was ensete, so-called false banana). Only after a certain point in the rituals of installation did a kati eat grain—and then only from special fields. On both counts, Irbano did not qualify as a proper candidate for the kingship. He had eaten an ordinary diet, and by the time he was installed, he had two children, including a son named Tonna.

Finally, in the nineteenth century, it was customary in royal installations for kings symbolically to create a transvestite, an *ashtime,* a biological male who became "female." The role was important in maintaining the lion house as a male preserve (ashtime provided much of the female labor there), a space that was therefore hierarchically superior to any ordinary Maale household. Irbano, perhaps as a result of his expe-

Figure 9. Bailosi (left), the last *ashtime* of Maale, Koibe, 1984.
Bailosi died in the early 1990s. Photograph taken by the author.

rience with Orthodox Christian northerners, discontinued this practice. Instead of tapping an ashtime on the back, he tapped a tree and proclaimed that the custom should be discontinued. Finally, Irbano did not complete the other rituals of kingship, including the culmination, his circumcision.

In these and other ways, particular aspects of what had constituted inequality in Maale fell away as imperial ideas began to overlay Maale ones, reinforcing certain features of local hierarchy, changing others. To northern soldiers and Orthodox Christian administrators in Bako and

Bulki, the Maale kati was a *balabbat,* in Amharic, literally, "one with a father," that is, a big man, above all, a landowner. And the twelve chiefs of Maale (by the early twentieth century, one chiefdom had been ceded to the Baaka) were chikashum, "mud chiefs," lower functionaries in the imperial state. It was through the balabbat and chikashums that the governors in Bako and Bulki ruled the Maale, through them, that he collected taxes and meted out a minimal level of justice.

Key to the imperial definition of legitimate hierarchy was the complex domain of land tenure. In the Amhara north, rights over land were basically of two types: *rist* gave peasants the hereditary right, through both fathers and mothers, of productive control over particular plots. The peasant owned his own field; he controlled production decisions. Superimposed upon such privileges was another called *gult*—the prerogative to collect tributes from rist-owners. Gult rights were usually not hereditary and were typically controlled by the Emperor at the center of politics. In the early twentieth century, gult rights were the principal means by which the Emperor supported state officials. With no salaries, local governors were sent "to eat" their respective provinces.[8]

The northern notion of what justified the inequality between gult lords and ordinary peasants was quite different from the Maale idea of the uneven distribution of ancestral forehead. To northerners, persons were not inherently different from one another; men were basically the same. What allocated persons to different roles was individual ties of clientage to powerful persons. With a little luck, any particular definition of hierarchy might well be reversed. But to Orthodox Christians, *someone* had to play the role of lord, otherwise, the inherently sinful nature of mankind meant that only chaos and the Devil would reign. Where the Maale notion of hierarchy drove its adherents to ritual involution, the northern one encouraged an explicit, rough-and-ready *real politik.* Given a better alternative, followers abandoned patrons and political factions reformed. It was this latter notion of politics that came increasingly to inform Maale struggles over succession.

After the incorporation of Maale into the Ethiopian empire, then, the chiefs and the king became gult holders. Because of their role in the state—not because of the rituals they performed for the fertility of the country—the Maale elite was given the right to exact tributes from peasants who lived on their lands. But the areas over which chiefs were granted such rights normally did not correspond to the old boundaries of their chiefdoms. The imperial administration required parts of local territory to support officials, and the Emperor allocated still others to private persons he wanted to reward (or sometimes exile). As both these processes wore on, the imperial presence in Maale increased during the 1910s and 1920s, and the Maale chiefs and the king were consequently squeezed into smaller and smaller tribute areas.

The three western chiefdoms (region 1 in Map 3) closest to the garrison towns of Bako and Bulki were affected first. There, the economic powers of the Maale chiefs were decisively undermined in about 1910, when the Emperor made personal gult grants of the chiefdoms of Bio, Lemo, and Ginte in their entirety to northern soldiers. In Bio, *fituarari* Turunih from Gonder settled with his band of approximately twenty soldiers, many from Gonder and Gojjam. Lemo went to *kanyazmach* Ayele, also from Gonder, and his soldiers, and Ginte to *kanyazmach* Gidi from Tigray and his followers.

These three, like the governor of the province (by the 1920s, the territories of Bako and Bulki had been combined and the governor lived at Bulki) was directly tied to the Ethiopian Emperor. All were said to be the Emperor's *karami*, "servants." Technically, the governor took precedence, but since the three gult lords in Maale also enjoyed direct access to the Emperor, this precedence was a weak one. The lords in western Maale could always go around their nominal superior to the Emperor himself.

Officials in the imperial administration settled in other parts of Maale, and for their support, they were given the right to exact tributes in kind and in labor, not from whole stretches of territory, but from particular Maale families, so-called *gabbar*. The governor of Bulki and Bako had posted a *mislenyi*, a "representative," to Goddo, a high and fortified point in northern Maale, where an Orthodox church was established in the early 1900s.[9] After Maale and its environs were pacified, the mislenyi in the 1920s, *fituarari* Dubala, moved his headquarters (with the church) down the mountain to the plain in Ginte.

Beside a *mislenyi*, the governor also established a small garrison of northern soldiers at Koibe (in region 2 of Map 3). There, at least six ranking soldiers lived, at least two of whom commanded as many as six ordinary soldiers beneath them (each of whom were given at least two gabbar, two Maale families to support them). Again, the Koibe soldiers were nominally under the direction of the governor's mislenyi in Maale, but because they were personally tied to the governor in Bulki, the Koibe soldiers enjoyed direct ties to their nominal superior's superior.

This complicated hierarchy—rather different from Max Weber's ideal bureaucracy—encouraged a rough frontier jockeying for power

and an ever-greater appetite for Maale families from which to take tribute. Since Bio, Lemo, and Ginte were allotted to private lords, that
meant expansion in chiefdoms farther to the east. There, by the 1930s,
strong tensions had developed between encroaching northerners and
the local Maale elite.

Artamu, the chief of Bunka, the district that contained the Koibe soldiers, had left Maaleland to live in Tsemai after virtually none of his
subjects were left to provide labor tribute. (Tsemai was located immediately to the south of Maale across a provincial border and was a lower
and drier area to which the gabbar system had not been extended.)
Next to Bunka was the chiefdom of Irbo, and there, the chief, Galshila,
took stronger measures. Alive in 1975, Galshila described what happened: "My servants' houses—this person [referring to my assistant] is
someone you're raising, right?—when people like that, people that my
father had raised, that I had raised, were counted as gabbar, I fought
back."[10] When the northern soldier, Kebbede, who claimed the chief's
subjects, came to Irbo, Galshila set out to kill him. When Kebbede sat
down to rest and quench his thirst in the courtyard of a Maale compound, the chief, who had been silently stalking him, took two shots.
One bullet killed the man sitting next to Kebbede; the other passed
through Kebbede's arm, permanently maiming it. The response from
the Koibe garrison was swift. The chief's house was burned and his
neighbors arrested, but he managed to escape to Tsemai.

THE CONFLICT BETWEEN TONNA AND OTTOLO

In Bala, kati Irbano was an elderly man by the early 1930s. His two
eldest sons by different wives, Tonna and Ottolo, lived separately. Tonna,
son of Irbano's first wife, lived in Kajo and took labor tribute from that
area; Ottolo continued to live with his father and took tribute from people around Bala. These men, Irbano and his sons, occupied a contradictory position as the twentieth century wore on. At once dependent upon
the imperial state for the recognition of their positions and in opposition to it vis-à-vis their rights as traditionally defined, they had to
learn to play imperial politics, to adopt the rough frontier methods, the
wheeling and dealing, of their opponents, if they were to survive as significant political actors.

By the 1920s, Tonna, the heir apparent, had turned himself into
something of a local strong man. For example, when the Maale commoner responsible for organizing labor on his fields, Kenokaza, did not

show up one day, Tonna went to the man's house and according to an elder in 1975: "He asked, 'Why did you stay away? Why did you cause the others to stay away?' Kenokaza answered, 'I had work of my own.' Then Tonna beat him and beat him and beat him. Afterwards, Kenokaza died."[11]

By the late 1920s, Irbano himself did not carry out government work; instead, his *inderase,* literally "like myself," was an Amharic-speaking commoner. In Irbano's place, the inderase heard court cases, collected taxes, and relayed orders from the governor in Bulki. According to my notes of a conversation with an informant in 1975:

> At that time, many people accused Tonna of various offenses in front of Barkare, the shum [Irbano's inderase]. When Barkare asked Tonna about these cases and remonstrated with him, Tonna became angry, wanted to hit him, even to shoot him. Then when Barkare ordered Tonna to come to the government, he refused. When Barkare came for taxes from his neighborhood, Tonna prevented him from taking them.[12]

In 1975 Tonna's half-brother, Ottolo, confirmed this description of political tensions in the late 1920s and grounded them in the expansion of the gabbar system: "Barkare and Shusha were the important shums in Maale at the time and they carried out a policy of making even the kati's people—those immediately around Bala—into gabbar for the Amhara. Because of this, Tonna and Barkare became enemies, and Tonna refused to carry out Barkare's orders."[13]

What Ottolo did not add was that Tonna had also come into conflict with his father, Irbano, and with Ottolo himself. According to a Bala elder in 1975:

> First Shusha was the shum in Maale country. He was the kati's inderase, the main one who worked under the kati, but Shusha got on the wrong side of the Amhara living in the country. When this happened, they said, "Let Barkare be the inderase." No sooner than Barkare had become shum than they began to divide the gabbar of the country here in Bala. Before, they had divided the country all around but had left the kati's people in Bala. Then Barkare approached Irbano and said that he had to divide the whole country. Irbano replied, "All right, if you know what to do, go ahead." When he said this, Barkare gave Goshe [as gabbar for a northern soldier-settler]. He gave the father of Elma. Then that one down there, Shonto, he gave as a gabbar. In addition, Haile's father and Kolko's father he gave. He gave Damo. Baki's father, Lungare, he gave. He gave the Gojo. The Turgati people down there, the ones who watch over the *ṭsozo,*[14] the main Turgati, he gave. The one up there, Koke, he gave. Then Tonna said, "My father! My father, why don't you give away the *doddo,* the *kobo basso,* why don't you give away

Yeberi, Galai?[15] What kind of office do you have? You and I won't live together in this land. I'm Alkamo's son, see if I don't refuse to take orders from
you!"[16]

Not long afterward, Irbano was ordered to convey taxes to Bulki.
After the people in Bala—Irbano's and Ottolo's tribute givers—had put
in their time carrying honey and flour and driving cattle, Irbano ordered
his servant, Sulunge, to have some of Tonna's men help. One of Sulunge's sons recalled what happened next:

> After he [Sulunge] had come home, Tonna confronted him, "How can you
> order my men!" Sulunge replied, "What can I do? How can I tell you the
> basis for my order? When I look at the sky, it is far away; when I look at the
> earth, it is far away. I ordered the people here. "Order the people up there!"
> So I ordered them. Well, well, if you want to ask the kati, then ask him. Or
> perhaps you will prevent the order. What can I do?"[17]

When Tonna went to Irbano and refused to let his men help, his half-
brother Ottolo became very angry and quarreled with him. Tonna in-
sulted his brother and threatened to hit him with a fence post, and the
two began to wrestle. The kati Irbano intervened:

> "Tonna, Tonna, Tonna, is it you? Are you coming to kill? To kill? Am I not
> the one who bore you? The two of you, didn't I bear you both? Am I not the
> one who bore you both? If you prevent your people, who will help me? On
> what basis do you prevent? Have you become kati? Have you killed me and
> become kati? This one I bore. That one I bore. Who is Sulunge? Who or-
> dered him to order the people? Wasn't it me? Don't come to my gate a sec-
> ond time [to Tonna]."[18]

In this context of threat and tension, an event occurred within a matter of weeks that was to reverberate through Maale politics for the next
four decades. Abegaz, one of the Amhara soldiers who lived at Koibe,
was visited by relatives from Kamba to the east, and as was the custom,
when his guests left, Abegaz escorted them for part of the way, to the
border of Maale, the Woito River. On his way back, Abegaz and his son
disappeared.

At the same time, Tonna's wife's father died, and Tonna, along with
low-caste servants, Baki and Zaude, went to the funeral across the
Woito—playing trumpets as they went.[19] Tonna's wife and children preceded them, and along the way they met Abegaz and his son returning
from the Woito. When Tonna and his party passed along the same path
a few hours later, they met no one but happened to see blood in the sand
where they assumed that an antelope had been recently killed. About a

month later, after Abegaz and his son had not appeared, the Koibe soldiers convened an *aucacin* in Bala (a forced meeting to ferret out the criminal). For four days, the Bala elders were held under detention and questioned. Finally, on the fifth day, people admitted that brothers of the chief of Bala had killed Abegaz and his son (the brothers lived close to the route that Abegaz had taken back).

What actually happened so long ago is of course difficult to reconstruct, but all of the information that I collected—including some from close relatives of the chief of Bala himself—suggests that the chief's brothers had in fact been the murderers.[20]

Barkare and the northern soldiers, however, refused to believe the Bala elders. They were convinced that the killing had been perpetrated by Tonna. As the days wore on, Barkare insisted that Tonna was the true culprit, and as the elders grew more frightened, some gave in and named Tonna, Zaude, and Baki as Abegaz's murderers.[21] Determined to make an example of anyone who dared attack one of their own, the Amhara soldiers put Tonna in handcuffs, tying him and his servants together by their genitalia.

Heartbroken, Irbano died within a year, but not before he had cursed the whole land: "If I cannot have my first son, then no one in Maale will have theirs!" The prisoners were taken from Maale to Bulki and from there to Addis Ababa for trial. Irbano visited Tonna in prison in Bulki before he was taken away, and Tonna swore to him that he had not killed Abegaz. Irbano is reputed to have replied, "My son, if you did not kill him, then the people have placed evil words on your body. This necklace [referring to the principal symbol of kingship in Maale] will not miss you. My son, this necklace won't miss you."[22] While Tonna and his servants were in prison in Addis Ababa, the Italians invaded the city in 1936. After some time of eking out an existence in Addis Ababa, Tonna apparently entered the Italian Army and eventually died in a battle at Mojole.[23] After many years, Baki and Zaude would return to Maaleland, but local people had difficulty believing that Tonna was actually dead.[24]

In 1975, I interviewed Baki. When asked why Maale elders had participated in naming Tonna as the murderer, he replied:

> What was the reason for people's accusing Tonna? Before, he was a powerful man. Awfully powerful. Very powerful. Compared to anyone else, really bad. No one could reproach him. He simply took people's cattle and goats, without his father's knowing. . . . Unthinkably strong, he wanted only white animals: "Bring me a white goat. Bring me a white cow." "Isn't your father

alive?" people would ask. "What's a father? I don't have a father," he would say. . . . And then there was the crime. His servants' crimes. Abegaz aside, his servants killed many people. . . . A lot of people died. Because Abegaz was a big man, his murder was pursued. But there were many little people in Maale who died and their deaths never came to light.[25]

With Tonna lost and his father Irbano dead, Maale was without a kati. By late 1937, the Italians had more or less pacified the countryside around Maale and had established a military station at Bako.[26] By that point, the chiefs of Bunka and Irbo had returned to their homes and offices, and the Italian administration called on the Maale to install a new kati.

As was customary, the chiefs of Bala and Makana, along with the elders of Bala, sacrificed animals and consulted their intestines for signs as to who should become kati.[27] Actually, the question was which of Irbano's two wives (with sons) should be considered his principal wife—Tonna's mother or Ottolo's. Even though Tonna had disappeared, he had left sons in Maale, including first-born Tolba, who by 1937 was approximately ten years of age. First, the elders sacrificed an animal for Tonna's mother. According to men who took part in the reading, including the chief of Bala, the results were very bad. Again they tried, and again the results were bad.

When asked to explain, the men remembered the pattern of veins and spots in the intestines in the technical language of Maale divination. Two other issues appeared in informants' conversations. One was the curse that Irbano had uttered when Tonna was taken away; installing Tonna's son might encourage the action of the curse.[28] The other, possibly more important issue involved an incident that had occurred early in Irbano's reign: Tonna's mother, had become ritually impure, berbene.

Once in the 1900s, Irbano had been imprisoned for about six months in Bako by dejazmach Biru until he produced tax. Biru apparently first wanted slaves. When Irbano refused, then the governor asked for ivory. Finally, when Irbano's brother-in-law managed to produce an elephant tusk, Irbano was set free. But not before his wife, Tonna's mother, had taken an Amhara soldier from Goddo as a lover. According to Maale custom, if a husband has relations with a wife who has been unfaithful, he will die. He must divorce her.

Irbano was furious. Bala elders restrained him from killing her ("Oh, kati, have you gone crazy? If you kill her, how will you live with your children?"), but he exiled Tonna's mother from Maale. It was only her children's insistence some years later when they had grown up, mainly Tonna's insistence, that brought Irbano's wife back to Maale:

When the children grew up, they said, "How can he [Irbano] send our mother to Baaka country? Let us bring back our mother. Our father, who is he? Our father, why does he insult us? As long as we are around, how can our mother be made to disappear? Let her come here." And they brought her back to Bala. But this became a *gome* ["transgression," "broken taboo"] for the entire country. People went back and forth, they argued, but they were afraid to confront the situation and did nothing. Consequently, Tonna was taken away. His father died. His mother died. It was because of this gome.[29]

It may have been that the mother's transgression and Tonna's ruthlessness were interrelated: the illegitimated son intent on forcing the respect and position that he thought was his due. In any case, when the elders slaughtered animals for Ottolo's mother, the results were good. According to Ottolo, speaking in 1975:

> Before, as everyone knows, I did not want the kingship. My brother [Tonna] was born first. He was born first. Although he was born first, he disappeared. My father died. Three elders came to me, but I refused. It was not the custom.[30] But then the chiefs of Bala and Makana came. "We have chosen you," they said. I replied, "You're putting fire on the top of a house."[31] "We're giving it to you. We're giving it to you," they said. I asked, "In the future, will you say something different?" "No," they said, "We will not." I said, "Yesterday, you were the ones who destroyed [the country] with a crime, and now you're coming to me?"[32] "What would you have us do? Shall we leave your father? Don't leave your father unburied," they said.[33] Then I gave in.[34]

For more than the next two decades, Ottolo—who took the name of Warko when he became kati—reigned. But Warko had few political ambitions. Warm, slightly inept in the affairs of the world, loved by his people, Warko carried out the ritual aspects of the kingship while his younger, full brother, Dobbo, carried out the political work. Dobbo, schooled in the ways of northerners, quickly became a powerful figure. To the outside world, Dobbo became, in fact, the Maale balabbat.[35] The Italians gave him the military title of *grazmach,* a title he continued to use after 1941, when Haile Selassie was restored to power and the Italians were expelled.

THE REVENGE OF TONNA'S SON

The combination of Warko as kati and Dobbo as balabbat managed to mediate the increasing contradictions in local notions of hierarchy until the early 1960s. By then, Tolba, Tonna's son, a middle-aged and wealthy man, began to contest the royal succession in government courts. That

Figure 10. Ottolo, king of Maale from c. 1937 to c. 1963, telling his story, Bio, 1975. Photograph taken by the author.

Tolba took this matter—what previously had been the most internal of Maale concerns, talked about and justified in the most esoteric language of intestine oracles—to a foreign venue, a government court, is itself significant. By then, Tolba was a thoroughly new man. Like any northerner, he was prepared to upset the accepted social hierarchy given the opportunity. And doing so depended upon the skillful manipulation of patron-client ties.

Tolba was in fact successful in 1963, and he became kati and balabbat, principally because *grazmach* Dobbo, the politician, died in 1962, and Warko, left alone, could hardly match Tolba's machinations. But there were other reasons as well, long-term processes that had undermined Ottolo's and Dobbo's rule. One involved their relationship with northern settlers in Maale vis-à-vis land ownership, and the other related to the rankling issue of who was responsible for Tonna's death.

After the Italian occupation, the Ethiopian state was reorganized with British assistance in the early 1940s. For the first time, a central treasury was established out of which all government employees were paid. This meant that the gabbar system could be abolished in the countryside. By the early 1950s, most of the chiefs and the king, along with many ordinary Maale who had themselves been gabbar, were given new titles to plots of land and were made directly subject to the government office in Bako as far as taxes were concerned.

In this way, one of the principal props that had previously supported northern settlers in Maale was removed; however, this new era did not mean the end of settler influence in Maale politics. Some northerners moved away into the developing towns of the south and some, especially ordinary soldiers, began to farm as most Maale peasants (marrying Maale wives and taking on more and more of Maale culture), but a few of the descendants of the first soldier-settlers held on to power by continuing to fill offices in the local administration during the 1950s and 1960s—and by claiming land in various, mostly technically illegitimate means.[36]

Such land claims necessarily came at the expense of ordinary Maale who had just received land. Dobbo had taken up the cause of these subjects, arguing against northerners' land claims in court, and his opposition had quickly brought him (and by implication, Ottolo) into conflict with various northerners living in Maale. For example, Danyi, the son of Dubala (the latter was the provincial governor's mislenyi in Maale during the 1920s), claimed a large tract of land in southern Bunka. Before the Italian occupation, Dubala had established an outpost of soldiers there to protect Maale from hunters coming from Tsemai across the provincial boundary. On this flimsy basis, Danyi, Dubala's son, claimed southern Bunka as his personal *kalad*, "measured" land. (Kalad was supposedly land unoccupied before the conquest that the government sold to private individuals). Because the area contained the only watering hole for cattle for miles about, Danyi was able to take taxes from most of the Maale who lived in the south.

Through such means, Danyi, along with two sons of higher-ranking

Koibe soldiers, Kebbede and Manakule, became wealthy in the 1950s and 1960s. These men spoke Amharic, of course, although with an accent, having been raised in Maale; and they were adept at influencing the courts in Bako, later in Jinka—giving bribes, currying favor, collecting information. At home in Maale, they spoke Maale and developed various ties with the chiefs and king. Danyi, for example, had married one of Dobbo's daughters. Since Orthodox Christians were supposed to have only one wife (and Danyi had a northern wife), the Maale woman was counted as his *gared,* "house servant."

Despite the marriage of his daughter, grazmach Dobbo refused to be swayed. I interviewed Danyi in November 1975 (after he had been arrested by the zemecha students and placed under detention in Jinka). Danyi was straightforward about the role he had played in placing Tolba in the Maale kingship. Here are the notes of my conversation with him:

> What caused Danyi to support Tolba [in the latter's drive to become kati] was the fact that *grazmach* Dobbo was registering land in Maale with a government official and not recognizing land that Danyi claimed. By that time, Dobbo's daughter, Kedishero, had long been married to Danyi and had borne him six children. Danyi asked Dobbo to stop taking land from him, but Dobbo refused. Finally, Danyi sent a Maale elder to Ottolo, pleading with him to do something. But Ottolo only sent back a message that Danyi and Dobbo should settle this affair themselves. Danyi, infuriated, set out to depose Ottolo and Dobbo. And he freely admitted that he was the one who made Tolba kati. I asked him point blank, "People say that you were the one who made Tolba kati," and he replied, "Why should I hide it? It was me."[37]

But the land issue, by itself, probably would not have unseated Ottolo. Indeed, three of the most important Maale chiefs themselves—those of Makana, Bala, and Bunka—testified in court on Tolba's behalf. What had alienated them from Ottolo?

The chief of Bala had himself participated in Ottolo's installation more than two decades before. He, with the chief of Makana at the time, had assured Ottolo of his permanent support. The Bala chief, interviewed in 1974, explained: "Ottolo was kati for twenty-nine years and during that time, everything became bad for Maale people: There was no water, the bees left Maale, and the crops were bad. Finally, we consulted the intestine oracle again, and it indicated that Tolba should become kati. After Tolba entered, everything improved. Now there is water. The crops are good."[38]

What the chief did not explain was that another issue had remained

Figure 11. Kansira, chief of Bala, in front of Dulbo's tin-roofed house, Bala, 1972. Photograph taken by the author.

unresolved for those twenty-nine years, namely, Abegaz's murder, apparently by his own brothers. Indirectly, these men had caused the death of Tonna. Shortly after Ottolo was installed, the chief of Bala sent the chief of Makana to the new kati in order to ask his forgiveness. When a Maale man kills another, the transgression can only be removed by a ritual in which heads of the two families wash their hands together in the blood of a sacrificed animal. Ottolo steadfastly refused to carry out this rite: "Why did he [the Bala chief] not approach us when my father was still alive? He made me kati and then expects that I would have less feeling for my half-brother?"

The issue of the tension between Ottolo and the chief of Bala recurred at each important step in the ritual cycle. As the intestine oracle was consulted, it revealed which outstanding gome had to be attended to before the next step. So when Ottolo was to build his lion house, the oracle pointed to the matter of Tonna. According to Ottolo:

They said, "Take a ritual helper for Tonna's house and finish the matter." I replied, "I'm in the hands of the Goji. The Goji is in the hands of God. Let the Goji finish the matter. I refuse." "No, you must finish it," they said. "No, I won't do it. You want me to finish the matter tomorrow, while yesterday, it was you who committed the wrong, you who condemned an innocent man to death. Now you extend your hand and want me to make these bad intestines right. Are you walking around with your eyes open?" I said.[39]

Work on the lion house lapsed. The raison d'être of Ottolo's office as far as the Maale were concerned—his role in ritual—was thereby undermined by his refusal to be reconciled with the chief of Bala. As a consequence, over the nearly three decades of his reign, he carried out even fewer of the traditional rites than his father had.

As the issue of Abegaz's murder soured relations between Ottolo and the chief of Bala, Dobbo's raw power began to alienate the other chiefs—particularly the family of the chief of Makana. The Makana chiefs had traditionally been leading figures in the Maale polity, but by the 1950s Dobbo's monopoly of power, given his sanctioned position in the imperial government, meant that all the chiefs were being shunted aside. During the Italian occupation, Dobbo had Baha, the eldest son of the Makana chief, publicly whipped for insubordination. Afterward, when they met on a path, the two passed insulting one another. By 1963, Baha, along with the chief of Bala, was Tolba's principal supporter. According to Ottolo:

> The reason that Baha and my younger brother didn't get along was that Baha resented a commoner [that is, Dobbo] becoming balabbat. He wanted the chiefs to have power. For him, a commoner had become greater than the kati. . . . My younger brother . . . heard them all [the court cases] himself, he ate the gifts, he made the decisions. My younger brother was a little crooked, but at least he didn't send matters outside Maale.[40]

Besides the political split between the chief of Makana's brother and Dobbo, marriage ties added a final layer of motivation for Baha's support for Tolba. Baha's mother and Tonna's mother had been sisters; hence, Baha was linked to Tolba in a way that he was not to Ottolo.[41]

Besides the chiefs of Makana and Bala, Artamu, chief of Bunka, also entered Tolba's coalition. By the 1960s, Artamu himself had taken up the methods of the northern settlers in Maale; that is, he had begun to expand his holdings in the new system of land tenure through court cases with Maale commoners.[42] Artamu saw his future in alliance with Tolba and Danyi rather than with grazmach Dobbo. As mentioned in the previous chapter, Artamu was the richest chief in Maale on the eve of the revolution, and he was the only one arrested. A son of Artamu described Tolba's eventual victory in court:

> Then the Amhara really helped. Also our father helped. During that time, the thing with which one talked was money. It was only the owner of money

who won court cases. If you had money, then there was nothing you were going to do except win. When did anyone win on the basis of their arguments? When the case went to Jinka, our father testified, "Yes, that's right, he is the rightful heir. It's true that Tonna was the first son." The chief of Bala testified. Baha testified. Then everybody coughed up money, money. Danyi gave the judge one hundred and fifty, on Tolba's behalf. Our father, one hundred and fifty. Then the Amhara, *kanyazmach* [Kassahun] and his bunch, they coughed up. Danyi gave the bribes. Then the court gave its judgment.[43]

The result—the deposition of a living kati—was unprecedented in Maale history. The judge in the case, Mitiku, came to Bala, gathered the elders together, and, like Pontius Pilate, washed his hands of the matter. A Bala elder recalled the speech:

"Hear what I have to say. The country has been ruined. You chiefs are ruining it. By Amhara custom, as long as a king is alive, his son cannot enter and be made king. . . . After he is dead, then the son can say that I am taking my father's things. Tolba, listen to me. . . . You've done something bad. However that may be, don't compound the evil. Don't send Ottolo from the country. After you've given him land and told him to live there, then the two of you should become as one. If you don't do this, you're going to destroy your country."[44]

After the speech, the police ordered Ottolo to break his necklace and hand it over. The same elder recounted what happened next:

Then they all came to Nukuso's father's house. We met together. No one was absent, Kababa's father was there. Dauco's father, all of the Bala elders. They said, "Kati, break your necklace." The kati replied, "I can't break it here. I have a place. And then, I don't break it. The person who breaks it is the Gojo." "Where do you break it?" "I have a place." "Take us there," the police ordered. "It's a sacred place. But it's too late today. If I break it now, my mother's bones are lying inside the place. We have customs to complete. Because of this, it's too late today. What can I do?" "You bastard! You're putting this off because of your mother? The people who watch over your mother's bones can sleep with them like birds in a tree for all I care. If not, then they can bury her tonight. Bury her now, your mother! . . . This is your trouble, it's not ours." Then they said, "Stand, let's go." Then we went up [to Dufa, the sacred grove]. We gathered up his mother's bones and brought them out. Then the kati entered and sat down on the stone where he usually sat. "Break it!" they said. He replied, "Here, Gojo, you break it." The Gojo said, "Ah, people, before his eyes have dimmed, while his eyes still see, this is against all our customs. It's something unknown. All right, if you're ordering it. . . . " As the Gojo slowly approached the kati, the police shoved him forward. The Gojo turned around, "Why did you do that?" "Break it!" they said. "All right, but have mercy on me." he said and he broke it. . . . Ottolo said, "I've been cleansed. Take a good look at me. Me, the son of the queen-mother. Before, you, son of Gudari and son of Babbo [the chiefs of Bala and Makana], you made me. But it doesn't matter." And he jumped up and rushed off. He had gotten to the edge of Nukuso's father's field down there when the Bala chief and the Makana chief came running after him. "Eh, kati, kati," they called. He said nothing and just went on. "Ottolo, Ottolo," they said. "Yes," he said. "Wait there. Say you have left the country for us [i.e. give us your blessing]." He replied, "Do whatever you like, I don't care," and he just went on. . . . Later, Tolba came and called the Gojo and told him to place the royal beads around his neck. Well, he did it. But then those beads became the thing that destroyed the country. Even though the person who wore the necklace was still alive, Tolba took it and wore it. When someone dies, his *geta* [ritual helper] breaks the necklace, his son breaks the necklace and takes the beads. But with Ottolo still alive, Tolba broke the necklace and took it.[45]

So Tolba became kati, taking the new name of Arbu. Reluctantly, the people participated in the first of the cycle of royal rites. The chief of Irbo refused to participate, and over the next few years, Tolba took revenge by accusing him of various misdeeds in government courts.

As fate would have it, Tolba's reign lasted for only seven years. Around August 1970, he apparently suffered a stroke and died within a matter of hours—still a middle-aged man. Tolba's unexpected death automatically reopened the Maale past for reinterpretation. To many, Tolba's death was a sign that he was not meant to be kati in the first place. One of his own younger brothers, another of Tonna's sons, conceded, "Well, whatever went wrong, our elder brother [Tolba] was killed. Whether he died because of a gome in his house or not, he died."

This complex and sedimented series of stories provides the web of meanings in which Maale traditionalists reacted to the first events of the revolution. When the zemecha students entered the sacred grove and took out the bones of the kati, it was Tolba's bones they buried. By that point, the office of kingship in Maale had been so transformed by northern politicking that Tolba was unrecognizable to many Maale as a traditional leader. At home, he wore the necklace that identified him as kati, but when he went to his house in Jinka to go to court and to socialize in the drinking houses, Tolba removed his beads.[46] In the Orthodox Christian milieu of the town, they marked him only as a backward pagan.

Far from the Kefa example in which traditionalist peasants burned zemecha students for desecrating their leader, some Maale elders saw the first events of the revolution—particularly, the burying of Tolba's bones—as an actual vindication of Maale tradition. Tolba was never meant to be kati. He *should* have been buried "down." It was only the alien Amhara government that had imposed him on the country in the first place. Now, some silently thought, Ottolo—still alive in 1975—could be returned to his rightful place.

CHAPTER 4

The Dialectic of Modernity in a North American Christian Mission

And this gospel of the kingdom shall be preached in all the world for a witness unto all nations; *and then shall the end come.*

Matthew 24:14

If some Maale peasants saw the events of 1975 as a way to restore tradition, this hope was to evaporate after a few years, as it became clear that the revolutionary state would not tolerate the installation of a new Maale king. For the entire revolutionary period, Maale would have no kati. The traditionalists' initial wait-and-see attitude explains, then, only part of the success of the revolution in Maale, and then, only the very first years of that history.

More critical, and of more lasting relevance, was the active and sometimes fervid support of many evangelical Christians in Maale. As we have seen, Christian converts made by the Sudan Interior Mission (SIM) became Maale's Jacobins. They provided crucial support and information to the zemecha students in Maale; they helped carry out the most radical actions of the revolution as it occurred locally; and they dominated the leadership of the new peasant cooperatives when they were established in 1975.

Why were Christians the principal supporters of the revolution in Maale? On the surface, this result is more than a little surprising, since as I shall explain below, the basic impulse that brought the SIM to Ethiopia was an uncompromising rejection of modernism in their own society, at least as far as religion was concerned. Even while rejecting, indeed defining, their very identities against modernist religious ideas at home, the missionaries also used other aspects of modernity, particularly technology and medicine, to propagate their Christianity abroad.

In the end, ironically, the missionaries' principal appeal to Ethiopians came to rest precisely on their ability to offer an entrance to modernity, as it was locally constructed. Imbued with a progressive sense of time and increasingly impatient with "tradition," mission converts dreamed of a better day.

The converts to these newly formed churches never represented more than two percent of the population [of Mexico]. This very uniqueness, however, was the source of their strength and their importance. . . . When the revolution erupted in 1910 . . . the [foreign] missionary response was not startling, strong, or immediate, but it was almost unanimously in sympathy with the revolution. . . . [Local] Mexican ministers were not so restrained in their actions. In the north, especially around Ciudad Guerrero, and in the Puebla-Tlaxcala region east of Mexico City, Protestant ministers took leadership roles in the revolt along with other members of their congregations.[1]

Eventually, the support of mission-educated Christians, like the wait-and-see attitude of the traditionalists, would evaporate, when the revolutionary state turned against Protestantism as a "foreign" religion in the late 1970s. But before it attacked Protestantism, the Derg appropriated virtually all of the institutions that the SIM and other evangelical missions had created in Ethiopia. As we have already seen, the structure of peasant associations was similar to existing church organization. These bureaucratic practices and procedures gave an altogether new point and modernist efficiency to social arrangements in Ethiopia—an efficiency that underlay the consolidation of the revolutionary state.

THE FOUNDING OF THE SUDAN INTERIOR MISSION IN CANADA

Let me return to the development of anti-modernist Christianity in North America. One man who rose out of this tradition to build a missionary empire was Rowland Victor Bingham.[2] Born to a large Methodist family in Britain, for a time a member of the Salvation Army, and a young migrant to Canada, Bingham, after hearing a series of sermons by A. J. Gordon in 1892, made a commitment to foreign missions. And a year later, he accepted, as he said, "the burden of the Sudan":

It was the impassioned pleading of a quiet little Scotch lady that linked up my life with the Sudan. She had invited me to her home for lunch, from a meeting where I had been speaking in the City of Toronto. . . . Then she commenced to talk of the Sudan that was calling her son. . . . and ere I closed that first interview in her home she had placed upon me the "burden of the

Sudan," a burden just as real as the burden that pressed on the heart of Isaiah in the Old Testament. . . . When I left that little mother, I went back to my room, but the burden would not be shaken off. . . . And so . . . I had found what I had been waiting to know. . . . I felt God laid His hand on me for the Sudan.[3]

For Bingham, the "Sudan" referred to whole area of Africa south of the Sahara:

There it was, a great, black belt, stretching for twenty-five hundred miles across Africa, steeped in the densest darkness. The whole land was divided between the Moslems in the northern half and the pagans in the vast stretches of the territory in the south. In my imagination I could then see what I afterward saw in reality. The habitations of pagan heathenism were the dwellings of cruelty. Every kind of horrible heathen custom was practiced.[4]

The whole area was, according to Bingham, "larger than India, a population of sixty to ninety millions without a single Christian missionary."[5]

In 1897, Bingham founded the Sudan Interior Mission in Toronto. Modeled after Hudson Taylor's China Inland Mission, Bingham's SIM was an interdenominational "faith" mission. That is, the mission was connected to no particular church, nor did it have any invested money of its own or the assurance of any future budget. It depended entirely upon contributions from a variety of developing fundamentalist groups, and its missionaries were considered volunteers, not employees.[6]

Missionaries themselves were expected periodically to raise a major proportion of their own funds. If they failed to do so, this was taken as God's indication that they were not meant for mission work.[7] After collecting moneys by speaking in local churches, summer gatherings, and so forth, missionaries went to the field for a few years at most—meanwhile writing circular letters, "prayer letters," to keep their supporters at home abreast of their work. Returning to Canada or the United States or Australia to raise still more funds, they supported themselves "by faith."

The SIM's combination of hierarchical organization from the top and decentralized financing from the bottom fitted hand in glove with the network of developing fundamentalist religious institutions in the English-speaking world.[8] Almost all of Bingham's missionaries and the great proportion of ordinary church people who supported them were premillennialists,[9] most dispensationalists.[10] And, although the evidence is sketchy, it seems that the largest proportion of SIM supporters, at least in Canada, came from churches with members predominantly of the lower middle classes.

During the depression of the 1930s, it was, of course, precisely these North American Christians who were most severely hit. In some respects, premillennialism, with its focus on degeneration and impending crisis— and ultimate salvation—made the experience of the depression easier to understand and perhaps to bear. In any case, it was Bingham's kind of Christian who responded to economic depression with increasing support of foreign missions:

> During the depression, American Protestantism in general and its foreign mission programs in particular were stagnating or declining. The Northern Baptist Convention, for instance, experienced a forty percent drop in its foreign missions program between 1930 and 1940. In the same period, Bingham doubled the number of SIM missionaries. In actual figures, by 1933, the mission had 230 members drawn from Britain, North America, and Australia. It had over fifty permanent stations covering three fields of work in Nigeria, French West Africa, and Ethiopia. It was operating hospitals, schools, and the Niger Press, a field-based publishing house that served some of the needs of other Protestant missions in Africa. Continued hard work for the remaining nine years of his life allowed Bingham to see the Sudan Interior Mission grow by another fifty percent to over 400 missionaries, thus making it the largest Protestant missionary force in Africa.[11]

In sum, Rowland Victor Bingham was an entrepreneur for Christ. He connected (and created) supplies and demands with the object of accumulating not capital but souls—souls first in Nigeria and by the 1930s in Ethiopia. In the discourse of his time, he spoke of "opening up"[12] new countries, of extending his work to "unoccupied regions."[13] In doing so, Bingham ever rejected modernist interpretations of Christianity, but in a complex dialectic, he welcomed modern technological advances to accomplish his own anti-modernist religious end: to hasten Christ's second coming. Looking back over his life as an elderly man he wrote:

> We are "speeding up" in almost everything in business and material things. In our days men make, by a single turnover in business, as much as our fathers used to hope to make in a lifetime. Then in the matter of locomotion the world has gone crazy on "speed" . . . [at] the time of our own first going to Africa, it took us twelve months of battling with tremendous difficulties to get eight hundred miles from the coast, and then my two companions reached that point only to find a grave. On my last visit to the field I flew right across from the Nile to the Niger in two short flying days, and since then one of our missionaries has made the whole journey in a day. . . . We are living in the days of speeding up in all these things, and Peter urges Christians to "speed up". . . . In the Epistle, ere he closes, he links the same word with the thought of "hastening the day of God". . . . And how can we hasten the day of God?. . . . our Lord was quite specific when He said, "This

Gospel of the Kingdom shall be preached in all the world for a witness unto all the nations, and then shall the end be." . . . God is giving us the facilities for speeding up this work in our day as never before. We can circle the globe with messages in ways our fathers never dreamed of. . . . Let us pour it [our offerings] out for God and for a lost world, and in five years we will finish the task which our Lord declared would bring in the great consummation of the age, bring in the everlasting kingdom and the righteousness of God.[14]

THE SIM ARRIVES IN ETHIOPIA

The first Sudan Interior missionaries reached Ethiopia in December 1927. In a matter of a few short years, the mission had become by far the largest in Ethiopia. By the end of its first decade, fifteen stations had been built, staffed by some seventy-five missionaries.[15] This expansion was doubly impressive, for on the North American side, the period saw the most serious economic depression of the twentieth century. And on the African side, Ethiopia, with a long-established Orthodox Christian church, would have seemed the most unlikely of countries for the rapid growth of evangelical Christian missions.[16] Traveler Charles Rey captured the atmosphere of Ethiopia for Europeans during the 1920s:

An Englishman coming to the country . . . is faced by conditions which need a complete mental *volte-face*. The country belongs to the native; he is the top dog; all power is in his hands. So far from having been conquered by the white race, he has defeated them in open field. He has been shut off from progress for centuries and he knows little of the white man; what he does know does not altogether redound to their credit.[17]

To understand how the Sudan Interior Mission came to flourish in this environment one must understand the relationship between two men: *ras* Teferi Makonnen (who became Emperor Haile Selassie on his crowning in 1930) and the first field director of the SIM in Ethiopia, Dr. Thomas Lambie.

From 1916, when he was appointed regent, *ras* Teferi shared power with Zauditu, daughter of the deceased Emperor Menelik. In this uneasy division of power at the center, Teferi became the leader of the "modernist" faction— the "young Ethiopians" who criticized "tradition" and maintained that Ethiopia had to adopt Western ways in order to prosper and progress in the modern world.[18] They were opposed by a conservative faction focused on the Orthodox church and Empress Zauditu:

Zawditu was the rallying point for all the forces of reaction in Ethiopia. The [Orthodox] priesthood were her especial friends and were fanatically opposed to the spread of education on which the Regent [Teferi] had set his heart. . . . But he found the priesthood adamant when he wished to extend his learning to the common people. "Books are holy things," said the Etchege when drawn into a discussion of printing, "but if you have many of them they will become so common that no one will consider as wisdom what is to be found within their covers." . . . One very interesting development of this argument was found among the priests. They said that there was holy power in the sacred books—that is, power to charm away illness and to protect against foes. Now either this holy power was not passed onto a copy—in which case why make a copy which was clearly a sham and a deceit; or the power was passed on. And this was serious—for if the power of a sacred book was to be shared among a thousand copies surely it would become so little that it would be of use to none.[19]

Against such thinking—not unlike, in a different context, modernist Protestant theologians in North America—Teferi maintained that Ethiopia had to adapt its religious thought to scientific progress. After traveling to Europe, Teferi became more convinced than ever that Ethiopia had to reform in order to maintain its independence and its place in the world.

Tafari believed that Ethiopia could learn much from Western lore and life, which fascinated him. He was an avid reader, and his study was filled with books in French on all subjects. His recently built modern home contained European furnishings. Its contrast with traditional dwellings could not have been more stark: "The electric light, gold plate, gold-lettered menus wreathed in roses . . . showed our host's appreciation of Europe." As one entered or left the regent's residence, one could not help noticing that the guard saluted smartly in European style, wore a khaki uniform, and was armed with modern weapons.[20]

How ironic that the leading Ethiopian modernist of the 1920s, *ras* Teferi, came to support the activities of the arch anti-modernist Sudan Interior Mission.[21] Or, was it? For Bingham, the dialectic between anti-modernism and its shadow, modernism, was always more than a simple opposition. These two stances toward the world seemed in fact to depend upon one another and at times to feed into one another.

So Dr. Lambie, the first field director of the SIM, was able to enlist *ras* Teferi's support. In retrospect, two sides of Lambie's character proved critical for the success of the SIM in Ethiopia. First, Lambie was a physician—a man of modern science. In Ethiopia during the 1920s, Western-trained physicians were extremely few. The assistance they were able to offer for some maladies must have seemed near-miracles. Second, compared to other missionaries, Lambie was an extremely flexible politician, able to play the game of give-and-take with the Ethiopian nobility.

If Bingham, the head of the mission in Canada, was a dour entrepreneur for anti-modernist Christianity, Lambie, the local field director in Ethiopia, was something of a slippery diplomat.

The role of modern medicine in Lambie's success in Ethiopia appears clearly in his writings. In the 1930s, he was often to recall a story of how his medical training had provided the key with which to unlock the door to Ethiopia:

> One night we were awakened from a sound slumber by the sound of loud knocking on the outside gate. His Excellency *ras* Nado [the local governor in Wellegga], with fifty armed men, was announced and shown upstairs. In his sleep an insect had crawled into his ear and was causing him great pain. Fortunately, I had an ear speculum and head mirror with me and discovered a small black beetle, which I extricated without much difficulty and put into a small glass vial to let him examine it. He passed it to his soldiers, who solemnly assured him that it was a wood-boring beetle and that if the *hakim* [physician] had not taken it out it would have bored through his head and killed him! I had to tell him this was not true, but the soldiers inferred that although I might know how to take them out I certainly did not know the nature of the pest. He chose to believe them rather than me, and wrote a letter to the regent—His Majesty, *ras* Teferi, saying that Doctor Lambie had saved his life, and a lot of other nonsense, which had the happy result of gaining us access to His Majesty a month later. Many things in after years seemed to hinge upon that event—upon the removal of the little beetle with the rhinoceros-shaped snout. It proved to be one of the little things that God uses to shape destiny . . . the little things of life that add up to a great sum.[22]

The event that Lambie describes above occurred before the SIM came to Ethiopia. At the time, Lambie was a Presbyterian missionary in the Anglo-Egyptian Sudan. In 1922, he returned home through Ethiopia, and in an audience with *ras* Teferi, Lambie was pressed to return to Ethiopia and to build a modern hospital in the capital, Addis Ababa. (The only previously built hospital, by the Russians, was in disrepair.) The request surprised Lambie, but he quickly saw the value of a hospital as an entry point for mission work in the country,[23] and once home in the United States, he proceeded to raise the money—outside regular Presbyterian channels—to build what became the George Memorial Hospital. In "Conquest by Healing in Ethiopia," Lambie stressed the value of medicine for evangelism:

> There is perhaps no country where a medical diploma acts more efficiently as an entrance passe porte than Ethiopia. . . . Ethiopia was then a closed land to missionary enterprise, in fact in all the land there was one single lone Protestant worker. Thus medicine was once again the spear point or the camel's nose or whatever you choose to call it. . . . Were there enough doc-

tors Ethiopia might be opened to the Gospel from end to end, for where a doctor goes several other missionaries can go.[24]

After the hospital was built, Lambie hoped to be able to extend Presbyterian work into the "unoccupied" south. At that point, the southern half of the Ethiopian empire had been conquered and incorporated by the Orthodox Christian north only a few short decades before, so that the entire area remained overwhelmingly "pagan" and Muslim. In 1926, the Presbyterian Mission board was unable to entertain Lambie's ambitious proposals, and he began discussions with others about the possibility of organizing a new "faith" mission. Those discussions eventually put Lambie into contact with Bingham and the SIM.

When he arrived as head of the SIM in Addis Ababa in 1927, Lambie came, then, not only as a physician but as a past provider and benefactor of the major modern hospital in the country. Under Lambie's direction, the party of nine adults and two children set out to establish stations in the south. A hospital was eventually built in Welaita and clinics at many of the other stations—the latter run by nurses and missionary wives who continued to use medical knowledge to reap their harvests. Marcella Ohman, for example, stationed at Gofa in 1931, reported that she had treated 295 patients in May (with 3 house calls), 119 in July (with 1 house call), 83 in September (with 3 house calls), and 103 in October (with 14 house calls).[25]

At times, medical technology became almost a modernist fetish in the hands of anti-modernist missionaries. In 1932, Mrs. Ohman wrote to Lambie:

> I should very much like to know if you could send me a stethoscope, as our Dejasmatch [Beyene Mared, governor of the province] thinks that a stethoscope is absolutely necessary. Everytime he calls us to visit a sick person he asks us to be sure and bring along the stethoscope, and he thinks we cannot give medicines without it. The very first time we saw him after we returned he asked if we brought one along. I am sure he would have far more confidence in us if we had one here at this station, as he is rather doubtful about one's knowledge if they do not use a stethoscope continually.[26]

If medicine was one indispensable basis of Lambie's and the Sudan Interior Mission's relationship to the Ethiopian nobility, it was not the only one. The doctor became, on a wider scale, a veritable "mediator of modernity" in Ethiopia.[27] For example, while in America in the early 1920s, Lambie received a letter from *ras* Teferi requesting that he bring back a threshing machine and tractor, sending along money for the pur-

Figure 12. SIM missionaries in Ethiopia, c. 1930. Lambie is seated in the middle of the second row. Photographic Collection, SIM International Archives, Charlotte, North Carolina.

pose. Before making his purchase, Lambie sought the advice of the Department of Agriculture in Washington, D.C. "Their advice was good, for the machinery proved a complete success."[28] Shortly afterward, Lambie imported a Ford automobile for his own use in Addis Ababa (this at a time when it was difficult to drive much outside the city),[29] and later in 1933, after he had returned to Ethiopia for the Sudan Interior Mission, he imported a car for *dejazmach* Abebe Demtau, son-in-law of then Emperor Haile Selassie and governor of one of the southern provinces in which the mission had just established a new station.[30] Beside the car, the *dejazmach* had also requested the ordering of "a large umbrella such as Dr. Lambie uses for shade purposes when eating morning lunch on trek; also . . . some large type of food kit (service of six) similar to Dr. Lambie's."[31]

The Ethiopian nobility was never the object of the SIM's attempts to evangelize. The elite was, after all, already Orthodox Christian. To have attempted to convert Ethiopian officials would have almost certainly meant expulsion. But Lambie and his charges were entirely dependent upon the Ethiopian nobility for permission to reside in the country. As might be expected, the mission's relationship with Ethiopian power was full of cross-currents. Bingham and Lambie had continually to tell themselves and their fundamentalist supporters in North America that Haile Selassie was a "real" Christian, or very nearly so.[32]

If Sudan Interior missionaries remained in the good graces of high Ethiopian officials by providing medical care, modern technology, and, later, schools, they also sometimes used these aspects of modernity in order to attract the interest of those Ethiopians they wished to convert: the "pagan" peoples of southern Ethiopia and its frontiers beyond. This becomes particularly clear in Lambie's writings when modernity failed to fascinate:

> The Dinkas [of the Sudan] are really a very hard nut to crack, as they are so self-satisfied. All foreigners are more or less barbarians to them. Instead of regarding such inventions as aeroplanes and motor cars with awe and wonderment they count them as inconsequential trifles. As for religion, their own they consider far better than that which any one else possesses. Their conceit is colossal and ridiculous, but it raises an almost insurmountable barrier between themselves and the missionary or any Christianising or civilising influence.[33]

In the Anglo-Egyptian Sudan, the religion that Lambie and the SIM offered was that of the colonial power. In southern Ethiopia, this was not the case. The religion of the "colonial power" was that of the Ethiopian Orthodox Church. It took some time, in fact, for evangelical converts in southern Ethiopia—when they appeared in the early 1930s—to realize that their new religion was at all related to the Christianity of their northern conquerors.[34]

If the Dinka of the Sudan remained resistant, the lure of modernity eventually worked its mystique in southern Ethiopia.[35] Decades later, after a strong, indigenous evangelical church had been established at places like Welaita, and after a few converts had been taken to the United States, a North American missionary would describe—with all of the complex pleasures that Lambie would have appreciated—the modern world through Welaita eyes:

> Markina told the Soddo [Welaita] believers some of the wonders of the New World. They laughed in disbelief when he said he had seen one cow give a bucket and a half of milk at one milking. In fact, he advised his father to sell his 50 cattle—which protestingly gave about a quart a day per cow—and buy one of the kind he had seen. "We traveled in subways and came out of the earth like moles," Markina told the incredulous people. "We went to the top of the Empire State Building—floor upon floor reaching into the clouds. We saw men playing ball in a big field where night was turned to day." Waves of laughter were the response to these tall stories. An astronaut re-

turning from Mars could not have told the people anything more unbeliev-
able. Most amazing was a flush toilet—"you press a lever and everything dis-
appears!" With unabashed Eastern frankness, Markina once confided to a
missionary that two thoughts had come to him at seeing this wonder: (1) if he
threw in his passport, perhaps he could stay in the USA; (2) the Lord had removed his sins as completely as the water flushed everything away.[36]

If one basis of Lambie's relationship to Haile Selassie was medicine
and modern knowledge, the other, as I have said, was his diplomatic
skills. For an evangelical Christian, Lambie showed a remarkable ability to adapt, without undue moral qualms, to whatever structure of
power that existed. This aspect of Lambie's character eventually led to
his downfall, but it was also one of the bases of his initial success. In the
Ethiopian state of the 1920s and 1930s, little business was transacted in
impersonal, bureaucratic style. Ambiguity was a finely pursued political
art, and things got done through shifting and ever fragile patron-client
relationships.[37]

In this political world, Lambie became the client of then *ras* Teferi.
As director of the Sudan Interior Mission, he arrived in Addis Ababa in
1927 without permission to undertake mission work, with only his past
relationships to the Ethiopian nobility. Early 1928 happened to be a
moment of intensifying strain between traditionalist Empress Zauditu
and modernist *ras* Teferi, and to Lambie's surprise, he was not immediately able to gain permission to travel south. Instead, he was called before a council of the Ethiopian Orthodox Church (in Lambie's phrase,
the "Abyssinian Sandhedrin"[38]) to explain himself. Lambie, writing
two months later, described the encounter:

> We started in by affirming our friendship for them and our appreciation of
> the fact that the Coptic Ethiopic Church had survived for many centuries the
> attempts of paganism and Islam to overthrow her. We said that we wished to
> help her in every God appointed way. We had heard of the need of the Mo-
> hamedans and pagans in southern Abyssinia and were desirous to bring
> them to the knowledge of Jesus Christ. God had moved the hearts of kind
> Christian people in America and other places to meet this need and had sent
> us out but more than that we believed that God had sent us out.
>
> To this they replied that their countries had been much troubled by war
> and that only recently had order been secured but that now the Kristiyan
> [sic] faith had gone to all parts of Abyssinia excepting Jimma province. . . .
> They said that they would send priests to Jimma and baptize the people and
> that the Mohamedans must first be baptized and then taught and that if they
> needed us to help them in this teaching they would let us know . . .
>
> This seemed very unpromising . . .

We believe in fasting said they and you do not . . .

Colossians 2:16. Let no man therefore judge you in meat or drink or in respect of an holyday, etc. . . . .

The Bible you teach is the Lutheran one and not the real one, it has been changed.

We know of course that it has not been changed and that comparisons with the original manuscripts prove the authenticity of our Bible . . .

We sought to emphasize that we were sent to preach the word rather than to baptize and that we were in no sense seeking to duplicate any denominational organization in America or any other country.

We said to them, If there are some differences between our practices in the matter of church government we believe that the Spirit of God will show [sic] to the people of Ethiopia after their conversion and wish them to do as God directs and not to follow the pattern of any American church for you are the people of another country.[39]

In a matter of five short years, the SIM (with Lambie's reluctant permission) *would* begin baptizing, and finally (in 1956) a nationwide "denomination," the Kale Heywet Church, *was* founded—a body that would count over three million Ethiopians as members by the mid-1990s.[40] There can be little confusion that these were Lambie's intentions from the beginning.[41] It was, in fact, this overriding commitment to evangelization and to an independent native church that set apart the SIM from virtually all other foreign missions operating in the country at the time. Others, even evangelical ones, were pledged, at least in theory, to shepherd any converts that they might receive into the Ethiopian Orthodox Church.[42]

Lambie, in the manner of a good Ethiopian politician, apparently chose to keep his long-range intentions hidden and to interpret his current promises as narrowly as possible. Realizing that the Orthodox Council would turn down his application to work in the south, Lambie quickly withdrew his request. Appealing to patrons at court, Lambie obtained permission from *ras* Teferi to travel south in order "to take the air":

We quietly went ahead with our preparations, buying mules and having saddle-pads made and getting everything shipshape for departure, and when at last everything was ready we received our permission to depart. The passport read that we were permitted to "take the air," or take a constitutional, or words to that effect. The Prime Minister told me confidentially not to ask permission; we could quietly visit a town, and if some good opening occurred we might slip a Mission station into it without making a fuss and probably everything would be all right. His Highness wanted to help us, but not openly.[43]

As it happened, Lambie discovered that many of the governors of the southern provinces in which he wished to settle were already acquaintances, but negotiating the political currents required to build permanent stations—two steps forward, one step back—took a politician of some skill, one who was willing to adapt himself to Ethiopian political culture.[44] Lambie was finally able to prevail because of his clientship to *ras* Teferi, who was, step by step, consolidating his power at the center of the Ethiopian state. Teferi was crowned *negus,* "king," in 1928 and finally, after Zauditu's death in 1930, *negus negist,* "king of kings."

The resulting relationship between Lambie and Haile Selassie contained its ironies. As it happened, the opposition of the Orthodox Church to foreign missionaries was, in the end, useful for the Emperor. His own modernist goal was, after all, to wring as many hospitals and schools as possible from the missionaries—not to mention threshing machines and Ford automobiles.[45] In the beginning, the missionaries had no intention of offering these—particularly the younger men without Lambie's previous experience in Ethiopia, those whose only thought seems to have been saving souls. The ambiguity and hesitation, the lack of clear bureaucratic procedure, provided the means by which all the missionaries were reluctantly forced to change their course:

> The government needed pliable change agents. Who better than expatriates that had no political ambitions, who believed in the saga of a Solomonic dynasty, who were willing to educate and carry on medical work? They required no money. The government was able to coerce the Sudan Interior Mission into becoming much more involved in institutional medical work than it had ever intended. The schools run by the Mission were small but highly significant. In each of the fifteen places [during the 1930s] these schools introduced the western educational model that Ethiopia was in the process of adopting . . . The government obtained an influence from the expatriate evangelists: the influence of modernity.[46]

On the part of the missionaries themselves, being pushed into providing modern services like hospitals and schools (and much later during the 1980s, economic development aid) set up complex ambivalences. In some ideal sense, anti-modernist missionaries expected that the word of God would be wholly sufficient to bring Ethiopians to the Truth. Nonetheless, to reside in Ethiopia, much less to carry out mission work, required governmental permission. Pressure from Haile Selassie's government—and later appeals from their own converts—meant that the SIM could hardly ignore modernity. Continually pushed back into some reliance on mediating modernity, the missionaries eventually reaped a harvest among southern peoples that they probably would not have enjoyed otherwise. For, being modern—in line with history, changing to fit with new times—was an important part of Christian identity in the south.[47] In other words, what Christianity offered to southern Ethiopians was a way of narratively repositioning themselves in relation to local and global forces, a way of becoming Ethiopian with links to a powerful world religion—but without adopting the religion of their conquerors.[48]

FROM NORTH AMERICAN ANTI-MODERNISM TO ETHIOPIAN MODERNISM

In the conversion process that slowly unfolded, the negative sign of anti-modernism was switched again and again.[49] Consider for example the Biblicism that the missionaries brought to southern Ethiopia, their emphasis on the Bible as the "inerrant" word of God. To North Americans, this doctrine protected religion from the modernist claims of science: whatever science professed to know, all that anyone *really* needed to know was the Bible: "[The SIM missionaries] felt duty-bound to have a Bible text for every religious statement they made. They believed that their interpretation of the Bible was that held by Jesus and his apostles; they believed in an authoritative Bible and took it with them to southern Ethiopia."[50]

In the context of southern Ethiopia, however, an emphasis on the Book had entirely different consequences than in North America. In Ethiopia, being able to read the Bible (and hence other books) in a society in which no one else could separated one, not from modernity—far from it—but from tradition. In the 1930s, the SIM was allowed to use local vernaculars, but after the Italian occupation had ended, it was required to use the national language, Amharic, both in preaching and in Bible translation. For southerners, being literate in Amharic opened a whole new world of the nation, courts, newspapers, radio—in short, modernity.

Another example of this process of inversion occurred in missionaries' notion of exactly what constituted conversion. Becoming a Christian, for fundamentalists, did not depend upon a mere rite like baptism; rather, conversion required a wholesale "separation" from the world and a basic behavioral change in converts' moral lives. In North America, this kind of separation meant detachment from tobacco, alcohol, and other sin and, more broadly, from all forms of (modernist) attempts to dilute religious

traditionalism. But in southern Ethiopia, an emphasis on so-called separation led to a radical rejection of tradition, one that, as one missionary
put it, would eventually "blast apart" customary assumptions:

> There was much criticism here recently when one of the baptized believers
> took a wife in a Christian way, leaving off the beer drinking and revelry and
> assuming his work after only a week's honeymoon. He and his wife should
> have stayed in from one to two months before appearing in public. This of-
> fensive conduct on the part of believers will eventually serve to blast the idea
> of the sanctity of customs from the minds and hearts of the younger genera-
> tions, for their customs must look sad indeed in the light of the glorious
> Gospel of Christ.[51]

The seemingly limitless self-confidence with which the missionaries
attacked local custom was no doubt undergirded by their belief that *all*
traditional rites were "Satan worship." Converts, to be accepted as
such, had to declare war on indigenous religion: "Conversion was a crisis experience and conflict was anticipated. As soon as a person indicated that he wanted to 'accept Christ' the evangelist would ask him to
undo his charms and throw them away. The evangelist would then go to
the home of the new convert and throw out all the paraphernalia connected with his former beliefs."[52]

Converts were expected not just to avoid traditional religion but to
carry the war on custom into the very hearts of their communities. One
of the missionaries in Welaita during the 1930s reported the following
example:

> One of the older believers has been taking quite a fearless stand against
> demon worship. His sister-in-law happens to be a witch doctor. He lives in the
> same house with her and as a consequence he is met with a considerable
> amount of scoffing and ridicule. The neighbors speak of her as God always
> addressing her in the plural. This lad has told her that if she continues to re-
> ceive this false worship that God will punish her in some terrible way. A por-
> tion of all food before being touched must be given as an offering to the tribal
> demon. This believer deliberately drinks out of her personal drinking vessel
> and sits on her special stool, regardless of the fact that it is generally believed
> that anyone doing these things will be killed by the demon. He has been faith-
> ful in testifying and is being greatly used of the Lord. It is largely through his
> endeavors that the demon meetings have ceased in this place. Pray for the
> strengthening of this brave lad and also for this demon-possessed relative,
> that even she too may be snatched as a brand from the burning.[53]

However ill-informed about Welaita society (it is difficult to know just
what was occurring in this case), this missionary account nonetheless
points to the kind of action that was expected from converts.

In the process of conversion, admission to baptism became a test of whether converts had in fact "separated" themselves from tradition. Leading up to the event, a whole series of practices ensued in which converts were examined and reexamined. To be accepted, a candidate had to demonstrate that he or she was truly leading a "new life." At first, this process of inspection and scrutiny, of confession and more confession, was presided over by expatriate missionaries. After the first baptisms, however, the examination of new candidates was taken over—probably more efficiently—by local Christians themselves. Surveillance and self-surveillance gave rise to strikingly new forms of organizational power in southern Ethiopia, forms with which "tradition" would not be able to compete in the coming decades.

The resulting sociological character of the new church groups appears in a description of the first baptisms at Welaita in 1933:

> For nearly a year the question of baptism was presented, considered, and discussed. For the last two or three months of 1932 it was a daily challenge. Who is suitable? Later the question was Who is willing?
>
> At first it seemed as if there were a score or two who would present themselves as candidates for baptism. Conference after conference was held. Examinations into hours were conducted. The process of elimination began in earnest. First on one count and then on another the work of separation took place. Some for inconsistent lives, others for unconfessed sins, and others for attachments to sinful customs, were regarded as unsuitable.[54]

THE GROWTH OF A LOCAL CHURCH IN WELAITA

Foreign personnel in the Sudan Interior Mission continued to grow into the mid-1930s, finally expanding to open stations even in northern Ethiopia, where Orthodox Christians predominated. But the personal relationship between Lambie and Haile Selassie that made this development possible was disrupted beginning in 1935, when Mussolini began his invasion of Ethiopia. By May 1936, Haile Selassie had fled the country to remain in exile for the following five years. Lambie, ever the diplomat, attempted to accommodate himself to the new structure of power. According to SIM missionary Brian Fargher:

> Lambie's efforts to please the Italian government seemed to go beyond what was strictly necessary. For some unknown reason (was it to please the government in the hope that it would allow him to remain in the country?) Lambie, ignoring thousands of witnesses and photographs, wrote a letter to the Red Cross headquarters in Geneva denying that the Italian air force had bombed Red Cross hospitals. He must have known that the bombings had

taken place repeatedly, in many different parts of the country, and at widely separated times.[55]

Haile Selassie was never to forgive this breach of loyalty, and after Lambie—who had previously gone to the length of switching citizenship from the United States to Ethiopia—left the country in August 1936, he was never to be allowed to return. By August 1938, all SIM personnel had been ordered to leave the Italian colony, some taking up work in the Anglo-Egyptian Sudan.

When SIM missionaries were finally able to return to Ethiopia after Haile Selassie was restored to power in 1941, they were amazed and overjoyed to discover that, *in their absence,* an explosion of Christian conversion had taken place in the south. This was particularly the case in Welaita, where the missionaries had left at most fifty converts in 1937, and where by 1944, some fifteen thousand existed.[56]

To understand this explosion requires finally some appreciation of the SIM policy with regard to the "indigenous church." In a book in 1942, Lambie set out its fundamentals:

> What is this method . . . ? In brief outline it is this: Missionaries go to a place where Christ is not known. They study the language, translate some of the Bible, and preach Christ crucified as the only way of salvation. In time they gather, or rather, the Holy Spirit gathers out a little group of true believers. They baptise these believers and form them into a church, ordaining elders. They give them all that the Bible says about church organisation as outlined in the Epistles of Timothy and Titus. Then the missionaries take their hands off and let the native believers carry on.
>
> The missionaries do not build any churches or pay any native evangelists, but from the very beginning they encourage the native believers to do these things for themselves. Thus the only expenditure for the work, aside from the missionaries' own support and allowances, comes from the native church itself. By this method the Mission aims not to make adherents but to form a really indigenous church.
>
> Most missions have gone along different lines. They have themselves built the churches and paid the native evangelists. They have been either at the head of the church or exerted a powerful influence in it and have often determined the exact line of procedure and organisation.[57]

As Lambie pointed out, this notion of the autonomy of the local church—from the very beginning, from the first baptisms—was indeed significant. There were, of course, limits to this autonomy, especially when local churches failed to separate themselves completely from drinking, smoking, polygyny, and traditional religion. According to Fargher, the principle of local church autonomy was perhaps infringed upon more in Ethiopia after the Italian occupation than before, and it was never really practiced to the same degree in other parts of Africa like Nigeria.[58] But the SIM's ideal of a native church in Ethiopia was no doubt critical in giving southerners a space within which to claim ownership of evangelical Christianity.

According to the formula, "self-supporting, self-governing and self-propagating," autonomy required, first of all, financial independence.[59] The indigenous church was expected to provide all of its own funds, even for evangelism. Lambie's associate, George Rhoad wrote:

> We are receiving enquiries from the people in this conference [the 1933 Moody Bible Institute Annual Conference], as to whether they could not make contributions to the support of our native teachers. Not one cent! We believe in the indigenous native church and the grace of God that can work transformation in native peoples as well as here. The natives are able to demonstrate their love, and are willing to accept the challenge to prove it. Those native converts have themselves determined that they would separate men who have approved themselves in their midst, and send them out to preach the gospel. One man will set apart one or two of his goats, and a woman will give her chickens, all to help forward the work of God. They do not need money. Already the native converts have gone out to build places of worship. They select hill tops from which the testimony may radiate and where people may see the place where God can be learned of. They do not come to us for designs, or benches or pews. Thank God that you can leave it to the life as it is in God and from God, expressing itself according to the temperament of a people, and already within five years in Abyssinia there are ten native churches supported by native people, with native evangelists.[60]

The theory of self-governance for the local church meant that expatriate missionaries did not consider themselves pastors of the churches they established. "The indigenous principle, as they [the SIM missionaries in Ethiopia] interpreted it, prevented them from exercising any control over the congregations once these congregations had elected their own elders. The missionaries saw their own roles as that of apostles, rather than simply as evangelists or pastors." Exactly how local congregations chose to govern themselves was not a major concern for the missionaries: "They did not place a great deal of emphasis upon the formal structure of the congregations; the transformed individual was the focal point of the new church."[61]

Once a group of believers had been baptized by missionaries, the indigenous church had been established. From that point onward, only the elders of the church baptized, not the missionaries, and only the elders, not the missionaries, dispensed the sacraments. "Once the local

group was established, the two, that is, the Mission and the congregation in the community, existed side by side as autonomous and independent organizations."[62] Once division had occurred, the elders of the
local congregation who had received communion from the hands of the
missionaries only once or twice before began serving the sacrament to
the missionaries.[63]

The final part of the formula, "self-propagating," was perhaps most
critical of all. To be a church, local groups had to expand:

> Without this [expansion] the SIM staff did not consider that their work had
> been successful. They viewed their own role as evangelists who used their
> mission stations to evangelize and establish churches and then move on to
> another place. This meant that the evangelizing task which had been begun
> in the first area was now taken over by the members of the new churches
> who used events like markets and funerals as well as the community event of
> house building to preach to the neighbours.[64]

It was this last aspect of the church that most impressed missionaries
when they returned to areas like Welaita in southern Ethiopia after the
occupation. According to Walter and Marcella Ohman writing in 1945:

> This mighty movement of the Spirit is not confined to Walamoland but has
> spread into neighboring tribes. Walamo [Welaita] men have sold their lands,
> taken their wives and children, and have moved into other areas or neigh-
> boring tribes where there was no witness. There they bought land, settled
> down and began preaching. Today four neighboring tribes have their
> churches from which the witness goes forth, and there are daily additions to
> all the churches.[65]

The fact that the missionaries were away during the initial explosion of
conversion was probably significant.[66] Nonetheless, the peculiar structure of the SIM and its indigenous church policy made it easier for Welaita to identity themselves with Christianity than it otherwise would
have been.

The SIM's policies also meant that the conversion process, quickly
presided over by local people, probably went deeper.[67] Unlike other
areas of Africa in which Christian beliefs were mixed with indigenous
ones, no space of easy coexistence was left in southern Ethiopia. Welaita
believers themselves attempted to exterminate traditional practices, root
and branch.

The result by the mid-1940s was an expansive and indigenous
church in Welaita. Five decades before, Welaita people had been sav-
agely defeated by northern Ethiopian armies. At that point, thousands
of Welaita had been killed and taken as slaves; the Welaita king was im-

prisoned and deposed. From something of a regional power themselves, the Welaita had been suddenly transformed into the lowliest of the low. Against this background, fundamentalist Christianity offered a new and powerful identity—a way to separate oneself from past Welaita tradition (that had offered no protection), to bypass their northern Orthodox Christian conquerors (who viewed them as little more than slaves), while becoming literate citizens of the nation (with links to prestigious and wealthy foreigners).

As I have shown, an important part of evangelical Christian identity was the commitment to take the "good news" to others. Welaita's regional dominance in the nineteenth century was thus spiritualized by the middle of the twentieth. By then, Welaita churchmen began to see themselves as the local center from which the Christian light would shine in southern Ethiopia. Welaita evangelists settled farther and farther afield, finally reaching Maaleland in the early 1960s.

There, as the following chapter will recount, Welaita evangelists would eventually produce new men and women in Maale, socially bound to small groups, constantly examining and reexamining their own and fellow believers' deportment, contemptuous of the past, and committed to a new and progressive future.

CHAPTER 5

The Cultural Construction
of Conversion in Maale

Missionary life is not easy. Our Lord never promised us ease in service. There will be times when we may feel forgotten, neglected, or
set aside. Our good may be evil spoken of, our wishes crossed, our
taste offended, our advice disregarded, and our opinions ridiculed.
We may have to be content in hard physical surroundings. The Bible
teaches clearly how to be victorious in these times: "Now thanks be
to God who always leads us forth to triumph in Christ, and who
diffuses by us the fragrance of the knowledge of him in every place"
(2 Corinthians 2:14, literal translation). "That is why, for Christ's
sake, I delight in weaknesses, in insults, in hardships, in persecu-
tions, in difficulties" (2 Corinthians 12:9, 10). "Christ will be ex-
alted in my body, whether by life or by death" (Philippians 1:20).
"In all these things we are more than conquerors through him who
loved us" (Romans 8:37).

SIM Manual, 1991 edition

If the first field director, Dr. Lambie, was never allowed to return to
Ethiopia, other SIM missionaries started coming back in the mid-1940s.
By 1947, the mission had regained its pre-Italian strength, and over the
next decade, the number of missionaries dramatically increased—by almost a factor of three (see Figure 13).

After the restoration of Haile Selassie's government, however, the SIM
came into increasing conflict with the culturally dominant Amhara. A
provoked and more sensitive, post-occupation nationalism demanded
that all non-Orthodox faiths be suppressed—since only Orthodox
Christians could be counted as "true" Ethiopians. Consequently, it took
the new government several years of discussion before a mission policy
could be worked out, and even then, missionaries (and much more
openly, mission converts) faced increasing opposition by local governors and local elites, no matter the national policy.

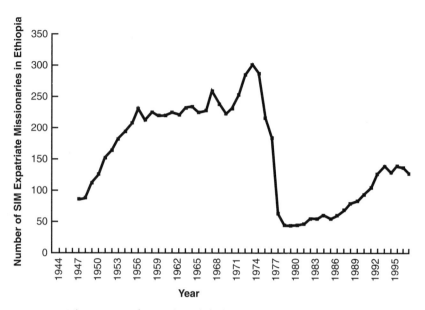

Figure 13. The pattern of growth and decline in numbers of expatriate SIM missionaries in Ethiopia. Data provided by the Library, SIM Headquarters, Charlotte, North Carolina.

After the Ethiopian Orthodox Church secured its independence from the Coptic Church of Egypt and appointed an Ethiopian as archbishop (previously the head of the Ethiopian Church had always been an Egyptian), this opposition hardened:

> The signing of the 1948 agreement [separating the Ethiopian and Egyptian churches] and the subsequent consecration of Abune Basilios as Metropolitan of Ethiopia on January 13, 1951, increased the Ethiopian Orthodox Church's self-confidence. . . . This Ethiopianization of the leadership of the church strengthened its critical attitude towards the evangelical churches, non-Orthodox and missionary dominated as they were. . . . The spring of 1951 saw new persecutions in different areas and among various evangelical groups. . . . 1954 and 1955 were especially difficult years.[1]

If Ethiopian nationalism was culturally connected with the Orthodox faith in the 1950s, it was also linked with an increasing demand for the country's modernization. The humbling ease with which the Italian army had invaded Ethiopia in the 1930s made modernization a crucial priority for the government elite. But the resources needed to accomplish this task were, of course, severely limited. Among church groups, it was only evangelical missionaries who were prepared to offer much help in this regard. Hence, the political logic of nationalism (modernize with whatever resources present themselves) came into collision with the dominant cultural definition of the nation (only Orthodox Christians could be counted as reliable Ethiopians).

Ever the political realist, Emperor Haile Selassie continued to take the lead in supporting foreign missionaries, and it was apparently his personal intervention in 1944 that finally produced a (relatively liberal) mission policy, after more restrictive ones had been mooted.[2] In the government decree, the country was notionally divided into two areas, "Ethiopian Church" areas, where missionaries were prohibited from proselytizing (but could run hospitals and schools), and "open" areas, where they could do both.[3] This meant that the bulk of mission activity was to remain concentrated in the non-Amhara south.

After the Italian occupation, Haile Selassie's government stepped up its pressure on evangelical missionaries to provide modern services— particularly schools in the late 1940s and 1950s. As before, some missionaries were reluctant to assume such responsibilities since they did not seem to contribute directly toward saving souls. But the SIM field director in Ethiopia understood very well the local political equation. In 1949, he wrote to all mission personnel:

> Regarding SIM Elementary Schools I have written you recently and much along the same lines as I am writing now, but I feel I must again impress you with the urgency of this matter. The Ministry of Education has made it clear, backing up the thought by action, to the effect that if the SIM does not produce schools and of a sizeable kind that no more stations or permits of Entry will be granted. . . . Here is a situation that will help you to understand matters: the Governor at Bale asked us to open a station at his district town of Goba. Mr. Davison and I, with his help chose the land, all necessary papers were sent to the Ministry of the Interior and Education, but the Ministry of Education refuses the permit for this station and the only reason is that we are not starting schools elsewhere. . . . This Governor begged the Vice Minister personally on our behalf to grant this permit but was unsuccessful in gaining anything. Being very concerned he came to me a number of times and talked the whole matter over for hours. I explained we could not get pupils to come. He replied, "That does not satisfy the Vice Minister."[4]

In the coming decades, the SIM would indeed establish schools on a wider scale. By 1970, a few years before the beginning of the revolution, the mission was managing 363 academic schools with nearly 30,000 children enrolled.[5]

THE CONSTRUCTION OF A SIM STATION AT BAKO

Just as the director believed, the expansion of schools would eventually allow an increase in the number of mission stations, hence work among "unreached peoples." Before the Italian invasion, the southernmost SIM post had been located in the Gemu highlands. As the mission expanded rapidly in the late 1940s and early 1950s, plans for new stations in the far south were drawn up. One of these was at Bako.[6] In 1949, a sketch for a hospital at Bako was completed (see Figure 14).

Unconstrained by accident and local reality, these architectural plans illustrate something of the missionary imagination: A patient approached the hospital via a long avenue flanked by a school and a doctor's house. Space was carefully portioned to control the movement of persons. A reception-and-fees office led directly to a waiting room, which led to an "inspection room." To the left were so-called first-class huts (presumably for important officials), to the right, those for the recently operated upon. Finally, arrayed in an orderly grid in the rear were the huts for ordinary patients.

This kind of rationalized spatial arrangement of dwellings was completely unknown locally at the time. Significantly, it would be used to lay out a new awraja or district capital in the 1950s, as government offices were moved from the mountaintop of Bako (where the mission station was being constructed) to the new town of Jinka located on a plain convenient for building an airfield (which the missionaries helped to choose). During the revolutionary period of the 1980s, the pattern reemerged as the state forced many peasants in the south to "villagize," to build houses in concentrated settlements on roads, laid out in a rigid, ninety-degree pattern of streets.

In the event, the missionaries' hospital was never constructed at Bako, but a new station was opened there on 19 January 1954.[7] The building of the first houses and clinic (the latter opened by the following June) was apparently made possible by a gift of $4,600 from a Mr. John Groeneweg in Minnesota. Just as the first missionaries were on their way to Bako, Mr. Groeneweg wrote to the field director:

> Sorry that I haven't taken time to write before this. Naturally I have been thinking a lot about how the station is coming along at Bako. Hope to hear that it is well on its way. I have retired from the farm and moved to Tyler. I would appreciate very much if you would remember to pray for me that I may get adjusted to the change and be a stronger witness for my Blessed Lord. I will be 70 years old May 1st and am enjoying good health. May the

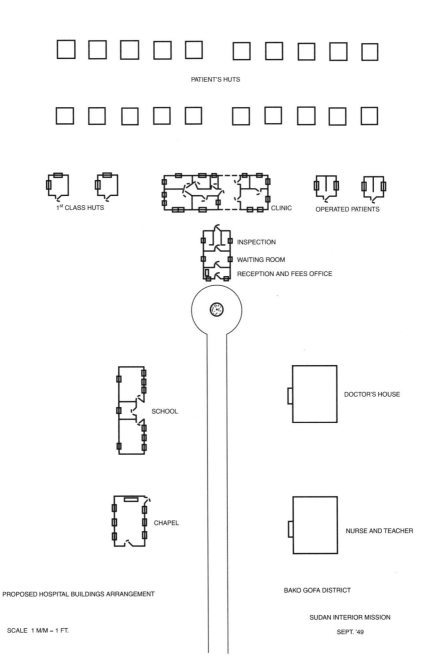

PATIENT'S HUTS

1st CLASS HUTS

CLINIC

OPERATED PATIENTS

INSPECTION

WAITING ROOM

RECEPTION AND FEES OFFICE

SCHOOL

DOCTOR'S HOUSE

CHAPEL

NURSE AND TEACHER

PROPOSED HOSPITAL BUILDINGS ARRANGEMENT

BAKO GOFA DISTRICT

SCALE 1 M/M = 1 FT.

SUDAN INTERIOR MISSION

SEPT. '49

Figure 14. SIM architectural plans for a mission station at Bako, 1949. Bako correspondence, SR-36, SR-37, SIM Archives, Charlotte, North Carolina.

lord richly bless you and all the dear missionaries there and give you many precious soles [sic] for your hire.[8]

In a matter of months, the governor at Bako was under medical treatment by the missionary wife[9], and by the middle of 1957, the missionary couple at Bako[10] reported that "three more evangelists have come from Walamo" [Welaita].[11] Welaita evangelists, with support from their own churches in Welaita, were a key component of the conversion process around Bako. If the expatriate missionaries had not enjoyed their help, the building of local Christian communities in places like Maale would certainly have taken far longer.[12]

The manner in which Welaita evangelists spread the gospel was described in a prayer letter from missionaries stationed in Welaita in 1952:

Eighty-seven evangelists (or shall I call them missionaries?) from the Walamo churches, and supported by them, are out preaching the gospel of God's grace in other areas. Just how do they do their work? Where do they hold their meetings? Do they have tents or meeting halls? Do they have great crowds to speak to? Let me tell you a little about them. First, they hear God's call, "Who will go for us?" to which they answer, "Here am I, send me." Then they wait upon God in prayer that they might know His place for them, and finally, two by two, they go forth to some untouched area. A Bible, some pencils, paper, alphabet cards, and an extra cloth over their shoulders and they come to say good-bye. We wish them godspeed, away they go, and we do not see them again for many months or a year. Entering another province, they try to make friends. No one knows them, and they know no one. Perhaps someone will allow them to sleep in his house, perhaps not, but they can always sleep outside, even if it is cold, as long as they have an extra cloth. They begin to tell the gospel story to anyone who will listen. Some will listen, the many will scoff and laugh. At last a friendly person will allow them to stay in his home a few days, and while there, the children are taught the alphabet. Father is now interested in seeing his son really able to distinguish one letter from another, and he becomes more friendly. More children join the group, and their parents come to see what it is all about. Soon they have a little group of day students and in the evening it is not hard to tell their parents as well as the children, the story of God's great love. One heart is touched and believes, and then another. They want to hear more and more. They build a small hut in which their children can gather for school work and they find it a good place to gather in the evenings to hear what God has said in his Word.

By this time the little school and the strange message is causing quite a stir, and the evangelists are called into court, asked why they have come and what they are doing. They are told that they must stop this teaching and leave the province. The first time they are only threatened as to what will happen if they do not leave. But the next time, they are put in prison, sometimes beaten and often suffer sickness. Relatives must feed their own people in prisons in this land, but these evangelists have no relatives to look to, for no one knows of their plight. Are they forsaken? No, for God has his ravens everywhere, and their new found friends and believers daily supply their needs. The persecution only strengthens the young believers, and they too become bold for Christ. Some of these suffer for His Name also, but count it all joy. After a long time the men may be released, again told to leave the province, and threatened with worse treatment if they return.

Now truly the leaving is hard. "What will we do without you? We know so little of God's Word. We cannot read it ourselves. Come back, come back and help us. Come back with your wives and children and we will help you to build you a house, and you can have a piece of land to plant. We will pray for you. God will help us."

Home again to their families, they tell them all, and their wives decide to leave all and go out for His Name's sake. But friends and relatives say, "Are you not afraid to return?" "No, God has sent us forth. He will take care of us." So the cow is sold, the house is sold, the land is sold—all, all for Him. . . . Money is given them from what we call the "Evangelists' Fund," and they often receive a gift from their church, and so with all they have left of their personal money they go forth.[13]

Eventually, many of these Welaita evangelists settled permanently around Bako and Jinka. One of these was Minote, who was to participate in the evangelization of Maale; the following is Minote's account of the early years:

Before I went to Maale I had been an evangelist in Gurageland for seven years or so. I came back home [to Welaita] sick. But then they wanted someone to take God's Word to Bako and Hamar, but I was reluctant. I wanted simply to raise my children. But finally, God's strength overcame my reluctance, and I decided to go. That was in 1961. A [mission] doctor in Welaita gave me some medicine to take if I got sick, and I came by plane to Bako. Balgizo Kunso, another Welaita evangelist, had already settled in Maale, and he chose me, "the tall one," to go to Maale with him. . . . When I arrived, I was told that there was nothing to eat in Maale, nothing to drink. They were selling grain by the cup. I asked about the Ari [Baaka] and I was told that they were eating people. I told myself that I was carrying God's word. If they ate me, then so be it. . . . When we left Bako, we didn't even take flour with us. Balgizo had a little sorghum. We prayed that it would last until the harvest. And indeed that little amount did last. Balgizo gave his wife a portion for me. We were all eating wokankaro [a kind of grass]. But that little amount wasn't finished, and we put the remains of it in a gourd after the new harvest had come in. . . . I was going all over Maale with Balgizo, evangelizing. We didn't sit down. We were always evangelizing.[14]

Even with help from Welaita evangelists from the 1950s—men and women who were culturally much closer to the local people than the expatriate missionaries[15] —almost a decade passed before the missionaries baptized any converts around Bako, in June 1962. The year before, a dedicated missionary couple had arrived who would stay for most of the following nine years. Because local people had difficulty in pronouncing their name, the new couple became known as Mr. and Mrs. Paulos (Amharic for Paul). The name was appropriate, for like Paul of the New Testament, the new missionaries became apostles to the churches centered on Bako.

> In 1962, there was a significant change in the way the work was carried on [at Bako]. At that time, the scattered believers that existed throughout the area were organized into their own evangelistic association. Each group of about ten converts was formed into a congregation, and the congregations were assigned to a parish. The parish representatives gathered for monthly meetings. This led to the formation of the Aari [and Maale] churches, which later became part of the Kala Hiywat church, the national Ethiopian denomination with roots in the evangelistic work of the Sudan Interior Mission.[16]

Just after the first baptisms, Mr. and Mrs. Paulos reported to their supporters in Australia:

> It was a jubilant day when nine were baptised here. This was the first believers' baptism in this area. . . . Now it will be possible to elect elders and get the groups functioning properly. Yes, four churches have been built, two more soon to go up and about 10 other meeting places where babes in Christ get together to pray and witness. . . . [Mr. Paulos] is out on another trek trying to encourage and to link up the groups. . . . there is a beginning of the showers to come [among the Maale]. It is among the Arras where the greatest movement has taken place.[17]

If the work of the Welaita evangelists was one key to the formation of the local church, so also were the labors of expatriate missionaries like Mr. Paulos "encouraging and linking up groups," creating modern organizations with representative practices, monthly meetings, and bureaucratic procedures. By themselves, the Welaita evangelists probably would not have set themselves these tasks—since nothing in the previous social and cultural organization of the south prepared people for these changes.

Mrs. Paulos: Recently, a prominent witch-doctor came fleeing to us from Satan. Oh, what a story and what a transformation! He went straight home, cleaned up his place (and himself of three years' growth of hair) and so great was his testimony that two wives, a brother and two others came to the Lord before our Christian Wallamo servant returned next day. The latter meets with them each

Lord's Day and seldom returns without a report of one new recruit added to the Lord's army. Just a week ago another witch-doctor from a different area came and was freed, though not without a bitter struggle. So on goes the work of the blessed Holy Spirit in our midst.[18]

CONVERSION BEGINS IN MAALE

The "showers" among the Maale that Mr. and Mrs. Paulos mentioned to their supporters began when an important lineage elder named Sime visited Bako in the early 1960s. Later, Sime was to fall away from the church, but I was able to interview him in 1984 about his experience of conversion some twenty years before. The following is a full text of Sime's narrative translated from Maale:

> At that time, I was really sick. While I was sick, my son died. Also, my wife died. All the women were finished. All the people I lived with were finished. After they had been finished, I left that house and built a new one up there. I went. But I was sick and sick and sick. When I had been defeated, I heard that a doctor had come to Bako. I went to Bako. Me and the one called Shambare. When we arrived, the white woman said, "Believe in God [*tsosi amane!*]"[19] "Believe in God!" I replied, "Where's God?" Listen well, I said, "Where's God?"
>
> "Believe in God! Believe in God!," she said again. I replied, "Where is God here that I can believe [witness him]?"
>
> "We believe in the God of Gods."
>
> "Where is God that one can believe?"
>
> By then, I had been circumcised and finished all the Maale rituals.[20] We said that *tsosi* [the Divinity] existed in the heavens. When we died close to that God, our flesh remained in the ground. God dwelled above—that's what I had heard since I was a child. "Where is this believer's God? He is a lie."
>
> "Believe in God! Believe in God!"
>
> "Oh, this God is not believable."
>
> "Then go away!" she said to us. "Get out! Get out!" We went out of the house and sat down. Sarka's wife, at that time she was still a young girl, worked with the white woman, and she came up to us:
>
> "Why don't you believe in God? Here you've come because you're sick. The sickness has gotten the best of you. When she tells you to believe in God, why do you refuse? She's sent you away to believe in God."
>
> "Where is God that we can believe in him?"
>
> "Medicine is like God. When you believe in God, the medicine works. If you don't believe, then the medicine won't work."
>
> "Then where is God here that we can believe in him?"
>
> "Oh! The thing that counts is your hand. When she says to believe in God, she doesn't mean that you have to see him. It's raising your right hand like this. That's believing."

"When I do my hand like that, does it mean that God is short? What does it amount to?"

"No, it won't do anything. Only the medicine will work."

I thought that raising my hand like that meant that God was short. Hear me well. I thought that raising my hand meant that God was short.

"Now shall I only raise my hand?"

"Yes, raise your hand and break your necklace."[21]

"Break it and do what?"

"Break it and give it to her."

"We'll take you back [to her]," that was the way that the children preached to us. Well, I wanted to get doctored. But she refused. She said that unless I believed in God, she wouldn't give me any medicine. What could I do? I told the girl to tell the white woman that I wanted medicine. She told her.

"Believe in God! What are doing for yourself?" She asked me like you are asking me now [about Maale life].

"Well, I was just lying sick and drinking alla [beer]."

"What is alla?"

"We brew it from finger millet."

"When you drink it, what happens?"

"It kills some people. Others get well."

"Don't many die?"

"They do."

"The reason that you came was for medicine, isn't that right?"

"Yes."

"To be doctored, no?"

"It won't be any trouble. Take your necklace and go. It won't be any trouble. Take your necklace and go. Take the necklace and throw it away like trash. Believe in God! I am going to doctor you."

"All right," I consented.

"Believe in Jesus Christ!"

I believed in Jesus Christ.

"Don't smoke tobacco. Don't drink beer. Don't drink anything that makes you drunk. Food, you eat food. Don't smoke tobacco. Stay away from prostitutes."[22]

In this way the woman made us believe. She said, "Listen to me well. Don't bear false witness. Don't go after another man's wife. Don't take a lover." That way she made us believe [in God]. "Don't steal."

She gave me a shot in the hip. Sleep took me and threw me. It put me to sleep. It didn't put Shambare to sleep. But it put me to sleep. When I got up the next morning, my leg could kick. Before, it didn't move.

I needed to pay my tax. I needed to go to Jinka. Shambare said, "I want to go home." "You go on," I said, "I'm going to Jinka." Before I thought that I owed the *wuzufe* tax. When I got there, I didn't have to pay the *wuzufe*, only the *wagonsi*. I wondered, "Is this because I believed in God?" After I got my receipt, I returned home feeling really strong.

Then I lived and lived. After that, I made Shole Gotsi in Bannati a believer. Then my son was small. Everybody I was making believe. I went to the lowlands, to Barindu, to Gastuka, by way of Bi always increasing the number of believers. Doisoma [his son] entered the mission [school]. Dubbo [another son] became the peoples' teacher.

I did that and I did that, and then I married, but the woman wouldn't listen to me. I tried sending someone as an intermediary, but it didn't work, and I divorced her and took another woman. That's how I remain [outside the church].[23] At the same time that I continue to live like a *museno* [mission convert] I am also drinking beer. I sit here like that.[24]

Also in 1984, I interviewed Mrs. Paulos, the missionary wife who had converted Sime in the early 1960s. The following are my field notes of the conversation. Instead of medicine and schools—which went unmentioned—Mrs. Paulos emphasized the themes of anti-modernist Christianity, in particular, the great struggle between God and Satan and the consequent urgency of conversion:

Mrs. Paulos was alone one day when Sime and another man came from Maale. "They wanted to know more about this Jesus who could deliver them from Satan's power and the bondage and poverty he always brought upon them." She asked them to come into her house (her husband was away) and to sit down on chairs. They were ill at ease because they didn't know how to sit on chairs (she also mentioned that later the men joked about wearing shorts on the journey to Bako that day—they hadn't known how properly to put them on). She asked the children to go out and play and closed the door. Sime and the other man looked at each other fearfully, for they had been told that white people eat people. She asked them whether they would like to accept the Lord Jesus Christ as their savior. They said yes. She explained that in order to shut everything else out, they should bow their heads and close their eyes to pray. Again, they were afraid, but they did so. "They accepted salvation in Christ Jesus." And they went back home rejoicing because they felt they were delivered from the power of Satan. They had believed that Satan had greater power than God, and they were making offerings to Satan to prevent misfortune.[25]

She said she and her husband had not had the time to study the traditional religion. . . . they had depended upon the natural seeking of the people. God gave a certain illumination to people apart from his Word. They had built on this natural illumination. They had so much to do, and no time to do it in. "We had really to get on with it."[26]

The conversion of Sime was a singularly important event in Maale, for he was the senior elder of what was probably one of the largest lineages in Maaleland. When Sime converted, the efficiency of the rituals carried out by all of his junior kinsmen was automatically affected according to Maale thought. It was not long then before all of Sime's "younger brothers" followed him in converting. A Welaita evangelist was soon posted to live near Sime's house in Koibe. In the years to follow, at least four other Welaita evangelists were to settle in Maaleland. Most brought their families for periods of five to six years.[27]

A SIM missionary: At every opportunity, the home of a believer became the residence of an evangelist whose task was to establish a church. The expatriate missionaries acted as catalysts in this process, providing no funds and doing very little of the preaching. Every Christian was encouraged to give what he or she could for the support of Ethiopian evangelists, and whatever was given was immediately passed on to the evangelists. . . . The work developed along four significant lines: (1) Local Bible schools were established so that students need never be sent out of their own area for training. The schools were as self-sufficient as possible, taught by local teachers, and supported by local money. (2) Visiting evangelists, both expatriate and national, were reduced in number so that the evangelistic outreach could be taken over entirely by local people. The church provided, trained, and supported its own evangelists. (3) Expatriate involvement in handling finances, teaching, and administration was gradually reduced. (4) The structure of the national Kala Hiywat church was strengthened.[28]

AN INDIGENOUS THEORY OF CONVERSION

The manner in which men like Sime understood conversion was inevitably conditioned by the long-established categories of Maale religion.[29] For the Maale, divinity or *tsosi* was the collective and abstracted representative of all the ancestors, almost the eternal principle of life itself.[30] The Maale referred, for example, to ancestral graves and to the quiver that contained body parts of all the past kings as *tsoso*. As a collective principle, *tsosi* was identified with the heavens, but it (to use a personal pronoun would probably misconstrue traditional thought) did not directly affect the lives of individual Maale. It was the ancestors, one might almost say, the divine principle in its separate and personal forms, who blessed and cursed. If a Maale correctly carried out his or her clan taboos, faithfully observed customs, then the ancestors' *baliti* or "forehead"—their power to affect fortune—meant that a person enjoyed health, fertility, and wealth. Persons with these characteristics were assumed to be in the correct relation to the Divine; in other words, outward material success was taken to index inward spiritual status.[31]

By the early 1960s, the missionaries at Bako lived at a level of wealth that no other person in the area managed, not even the highest official, the governor of the awraja of Hamar Bako. To the missionaries, of course, their standard of life represented a major sacrifice; the priva-

Figure 15. An island of modernity. A typical SIM mission compound in the south in the 1960s. Photographic Collection, SIM International Archives, Charlotte, North Carolina.

tions involved must have demanded considerable religious commitment over the years. But affluence and abundance are relative concepts, and locally, expatriate missionaries commanded great resources—electric generators, modern houses, and access to medical knowledge and air transport being only some.

Because riches and power automatically indexed spiritual status for the Maale, old categories of understanding opened the door to the new religion, as it were. Certainly, most of the early Maale Christians expected that conversion would mean health and wealth. These themes appear clearly in Sime's narrative and in almost all others that I collected.[32] In one case, a man living in the lowlands consulted the intestine oracle to see whether conversion would be advisable. According to the reading of the goat entrails, he and his five brothers—all very poor— would become rich if they converted. After he and his brothers converted and moved from the lowlands to Bunati, they did indeed become wealthy.[33]

By the 1970s, young men who had been through several years of Bible school began to preach against this too-worldly understanding of the gospel: "Don't believe in order to become wealthy. May God give us

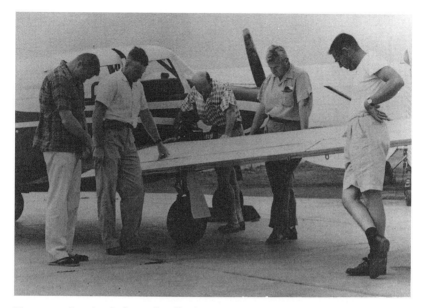

Figure 16. Praying before takeoff. The Mission Aviation Fellowship provided services and communications connections for SIM mission stations. Photographic Collection, SIM International Archives, Charlotte, North Carolina.

what he wills. Your property will remain on earth, but you will go to heaven." Despite this teaching, older believers remained skeptical: "Well, if that is so, then why should I be a Christian?"[34]

But conversion cannot be understood only as a set of abstract cultural themes. It must be placed also in the context of practices. In case after case, Maale reported that they had believed in Christ during a moment of great misfortune.[35] In Sime's case, his wife and children had died. He was ill. Such circumstances were the result, according to Maale thought, of one's own transgressions, *gome*. These ranged from inadvertently breaking any of a set of intricate taboos such as eating finger millet with milk (for some clans) to letting breast milk fall on the grinding stone (for many women), to deliberate transgressions such as eating new crops before they had been tasted by an eldest brother, and finally to wrongs like stealing or murder. When misfortune struck, a person had to determine the gome that was affecting his or her life and then "confess," *butsane*, literally separate himself from the transgression.

When calamity piled on top of calamity, when the confession of one gome after another failed to provide relief, the limits of Maale religion were reached. Sometimes, the misfortune that tipped the scale was simply a reading of the intestine oracle that was so bleak that one did not know what to do. In any case, all Maale—both Christians and non-Christians—maintained that a person could escape the effects of Maale *gome* by converting to another religion.

This belief, striking in and of itself, underlay what one might call an indigenous theory of conversion. In other words, the Maale already possessed a theory of religious change before the missionaries arrived. When disaster struck, it was not unusual for men to move away from ancestral homes (even though they contained the graves of many ancestors) or to adopt new taboos (it was apparently such situations that gave rise to taboos in the first place) or, in the most extreme cases, to move outside Maale or to accept the teachings of prophets who taught fundamentally new beliefs (at least one revitalization movement occurred in the area around Maale during the early twentieth century).[36] Such openness to change in severe situations—the accepted practice of escaping the consequences of one religious regime by converting to another—became an essential element in the formation of Christians communities in Maale.

Besides the cultural construction of conversion, it is also important to understand its sociological underpinnings. As the process wore on, the social roles that mapped onto conversion changed. The first converts like Sime had often been influential lineage elders. By the early 1970s, however, nearly all new male converts were younger brothers.

As I have explained, an intricate and complex system of taboos had upheld the power of eldest brothers in Maale lineages. When a younger brother's cow had a calf, for example, a ritual had to be performed by the eldest brother (presenting the new milk to the ancestors and then tasting it himself) before anyone else could come into contact with the milk. If this taboo was somehow broken, then the cow had to be traded for another; but if it were broken twice, the eldest brother simply took possession of the cow. Similarly, when bees first entered a younger brother's hive, he had to take the new honey to his eldest brother for presentation to the ancestors and for his tasting. If any fell on the ground along the way or if, say, he absentmindedly put his hand in his mouth without first washing it (thus consuming the honey before his eldest brother), the hive had to be given to his eldest brother. These prohibitions were onerous for younger brothers and upheld a system not only of unequal status but of differential power and wealth as well.

Interviewed in 1984, elders in the church at Gasiwatsi explained the attraction of Christianity for younger brothers:

Christians were simply eating and drinking. With something as good as this, why should we kill ourselves [attempting to keep the old taboos]? Everyone believed in Christ. . . . But did eldest brothers like the new religion? All of us are younger brothers here. Whatever we farm, we can use it ourselves. Whatever we own, we can control it for our own use. . . . When we became Christians, *tsosi leli kashkane,* we made rituals only to God. When we studied the Bible we found nothing that was taboo. The things that we had thought were taboo, we found were permissible. . . . When we really opened the Bible and looked at it, we saw that according to God nothing was *ketse* [taboo].[37]

THE CONFLICT BETWEEN CHRISTIANS AND OTHERS OVER LAND

The local understanding of conversion, set within an array of particular religious practices, underlay the formation of new churches in Maale. A final factor in the conversion process was the political economy of land.

By the early 1960s, there were three categories of landowners in Maale: first, *neftenya,* northern soldier-settlers who claimed that they had been given or bought land in Maale; second, the Maale chiefs and king; and third, Maale commoners, usually lineage elders. Increasingly, the first group and part of the second (particularly the new kati Arbu installed by government fiat in about 1962 and chief Artamu) began encroaching upon the land claims of the third—ordinary Maale commoners. Because of northern settlers' familiarity with the language and customs of the Bako courts (later Jinka) and their ability to influence and to give bribes to officials, coupled with the corresponding difficulties experienced by Maale commoners in fighting these stratagems, northerners were able to invent land claims out of very little and thus to reduce Maale commoners to the status of tenants, at least as far as the government was concerned.

As it happened, Christianity offered one of the few means whereby commoners could fight this process by the mid-1960s.[38] The SIM offered schooling in Amharic, the language used in courts, and second, the Welaita evangelists who settled in Maale offered a wider knowledge of national Ethiopian law and how to go about getting things done vis-à-vis the government. Finally, in a few examples, expatriate missionaries seem to have helped Christians in court cases —even though official SIM policy was not become involved in "political" issues.[39]

Two years after the first baptisms, in May 1964, Mr. and Mrs. Paulos wrote to other missionaries in the SIM asking them "to pray for Christians with land matters, etc. in court."[40] The first convert in

Maale, Sime, was involved in a long and bitter dispute with a northern landlord who lived in Koibe, Manakule. According to Sime, he received help from Mr. Paulos himself in appealing his case all the way to Addis Ababa.

Manakule, interviewed in 1984, described the coming of the Welaita evangelists to Koibe in the following way:

> Before they [the first Welaita evangelists] came, landlords were getting cows, money, honey. . . . The evangelists told the Maale that they should only pay money; they advised them that they should legally pay only 10 birr when they had been paying 20 or 30. One day I went to Sime's house to collect rent. [Sime contended, of course, that the land in question belonged to Sime, not to Manakule], and the evangelists gave me tea. I jokingly told them that they would have to pay rent next year. That very night, the evangelists went to Bako and told the white missionary there that I had threatened to kill them. The white man went to the awraja governor in Jinka and reported this. I happened to be present in Jinka at the time, and when the governor called me in, I explained that I had never threatened them. On examination, it turned out that what had happened, after I had left, was that the Maale had told the evangelists that I might try to kill them in the future. The white man apologized to me.[41]

Sime eventually settled outside of court with Manakule, buying the land that his ancestors had farmed for generations for eight cattle and five hundred birr, plus another five hundred in bribes to government officials. Others, like Sime's lineage mate, Beyene, also a Christian, refused to accede to Manakule's demands and pursued their claims in court, some of them for over a decade, eventually winning. In all of this, Christianity was to provide the social networks and some of the resources with which Maale commoners resisted northern landlords and Maale chiefs. Without such means, it is difficult to imagine that men like Beyene, stubborn to the end, would have been as successful as they were.

Conversion reflected, then, a complex interplay of factors. The preaching of the Welaita evangelists, plus the visits to Maale of Mr. Paulos every three to four months, eventually produced a network of churches in Maale. Consequently, on the eve of the revolution, congregations were to be found in region 1 at Gudo, Bio, Lemo, and (just forming in 1974) Ginte; in region 2 at Bunati, Koibe, Mela, and Gasiwatsi; in region 3 at Doiso; and in region 4 at Ajo and Buli.

Koibe, at the center of this network, and the home of the first convert Sime, was the local religious center. At Koibe, there was a two-year academic school run by the church, plus a one-year Bible school. At Bunati, Mela, and Lemo, there were one-year academic schools. (The only gov-

ernment school in Maaleland at the time was located in the police-
station village of Bushkoro in region 1.)

The Maale churches were organized into wider associations called
mahabirs centered on the mission station at Bako.[42] By the time of the
revolution, churches in Maale were divided into two or three districts.
Each church sent four representatives to a monthly district meeting. In
turn, there were approximately ten districts reporting to the Bako area
(most of which were Aari-speaking). Each district sent two representatives to the monthly area council.[43] Once a year, all Christians were encouraged to attend a "conference" with preaching, baptisms, and business meetings. A conference of the women's association in the Bako area
drew five hundred women as early as 1968.[44]

Meanwhile, the mission station itself was becoming a center of activity, with students and evangelists coming and going, the expatriate missionaries trekking out to organize and to encourage, and sick people
from all around coming to seek treatment. During the month of December 1971, for example, there were 55 students in the Bible school at
Bako (the school having been in operation since 1962). An academic el-
ementary school had been started in 1963, and by 1971, it comprised
four grades with 116 students (many of whom lived on the mission
compound, walking home periodically to bring their own food). Finally,
the clinic dispensed a total of 428 treatments during December 1971.[45]
All of these activities involved new social patterns. Patients had to be
taught how to wait at the clinic, students how to arrive at school on
time, and everyone how to respect Western notions of privacy for expatriate missionaries. Mrs. Paulos recalled how difficult it was to teach the
modern discipline needed for a Bible School: "When you think of Bible
School you think of students who already know how to read and write.
But for Maale, they had never seen a pencil or pen. They had never sat
at a desk or bench. It was rough going both for them and for us."[46]

Mission records contain no indication of the overall numbers of new
Christians, but surely by the late 1960s the Bako area and Maale could no
longer be considered an "unreached" area. Missionaries in Bako were, in
fact, making plans for a new station farther south and for evangelizing
other ethnic groups well beyond the Aari and Maale. Until the revolution,
the conversion process continued in fits and starts. In October 1967, for
example, Mr. Paulos asked others in the mission to pray "that nearly
1,000 confession of faith last month that they will be genuine."[47] Less
than a year later in May 1968, he reported, "After months of no profes-
sions, now eight patients have accepted Christ in the clinic."[48]

As Robert Hefner has usefully emphasized, Christian conversion is fundamentally about the assumption of new identities—often in situations in which macrohistorical changes have undermined old systems of status and self-validation.[49] These new identities are enacted primarily through the adoption of new narratives that reposition persons by making new sense of local situations, that promise new dignity and access to wider values.

When the zemecha students arrived in 1975, they hardly initiated the Maale conversation on what one might call "modernity." After thirteen years, after thousands of classes and meetings, after what must have been millions of micro-encounters—sitting at a desk, voting for a church candidate, learning the Amharic alphabet, listening to the Ethiopian radio—evangelists had produced a small but committed vanguard in Maale. It was young men from this group, impatient with Maale tradition, who helped the zemecha students bury the king's bones. And it was the same young men, oriented toward an ever progressive future, who assumed most of the leadership roles in the newly organized peasant mahabirs—organizations similarly named and structured as their own church groups.

This was the "pre-revolution" in Maale upon which the revolution of 1975 came to depend. It was partly on this basis that the revolutionary state penetrated ever deeper into local society in the 1980s. For the first time in Ethiopian history, relatively accurate lists of household heads in Maale would be drawn up. Taxes would be collected much more extensively. And tens of Maale young men would be conscripted into the Ethiopian armed forces. None of this would have been possible without the local, Christian-educated vanguard.

The saints saw themselves as divine instruments and theirs was the politics of wreckers, architects, and builders—hard at work upon the political world. They refused to recognize any inherent or natural resistance to their labors. They treated every obstacle as another example of the devil's resourcefulness and they summoned all their energy, imagination, and craft to overcome it. Because their work required cooperation, they organized to carry it through successfully and they joined forces with any man who might help them without regard to the older bonds of family and neighborhood. They sought "brethren" and turned away if necessary from their relatives; they sought zeal and not affection. Thus there arose the leagues and covenants, the conferences and congregations which are the prototypes of revolutionary discipline. In these the good work was carried forward; at the same time, new saints were trained and hardened for their unremitting labor. The results of that labor can best be seen in the English Revolution of 1640.[50]

Looking back, it is indeed ironic that one of the architects of these results in Ethiopia is none other than Rowland Victor Bingham: that dour Canadian believer in angels and demons, lakes of fire that burned forever, and a Jesus Christ who would be returning—any day now—to rule the world. It was Bingham the missionary who took up, as he said, "the burden of the Sudan," that "great, black belt, stretching for twenty-five hundred miles across Africa, steeped in the densest darkness."

But darkness and light have always been interconnected in modernities the world over. And as modernization has proceeded, such connections have become farther and farther flung across the globe. Retracing these paths is, I take it, one of the principal goals of historical ethnography.

CHAPTER 6

Marxist Modernism
at the Ethiopian Center

Cold War Deterritorializations

The strength of communism is found not in its economics—which
is hopelessly antiquated—nor in its character as a secular religion,
where it can be easily outclassed by the appeals of nationalism. Its
most relevant characteristic is its political theory and practice, not
its Marxism but its Leninism. In the socialist intellectual tradition,
Marx is usually thought of as the peak; before Marx there were
precursors, such as the utopian socialists; after Marx there were
disciples and interpreters, such as Kautsky, Bernstein, Luxemburg,
Lenin. In terms of the political theory of Marxism, however, this is
quite inappropriate—Lenin was not a disciple of Marx, rather Marx
was a precursor of Lenin. Lenin made Marxism into a political theory and in the process stood Marx on his head. The key to Marx is
the social class; the key to Lenin is the political party.

Samuel P. Huntington,
Political Order in Changing Societies

By 1976, virtually every major political faction in Addis Ababa had become "Marxist." This shift eventually made possible a complete about-
face in international alliances, with the Soviet Union replacing the
United States as Ethiopia's principal foreign backer. As the switch occurred, any number of consequences followed—most importantly, massive amounts of military aid with a resulting "deterritorialization" of
the revolution. From then on, what would happen in Ethiopia would
have as much to do with events in Moscow (and Washington) as with
those in Addis Ababa.

The sudden and dramatic adoption of Marxism—coupled with the
fact that few Ethiopians appeared to Westerners to be "real" Marxists—has often puzzled analysts of the revolution.[1] The paradox begins
to lose some of its force when one places Marxism within the particular currents of modernist discourse in 1976. There had been a time,

perhaps until the early 1950s, when Haile Selassie was Ethiopia's unquestioned modernist, the progressive emperor who would guide his
country into a new era. By the 1970s, the sign of this association, at
least for educated Ethiopians, had been decisively shifted. By then,
Haile Selassie and his elite were identified as the very cause of Ethiopian backwardness.

For potential opponents of the Derg after it had deposed Haile Selassie, this meant that there was no ideological position available from
which to undermine the military committee from the right. The pattern
of the Ethiopian past rendered such an option difficult: Liberalism, the
United States, and capitalism—through their association with the Emperor—had all been coupled with Ethiopian backwardness and corrup-
tion.[2] If any opponent were going to be effective in attacking the Derg,
he almost had to do so from the left. This set up a steady discursive
pressure on all civilian groups, no matter their "politics," to move further and further to the left. In its attempt to undermine its enemies, the
Derg followed, proclaiming its attachment to the "science" of Marxism-
Leninism in April 1976.

In this discursive context, the meaning of Marxism in Ethiopia came
to be contained not so much in its utopian vision of human liberation—
a theme familiar to Western Marxism—but in a story of how a weak
and backward collection of nationalities, located outside of Western Europe, attained unity, wealth, and international respect: the allegory of
the Russian and, later, the Chinese, revolution:

> The Bolshevik revolutionary model has been decisive for all twentieth-
> century revolutions because it made them imaginable in societies still more
> backward than All the Russias. (It opened the possibility of, so to speak, cut-
> ting history off at the pass.) The skilful early experimentation of Mao Tse-
> tung confirmed the utility of the model outside Europe. One can thus see a
> sort of culmination of the modular process in the case of Cambodia, where
> in 1962 less than 2.5 percent of the two-and-a-half-million-strong adult
> work-force was "working class," and less than 0.5 percent "capitalists."[3]

As the model of revolution was passed on to yet more "backward"
countries—ranged along the great chain of modernity—Marxism-
Leninism offered to each an apparent way of "cutting history off at the
pass." Levenson captures, in a particularly telling way, the ambivalences of this process for the Chinese:

> In the early nineteenth century, foreign intrusion could nurture only resent-
> ment—against others, and against the self—not self-esteem. From its begin-
> nings in the May Fourth Movement of 1919, Chinese Communism reflected

that resentment, with both its targets. Anti-imperialism struck at the foreign foes of the new or would-be nation; anti-feudalism hit the domestic foes of the new culture. The combination released Chinese feeling against the Confucian past, which, though moribund, had still invited acceptance, as Chinese; and against a western present, which, though, rejuvenating, had still invited rejection, as alien. To be both Chinese and fresh instead of either foreign or stale: that was the Communist promise.[4]

To be both Ethiopian and fresh was the basis for the excitement about, commitment to, and celebration of Marxism in the early days of the revolution. (Never mind that the very definition of Ethiopianness itself would become more and more problematic into the 1980s.) In this chapter, I shall outline how Marxism-Leninism was adopted as the legitimating ideology of the Derg and how, concomitantly, one man, Mengistu Haile Mariam, rose to dictatorial power.

THE MEANING OF MARXISM IN ETHIOPIA

Exactly how Westerners had "intruded" on Ethiopia (to use Levenson's term in the quote above) is important to understand. Unlike the rest of Africa, Ethiopia defeated its would-be European master, Italy, at the Battle of Adwa in 1896. This defeat added a distinctive edge to Ethiopian historical consciousness. From the Battle of Adwa until Mussolini's occupation of Ethiopia during the late 1930s, many Ethiopians shared perhaps a rather smug confidence in the future.[5] A small minority, particularly those like *ras* Teferi (later Haile Selassie) who had traveled to Europe, realized that Ethiopia's political independence meant little in the context of her relative economic "backwardness." As early as 1912, this theme appeared in an Amharic book published by Gebre Heywet Baykadagn. Gebre Heywet warned that Ethiopians "would be ruined if they did not adopt European culture."[6] Acutely consciousness of the gradations of the world around him, Gebre Heywet held up Japan as a model for Ethiopia to imitate. Japan was a feudal empire outside of the West that had not only maintained its political independence but had adopted Western ways to escape feudalism and to leapfrog ahead to modernity.

As I have mentioned, the Ethiopian elite's consciousness of being "behind" grew steadily after Mussolini's occupation of the country during World War II. After Haile Selassie was returned to power, first with British and then with United States assistance, Ethiopian political independence was restored. But nationalist pride in that independence (celebrated by black people throughout the world in the twentieth century) was undermined by the increasing realization, particularly by educated Ethiopians, that even African colonies in the 1950s were economically "ahead" of Ethiopia. This grating contradiction helped to produce a crisis in December 1960, when Girmame Neway led an attempt to overthrow Haile Selassie.[7] For the first time in their history, university students organized a demonstration. Supporting the political change, they marched under signs emblazoned with, among other slogans, "liberty, equality, and fraternity."[8] With the Emperor out of the country, leaders of the coup ordered Haile Selassie's son, the Crown Prince, to read a statement over the radio that included the following:

> The Ethiopian people have a history of more than 3,000 years, but in that long history no progress was made in agriculture, commerce or industry. . . . The Ethiopian people manifested patience, such patience as is unknown in any other nation. . . . Nevertheless, there is no nation which, in time, would not extirpate ignorance from among its people and not aim at improving the standard of living. While the newly formed independent African nations are making progress, Ethiopia is lagging behind, and this fact is now realized.[9]

When Haile Selassie returned home to the support of part of his army (backed by U.S. military personnel), the coup failed.[10] But the contradictions posed by the unevenness of the modern world remained, indeed intensified, in the consciousness of Ethiopia's new elite. According to Donald Levine, writing in 1965:

> The discrepancy between the growing desire for aspects of modern culture and the persistence of many old customs and problems has generated much impatience, anxiety, and ennui among the modern-educated. Their sense of inadequacy vis-à-vis Western "metropolitan" standards is no less painful for their having escaped a long heritage of colonial domination, and combined with a sense of failure to move rapidly toward aspired goals has created in many of the modern-educated marked self-destructive tendencies. Insofar as their destructiveness has not turned inward it has been projected outward against other elements inside Ethiopia and without. One of these targets is the uneducated mass of the people, who . . . are often regarded as so backward that the only way one can bring progress to them is through coercion and authoritarian manipulation.[11]

In the rest of Africa, colonial elites, in their struggle for political independence, often valorized aspects of rural tradition in creating new notions of national identity.[12] In Tanzania, for example, the idea of an indigenous African socialism, spoiled by British colonialism, but called forth and developed by authentic leaders of the new state, was an important part of nationalist ideology. In this way, cultural identity for colonial elites was partially submerged with that of traditional country-men; and this unity was sometimes reinforced in actual political struggles in which peasants played important roles.[13]

Ethiopian history was different. Rural tradition was not valorized to the same degree as in Tanzania.[14] Without an immediate common colonial enemy, modernist intellectuals and their rural countrymen had less to unite against. Consequently, educated Ethiopians came to define themselves not only in opposition to Westerners but also in relation to their own more "backward" countrymen—many of whom were ethnically distinct. This fact gave Ethiopian modernism a particular edge. As Levine noted, educated Ethiopians sometimes felt entitled to drag, so to speak, their traditional countrymen into the twentieth century.

In Ethiopia, too, elite ideas developed in a different social setting compared to some other parts of Africa. Removed from the kind of rural villages that supported the Zimbabwe African National Liberation Army, for example, Ethiopian modernism was formulated by students studying in Addis Ababa, and even more so by those in New York, London, and Paris.

> Once the Ethiopian Students Movement came into existence . . . it was swept off the ground . . . by European ideologies and organizational models. . . . while the literature most widely read was the works of Marx, Engels, Lenin, Stalin, Mao as well as the *Peking Review* and an assortment of pamphlets written in the name of the Chinese communes, the bulk of these books and articles came, interestingly enough, not from the East but from the West. The channels of ideological transmissions were the classrooms, conversations with the Western instructors who fancied themselves radical, the libraries and the journeys by Ethiopians mostly to the West.[15]

After the upheavals in the West of the late 1960s, virtually every Ethiopian took up Marxism.[16] According to Dawit Wolde Giorgis, an unsympathetic observer of the process:

> The role played in the Revolution by Ethiopian students in the United States and Europe has never been fully appreciated. . . . All Ethiopians students were under great pressure to study and profess Marxism. . . . Marxism was presumed to be an unchallengeable truth, even if it was not understood. It generated mass hysterical loyalty. The student leadership recast Marxism into its mold, and every element of youth discontent was defined in Marxist terms. Many did not read about it, but that was beside the point. They were obsessed by it. Most accepted it as true even before they read about it, and when they did read they found the "self-evident" truth. They were not seeking to establish truth. It was there already.[17]

For Ethiopian students abroad, Marxism-Leninism not only provided a principled way to reject the West that had supported Haile Selassie and hence Ethiopian backwardness but also afforded a way of appropriating the West's wealth and power through the Russian and Chinese revolutions. In this respect, Ethiopian students mapped Marxism onto the complex ambivalences of late nationalism. As John Plamenatz has argued, late nationalism "is both imitative and hostile to the models it imitates." Such hostility involves an intricate double rejection: "Rejection of the . . . dominator who is nevertheless to be imitated and surpassed by his own standards, and rejection of ancestral ways that are seen as obstacles to progress and yet also cherished as marks of identity."[18]

The product of the most abstract discussion, grounded only in the internecine struggles of student politics yet reverberating with deeply felt concerns, Marxist ideas became more and more influential among intellectuals. As early as 1971, for example, each of the ten candidates in a Union of University Students election in Addis Ababa professed that "Marxism-Leninism was the only possible ideology for Ethiopia."[19]

> The absence of political parties, strong organizations, and an indigenous class of traders and entrepreneurs gave the rapidly expanding numbers of university and secondary school students a crucial position because they constituted a disproportionately large section of what could be called the bearers of public opinion.[20]

When the *ancien régime* collapsed in 1974, there were few previously organized social groups, besides the military, to step into the fray. And in the military, it was a relatively uneducated and previously nonpolitical group of lower-ranking officers, like Mengistu, who rose to power. In the political vacuum that ensued, the students' Marxism—the only reasonably coherent position that could be seen to promise modernity in the context of 1976—was immediately sucked into the Derg. In this way, what had been the tortured concern of only a handful of intellectuals eventually became the ideology of the revolutionary state.

MARXISM, ETHNICITY, THE NATION, AND MODERNITY

Ethnicity, the nation, modernity: this triad had interacted differently, as I have pointed out, in Haile Selassie's Ethiopia than it had in much of the rest of Africa. For colonial Africa, it is commonly realized that some ethnic groups were able to accumulate more power than others because of differential access to modern institutions like international markets and Western education.[21] In such cases, however, the association between ethnic identity and the nation (that was to be created by anticolonial struggles) was typically indirect: some groups happened to be at the right place at the right time. But the cultural definition of nationhood itself was, at least ideally, disassociated from ethnic hierarchies: the nation was created by a common African struggle against a European colonial power.

The creation of nationhood in Ethiopia had been different. One group comprised of the mostly Orthodox Christian peoples of the highlands, the Amhara and the Tigreans, had founded the state, and it was an Amhara emperor in particular, Menelik II,[22] who had defeated the Italians and preserved Ethiopian independence. During the twentieth century, Amhara officeholders, particularly those from Shewa, dominated the imperial state, their language becoming the national language of schools (even foreign mission schools), newspapers, courts, and government offices. Broadcasting, teaching, and printing newspapers in other languages was illegal.

In the nineteenth century and before, the dynamic of imperial political economy had encouraged a slow conversion of pagan peoples on the periphery to the core, Orthodox Christian identity.[23] Modernization, the increasing concentration of power in institutions that required literacy, greatly increased this pressure.[24] Becoming modern, "of the times" (*zemanawi*), "civilized" (*siltanē*), "educated" (*yetamarē*), required one, to some considerable degree (especially if not a Protestant or a Muslim), to adopt Orthodox Christian customs. An Oromo man in Wellegga (later to convert to an evangelical Protestant church) described how he had been converted:

> I was baptized as a young man in the Ethiopian Orthodox Church. It was not because I believed in Jesus. Many people were baptized at the time. It was modern or should we say civilized. The Amhara were Christian and civilized. We were pagan and uncivilized. We wanted to be like the Amhara. They were the rulers. We were peasants. We tried to look like them.[25]

By the time of the revolution, significantly large groups of assimilated Amhara existed, particularly in the towns and especially in Addis Ababa.

Since the metanarrative of modernity was channeled into Ethiopia through the political center controlled by Amhara, the notion of progress, as I have already noted, was mapped onto ethnic differences. Some, namely the Amhara, were seen as "ahead," followed by others like the Oromo and Gurage, followed by still others, the truly "back-ward," *hwalaker*—those groups on the periphery that had been slave-raided in the nineteenth century.

The revolution's stress on equality unhinged the old equation of Or-thodox Christian Amhara-Tigrean identity with Ethiopian nationality, and in doing so it let loose a veritable deluge of new ethnic discourse. On the one hand, the revolution glorified and redeemed the nation. Now, at last, Ethiopia would be liberated, would come into her own. On the other hand, how the nation was to be defined was by no means clear. Just what was "Ethiopia"?

> In the early years of the revolution, some people—Amharic speakers, with Amharic names—surprised even their closest friends by declaring them-selves to be Oromo, or as "having an Oromo side." In some cases this iden-tity was maintained, in other shamefacedly suppressed as events took a course which placed increasing emphasis on centralisation and national unity. Sometimes, the contradictory demands of national and local or ethnic identity resulted in mental breakdown.[26]

The ambivalences of ethnic and national identity can be summarized in the history of Mengistu Haile Mariam himself.[27] The details of Men-gistu's background have never been clearly established, but as Lefort argues, the myths that grew up around him assumed their own reality:

> What does it matter if Mengistu's past remains unknown: the stories about him are much richer in symbols that speak to the crowds than the little noth-ings that he could have dragged up and embellished. . . . What do the precise facts matter, the ones reported by the radio, the television, the newspapers: there they only reach a handful. . . . Far more powerful and more effective is rumour, which runs from one street to the next, from village to hamlet, so big and exaggerated that it becomes the truth.[28]

At least three aspects of rumors about Mengistu's background are im-portant: As he grew up, he was said to have had an important social tie with and probably also a link of kinship to an important Amhara lord, *dejazmach* Kebedde Tessama (one story claimed Mengistu as the son of an illegitimate daughter of Kebedde). Second, he was clearly from a poor background; his father was said to have been one of Kebedde's ser-vants. And finally, part of Mengistu's parentage was said to be non-Amhara, possibly through one of Kebedde's slaves from the south. Often identified as physically distinct from northerners, Mengistu was widely perceived as a "slave," *baria*.[29]

These rumors and stories place Mengistu as a representative of a real category: the important stratum of assimilating Amhara during the

1950s and 1960s. According to the former revolutionary insider, Dawit Wolde Giorgis, "The fact that he [Mengistu] was not an Amhara, but seemed an outsider, was in his favor. But Mengistu, trained in an Amharised Ethiopian military tradition, is not really an outsider at all: He plays the feudal intrigue dressed up as Ethiopian nationalism."[30]

To no small degree, the story of the revolution in Ethiopia, the attempt of a nation "to cut history off at the pass," was to become the story of the rise of assimilating Amhara like Mengistu—a rise that "cut society off at the pass."[31] Fiercely committed to the old Orthodox Christian demarcation of the nation but proclaiming the equality of ethnic groups with those boundaries, relatively uneducated, distrustful of experts, occupying positions of power unthinkable only a few years earlier, Mengistu and many Ethiopians like him needed some way to resolve the tensions between ethnicity and nationality, some way to preserve the nation while transforming ethnic hierarchies. In this context, Marxism—or, more accurately, Leninism—offered more than a metanarrative of modernity. The model of the Russian revolution provided a way both of understanding the explosion of ethnicity that was occurring in 1975–76 and of controlling and repressing the tendencies that threatened the nation. In other words, Lenin's and Stalin's examples offered a narrative of how to weld together (or so it seemed in 1976) disparate ethnic groups into a unitary state defined by the boundaries of a previous conquest—by Russians in the Soviet Union and by Amhara and Tigreans in Ethiopia.

MENGISTU HAILE MARIAM
ADOPTS SCIENTIFIC SOCIALISM

Let me return to around the time of the first anniversary of the revolution, September 1975. Having earlier been outpaced by the Derg's movement toward a homegrown Ethiopian socialism in late 1974,[32] civilian opponents began to steal the military's ideological fire toward the end of 1975 by staking out a position to the left based, in their words, on the international science of Marxism-Leninism. Ethiopian *hibrettesebawinet* was apparently no match for a science. Despite the effects of the land reform, the Derg's position had begun to look embarrassingly passé by the time of the first anniversary of the revolution. Once again, the military committee was isolated and was forced to look to its opponents for support.

In the context that ensued, students took up a central role in struggles thrown up by the revolution, both those disillusioned local students recently returned from the zemecha and those returning excitedly from abroad. For both groups, Marxism-Leninism provided a grid for understanding Ethiopia's place in the metanarrative of modernity—even if the categories and distinctions of the political discourse that ensued had increasingly little to do with Ethiopian realities. At times, it seemed as if Ethiopians were fighting over *other* revolutions more than their own.

> There have been few, if any, countries where so many young and politically inexperienced intellectuals were catapulted so suddenly from student to national politics and to the highest positions of power. . . . Former student leaders were unprepared for the task at hand. In political discussions, they had dissected theoretical problems of socialism but not such practical ones as how to implement sweeping changes in feudal Ethiopia. As a result, they tended to continue debating theoretical issues that had also split the student movement, fighting the same old battles among themselves rather than discussing the new problems facing the country. Indeed, what was most striking in the Ethiopian revolution was not the factionalism of the leftist intellectuals *per se* or the acrimony of their debate, but the fact that *they seemed largely disconnected from reality.* [my emphasis][33]

As the Derg and the intellectuals moved leftward, both were divided. One section of the military committee held out the immediate possibility of forming a party, one composed of all anti-feudal elements and built on the basis of the institutions created by the great reforms of 1975, namely, the *mahabir*s, or peasants associations, in the countryside and the *kebele*s, or urban dwellers' associations, in the cities. But other members of the Derg, those gathered around Mengistu Haile Mariam—what might be called the radical or Leninist faction—opposed any attempt to build a party that was not firmly led by a (military) vanguard from above.

The increasingly vocal civilian left was also divided, mainly between two recently organized parties: the All Ethiopian Socialist Movement or MEISON (its Amharic acronym) and the Ethiopian Peoples Revolutionary Party or EPRP (its English acronym). Both were avowedly Marxist, as were a number of other, smaller parties.[34] The two dominant groups differed—ostensibly at least—on the question of whether an immediate transition to socialism was possible. According to the MEISON analysis, the Derg was progressive, if not yet socialist, and a tactical alliance with it—in their words, a "critical" alliance—could provide the basis for the construction of socialism in Ethiopia. In fact (as it became increasingly clear), MEISON intended to use the Derg and eventually to displace it. The EPRP position, in contrast, rejected any such shortcut and insisted that no military government could be revolutionary. The Derg was "fascist"; it had arrested true revolutionaries. Only a period of "unlimited democracy" could allow a return to the revolution. There were other differences between the two parties that were apparently rooted in the tangled history of student politics. A portion of MEISON's leadership was drawn from the recently conquered south, mainly from Oromo groups, and several had been trained in Western Europe, France in particular. The EPRP, in contrast, was overwhelmingly based in the traditionally dominant ethnic groups of the north, the Amhara and the Tigreans, and most of their leaders had been educated either locally or in the United States.

> On the theoretical plan, it could be argued that EPRP espoused Maoism and AESM [MEISON] Stalinism . . . Nevertheless, it is doubtful if these theoretical questions were at the bottom of the differences between the two organizations. . . . the real differences between ERPM and AESM [MEISON] remain deeply embedded in the annals of the Ethiopian Student Movement of the early 1970s: in the differences of going abroad at different times, in personal rivalries, and in group competition for leadership of student bodies.[35]

In early 1976, in a show of openness designed to win over its enemies, the Derg allowed an uncensored debate on Ethiopia's future in *Addis Zemen,* the government newspaper. The main question argued was not what political philosophy should guide Ethiopia. By that point, almost all educated Ethiopians in Addis Ababa assumed that it should be Marxism. Rather, the principal issues addressed was the correct interpretation of Marxism. The debate was taken up with such an abstractness that sometimes it seemed that political discourse itself had been deterritorialized:

> For most Ethiopians, even educated ones, the debate . . . was their first exposure to any kind of open political discussion. While many became highly politicized, many others became confused. The theoreticians . . . all wrote with lofty disregard for the common level of political education. They talked in terms of fine ideological points taken from the Soviet and Chinese revolutions. . . . For months there was an *unreal* quality about the whole debate, as if intellectuals played revolutionary games and imagined themselves as modern-day Maos, Lenins, and Marxes. [my emphasis].[36]

These differences in how Ethiopia Modern was to be constituted—and therefore which ghosts from the world-past were to be invoked and propitiated—interacted and reverberated in complex ways over the next two years. The result, finally, was the physical elimination of one faction of the Derg and the death and suppression of thousands of young intellectuals. The first step toward this bloody conclusion was the official adoption of the science of Marxism-Leninism as the legitimating ideology of the state.

In April 1976, after several months of open debate, Mengistu moved to consolidate his power within the Derg by attempting to reconcile the Derg's civilian enemies. In a last move leftward to embrace the ideology of his opponents, Mengistu pushed through the Derg an announcement of the beginning of a "national democratic revolution." (The phrase had been Mao Tse-tung's when he attempted to form an alliance with non-communist groups on the eve of Japan's invasion of China.) Both MEISON and the EPRP had called for such a front. Mengistu proclaimed that scientific socialism would henceforth be the guiding ideology of the state and that an agency to choose and train cadre (in fact already established in secret and presided over by MEISON personnel) would be formed. A party would eventually be forged by these cadre to assume power in a "people's democratic republic":

> To facilitate these steps, to coordinate the dissemination of the principles of scientific socialism, to aid the anti-feudal, anti-imperialist and anti-bureaucratic capitalist struggle of the broad masses of Ethiopia, and in general to help all efforts of the masses to be organized in order to form a popular revolutionary front, to find ways of advancing the revolution, a Provisional Office for Mass Organizational Affairs [POMOA] is hereby established.[37]

Despite the virtual identity of Mengistu's rhetoric with that of both MEISON and the EPRP, the latter rejected—out of hand—any common front with the military. By the middle of the year, many members of the EPRP had begun to drop out of their jobs in Addis Ababa and to go underground in preparation for the struggle against the Derg. As the official power of MEISON grew, tensions with the EPRP escalated. In October 1976, the EPRP began an outright program of assassination against top MEISON leaders, and the latter retaliated, "first by quiet executions, carried out by commando units . . . then by massive and official executions."[38]

Mengistu's rise to power within the Derg took place against this backdrop of killing. After Mengistu and his faction brought MEISON into the government in early 1976, officers in the Derg who opposed his leadership were forced to look in the opposite direction—toward the EPRP. Tensions rose. Conflicts sharpened. On 10 July 1976, one section of the Derg attempted to remove Mengistu from power. Three days later, he struck back by executing the plot's instigator, one of his main competitors in the Derg—Sisay Hapte—along with two other of its members and seventeen civilians and military men.[39]

The July executions did not consolidate Mengistu's power, and indeed after a reorganization of the Derg during the following December—a restructuring that copied the party in the Soviet Union—he lost influence. In late January 1976, Teferi Benti, the titular chairman of the Derg and a member of the anti-Mengistu faction, went on the offensive with another appeal to all so-called progressive groups (including the EPRP) to form a party. This plea was made even while the EPRP was engaged in a program of assassination against POMOA, the agency the Derg had created to organize the party.

Like Sisay Hapte before him, Teferi was a spokesman for the anti-Leninist faction within the Derg. Mengistu and his men struck back on 3 February 1977, murdering Teferi in a shoot-out at Derg headquarters, along with seven other top members of the military committee.

As Mengistu declared an all-out war against the EPRP the capital was gripped by the so-called red-white terror—a terror understood on the model of the Russian revolution.

> Defense squads in each neighborhood set up roadblocks and began visiting homes. The operation [in late March 1977], however, was carried out in an anarchical manner, each squad a law unto itself. . . . While house searches led to relatively few incidents, the city was tense, and by nightfall an orgy of shooting broke out which continued into the early hours of the morning. Long before the official curfew hour of 10 P.M., anyone moving about the streets became a target for the defense squads. People were taken from their homes in the middle of the night and often families did not know whether they had been abducted by defense squads or the EPRP. No one will ever know how many died during that one week, but the toll was certainly high.[40]

All the houses were watching each other, spying on each other, sniffing each other out. This is civil war; this is what it's like. I sit down by the window, and immediately they say, "Somewhere else, sir, please. You're visible from the street. It would be easy to pick you off." A car passes, then stops. The sounds of gunfire. Who was it? These? Those? And who, today, are "these," and who are the "those" who are against "these" just because they are "these"? The car drives off, accompanied by the barking of dogs. They bark all night.[41]

Urban guerrilla warfare against a determined government is rarely successful, and Ethiopia was no exception.[42] The appropriation of May Day celebrations by the Derg became a crucial site in the struggle with the EPRP. Each year, the Derg attempted to enact its narrative of the revolution and therewith to place itself at the head of a metanarrative of communist progress. And each year, the EPRP attempted to disrupt this display and to assert its own ownership of Marxism. By 1977, this struggle reached a climax:

> The May Day rallies of 1975 and 1976 had resulted in the arrest of many and in the death of some EPRP supporters; the rally of 1977 in Addis Ababa, on the other hand, led to the most horrifying carnage in the history of the country. An anti-government demonstration organized by EPRP to undermine the government's May Day rallies was launched on the evening of 29 April; well over 500 of the demonstrators were gunned down during the same evening while marching, running for cover or in the houses they had fled to for refuge. The massacre continued in the following days; according to the Secretary General of the Swedish Save the Children Fund, over 1,000 youths had been executed by 16 May and their bodies were left in the street and ravaged by hyenas at night. School children of eleven years of age and above were at the forefront of EPRP demonstrations. It is widely reported that hospitals often refused to treat the wounded on the grounds that they were reactionaries, and charged anything up to 100 US dollars and 25 dollars for the release of students' and workers' bodies, respectively, to cover the cost of bullets wasted in killing them.[43]

By the middle of 1977, the EPRP had been smashed. One section of the party gave up the urban struggle and escaped to carry on their struggle in rural Tigray. But the terror in Addis Ababa did not cease, for now the Derg and MEISON came to a falling out. By August, the head of MEISON, Haile Fida, and many of his comrades went underground; Haile Fida attempted to escape Addis Ababa but was caught and executed. Other members of MEISON remained loyal to the Derg and betrayed their former comrades. "In the final phase of the red terror, culminating in December 1977 to January 1978, it was often hard to tell who was being killed by whom; assassinations routinely ascribed to the EPRP may well have been the work of rival factions of MEISON, or even of the Derg seeking to rid itself of untrustworthy officials while blaming its opponents."[44]

By 1978, the terror was over. Conflicts within the Derg had been resolved: Mengistu Haile Mariam held unquestioned power. And conflicts within the cities had been settled: All urban opposition to the Derg had been brutally destroyed. For the Derg's supporters, the terror provided a litmus test of their revolutionary credentials. For others, it provided a set of horrible memories that made the expression of any further dissent difficult:

This terror served, in gruesome fashion, the classic functions of violence in a revolutionary state: it produced a political *demobilisation,* matching the mobilisation of the early years, which made it possible for the new regime to organise and impose itself on a cowed population. Popular acquiescence in a multitude of later restrictions, from the institution of national military service to the compulsory wearing of uniforms, comes down to the fact that no one is prepared to go through such an experience again.[45]

DETERRITORIALIZATION OF
THE REVOLUTION AFTER THE LATE 1970s

An internal status quo was eventually undergirded and stabilized by the external realignment of Ethiopia that had begun in early 1977. As it turned out, a number of developments in the mid-1970s—Angola, Mozambique, Madagascar, along with Ethiopia—had intensified the Cold War in Africa.[46] To American policy makers, communism seemed to be on the march virtually everywhere on the continent.[47]

To the Cold War imagination, both North American and Soviet, the Horn of Africa was a critical strategic point—a fulcrum from which to exert world power at the meeting point of continents. A Soviet publication of 1978 claimed:

> The area has been allotted an exceptionally important place in the imperialist strategic plans because of its geographical location at the junction of two continents, Asia and Africa, its first-class ports in the Gulf of Aden and the Indian Ocean and, above all, its proximity to key sea lanes linking oil-producing countries with America and Europe. Some 70 per cent of the oil and other raw materials imported by Western Europe is carried over these sea routes.[48]

A projection, in fact, of how the Soviet Union itself saw the Horn of Africa, this view was reflected back and forth between Washington and Moscow, as between two mirrors, until it attained its own complex reality.

In the Cold War imagery that resulted, there was a constant slippage between signifier and signified, between political symbol and referential reality. While the United States spoke of the importance of "democratic freedoms," it increased sales of arms to military-led Ethiopia in 1975 and 1976. Two years later, the Soviet Union, upholding the values of "proletarian internationalism," cut off aid to a secessionist group in the north, the Eritrean Peoples Liberation Front (EPLF)—surely a more genuinely Marxist movement than any in Ethiopia, one that the USSR had previously supported. Now the USSR provided the Derg with the equipment and advisers to attack those (the Eritreans) whom they had so recently called comrades.

As Ethiopian political actors attempted to reenact this or that portion of Soviet or Chinese history, the material flows turned on by the switch in Ethiopian Cold War alliances, from the United States to the Soviet Union, dramatically expanded what local actors could accomplish. In effect, the massive shipments of arms and military personnel that ensued deterritorialized the revolution and helped to isolate the Derg from grass-roots pressure after 1977. The result, particularly after Ethiopia was invaded by the Somalis, was cultural reaction, in which an official Marxism-Leninism was overlaid on old Orthodox Christian notions of the nation. How did this occur?

The United States had invested heavily in its alliance with Ethiopia during the 1960s. By the 1970s, it was beginning to distance itself from the elderly Haile Selassie, in preparation for the political transition that would inevitably follow with his death. But political leaders like Secretary of State Henry Kissinger continued to emphasize Ethiopia's strategic importance so close to the oil-rich Middle East—particularly given the Soviet Union's buildup of power in neighboring Somalia.

Consequently, the first years of the Ethiopian revolution, despite its escalating leftist rhetoric, did not disrupt the relationship with the United States. Indeed, while U.S. military aid to Ethiopia declined, outright sales increased dramatically: "From an average of about $10 million a year between 1969 and 1974, U.S. military deliveries reached a total value of $18.5 million in 1974–75, $26 million in 1975–76 and almost $135 million in 1976–77."[49]

The Soviet investment in Somalia followed a similar logic, but from the opposite point of view. In the early 1970s, the Soviet Union had suffered a number of setbacks along the Red Sea. Moscow had lost influence in Sudan by backing an abortive communist coup in 1971, and the following year Anwar Sadat of Egypt had expelled all of the approximately 15,000 Soviet military advisers and experts.[50] A Soviet presence in Somalia was, in this context, attractive.

After Mohammed Siad Barre led a military coup in Somalia in 1969, the new regime had somehow to produce a credible alternative to the old. As happened later in Ethiopia, that pressure introduced a strong tendency within local political culture to turn to the left. "The natural choice," according to I. M. Lewis, "was some form of socialism."[51] After the newly organized Supreme Revolutionary Council proclaimed its allegiance to "scientific socialism," relations with the Soviet Union quickly warmed, particularly after the latter's expulsion from Egypt. From 1971 to 1974, the years leading to the Ethiopian revolution, Soviet economic assistance to Somalia increased to a total of $100 million, and military assistance multiplied by a factor of ten, as Soviet advisers began to pour into the country.[52]

Until the mid-1970s, then, the Cold War upped the ante in the Horn of Africa, but international alliances remained stable: Ethiopia with the United States versus its regional rival, Somalia, with the Soviet Union. Both the Americans and the Soviets understood this local stand-off in terms of the most abstract, political rhetoric—the freedom of the capitalist world versus the progress of global communism. In local terms, however, the basis of the rivalry between Ethiopia and Somalia (and hence their opposite alliances) had everything to do with notions of national identity: Somalia claimed the Somali-speaking Ogaden, part of southeastern Ethiopia, at least as the latter had been constituted by agreements with colonial powers at the turn of the century.

The Ethiopian revolution eventually deconstructed this network of symbols and material flows. The "revolution" in Somalia had involved no social upheaval; a military council had merely proclaimed its allegiance to socialism. But Muslim Somali-speakers had historically seen themselves as descended from Arabs, and in 1974, Somalia joined the Arab League, sponsored by conservative Saudi Arabia. For all these reasons, Somalia never appeared entirely reliable to Marxists in Moscow.[53] The revolution in Ethiopia, on the other hand, *did* involve social upheaval. Imperial Ethiopia, like Imperial Russia, had been a multi-ethnic empire presided over by an aristocracy of large landowners and an indigenous Orthodox church. By 1975, the old order was being torn up by its very roots. As the Ethiopian revolution radicalized—in the process appropriating symbols and phrases from the Russian revolution—Soviet Marxists, even while allied with Somalia, were increasingly intrigued.

Having been disappointed by seemingly radical movements in other countries, and realizing that aid to Ethiopia might jeopardize their position in Somalia, Soviet strategists remained at first distantly sympathetic. After the deposition of Haile Selassie, Radio Moscow announced that the changes in Ethiopia were "not just an ordinary military coup."[54] And after the land reform of 1975, *Pravda* noted the true revolutionary implications of the demise of a "centuries old feudal system."[55] But when the Derg asked for arms later that year, the Soviets temporized and hinted that the presence of "pro-Western" members in the Derg made such a decision difficult.[56]

As Mengistu began to consolidate power within the Derg by murdering, one by one, his supposedly pro-Western opponents,[57] Mengistu's interests and those of the Soviet Union began to coincide. For the Derg, the very sine qua non of the revolution had been the strengthening and redemption of the nation. By late 1976, the unity of the nation was being threatened on all sides: to the west, the Ethiopian Democratic Union controlled a swath of territory along the Sudanese border; to the north, Eritrean secessionists grew increasingly stronger; and to the east, Somalia—with claims on the Ogaden—was rapidly arming.

Everywhere, ethnic consciousness was blossoming, and it was no longer certain that the old imperial center could hold. Even though the United States had reluctantly increased sales of arms to Ethiopia, it was clear, especially after the terror commenced, that the United States would not provide the magnitude of force needed to repress the dissidence and to keep the military in control.[58] In the bipolar world of the Cold War, there was only one other possibility: the Soviet Union.

> Confronted with the social and ethnic convulsions created by the revolution, Mengistu coolly grasped the need for an ideological rationale to preserve Ethiopia's territorial integrity and, in doing so, legitimise his own political ambitions. The solution he found was Marxism-Leninism. This doctrine established Mengistu's revolutionary credentials at a time when his main rivals inside and outside the PMAC were Marxists, provided a ready-made scapegoat for existing troubles ("U.S. imperialism") and held out the promise of a new source of external aid which was both more reliable and more interested than the U.S.[59]

This statement probably rationalizes into one Machiavellian plan considerations that were actually more haphazardly brought into conjunction. Ethiopia's initial shift leftward—the great reforms of 1975 and its commitment to scientific socialism in early 1976—were carried out with virtually no outside encouragement. At the same time, however, it is clear, at least in retrospect, that the Derg would not have survived the year 1977–78 without the massive military aid that the Soviet Union and others eventually gave.[60]

By April 1977—when Mengistu expelled the U.S. military mission and other U.S.-supported institutions in Ethiopia—the change in alliances was well under way. Additional arms agreements, trade pacts, and cultural exchanges with the Soviet Union quickly followed. For Somalia, the switch took slightly longer. Six months after the Ethiopians evicted the Americans, the Somalis expelled the Soviets. The result was an exact reversal in international allegiances: Ethiopia looked now to the Soviet Union, Somalia to the United States and conservative Arab countries.

This 180-degree turn unhinged local politics. The Derg's enemies, both inside and outside the country, realized that switching military patrons had created a temporary weakness for the revolutionary state. It would take time to rearm and retrain the Ethiopian army. Somalia had already begun to support a liberation movement in southeastern Ethiopia,[61] and in June 1977, frightened by the Soviet supply of arms to Ethiopia and gambling on future U.S. support for itself, Mogadishu commenced an outright invasion of Ethiopian territory. Before the invasion stalled, the Somalis pushed deep into Ethiopian territory. Now, all Ethiopians were threatened.

This ill-conceived move on the part of the Somalis set in motion a train of events that led, finally, to the consolidation of the Ethiopian revolution:

> The Somali rulers had no long-range plans to secure the captured territory against the inevitable Ethiopian counterattack. They gambled on the disinte-gration of the military regime in Addis Ababa, and on Western assistance to balance the military superiority of the enemy. In the event, neither calcula-tion proved correct. In fact, the invasion was a great political boon for the Derg, which was able to capitalise on the patriotic fervour the war provoked to put all its domestic opponents at a great disadvantage.[62]

After Somalia expelled Soviet military personnel in November 1977, nothing remained to restrain Soviet support for Ethiopia, and toward the end of the month, the Soviets launched an immense airlift:

> The operation lasted for about six weeks. It involved some 225 Antonov-22s and Ilyushin-76s—about 15 per cent of the entire Soviet air transport fleet— in simultaneous flights to Addis Ababa from bases near Moscow, Tbilisi, Tashkent and Georgievsk. . . . Overall, the USSR ferried in over $1 billions worth of armaments . . . ;dispatched about 12,000 Cuban combat troops, 1,500 Soviet military advisers, 750 soldiers from South Yemen and "several hundred" East German technicians; and sent four Soviet generals . . . to su-pervise the integration of sophisticated Soviet weaponry into the Ethiopian Army and direct the war against the Somalis.[63]

By March 1978, the Somalis were decisively defeated. Soviet support was crucial to the result. But Mengistu was also able to mobilize strong internal support for the war from virtually all sectors of society.[64] As nothing else could have, the invasion allowed Mengistu to take upon his shoulders the sacred mantle of national preservation. "The Revolution-ary Motherland or Death!" Thousands of peasants, many from south-ern Ethiopia where the land reform had made the Derg popular, were called into service, trained, and armed.

Figure 17. Socialist symbolism. Fidel Castro in Ethiopia. Press photograph,
Archives, Institute of Ethiopian Studies, Addis Ababa University.

Wrapping himself in the Ethiopian flag, Mengistu lashed out even
more ruthlessly at the internal opposition. By the end of the Red terror,
according to Lefort, "of ten civilians who had actively worked for a
radical transformation of Ethiopia, only one escaped arrest, imprison-
ment, torture, execution or assassination."[65]

By the fourth anniversary of the deposition of Haile Selassie, 12 September 1978, Mengistu Haile Mariam's position was unassailable.[66]
Supported by the world socialist system, Mengistu's power was no
longer simply internally based; this fact was signaled by the fourth anniversary celebrations:

> At the top of the dais overlooking the vast Revolution Square, under a flam-
> boyant canopy protecting him from the fierceness of the sun and from the
> bursts of rain, Mengistu Haile Mariam was enthroned on a gilded armchair
> covered with red velvet. Alone. And, for the first time at an official occasion,
> all the other members of the Derg were relegated to the side-stands, lost in
> the crowds of dignitaries of the regime and invited guests from abroad. On
> Mengistu's right, Fidel Castro, who had arrived very late, sprawled in his
> armchair, very listlessly watching the endless march-pasts. What did it mat-
> ter? His presence alone consecrated the entry of Ethiopia into the great fam-
> ily of socialist countries.[67]

THE DERG APPROPRIATES
ORTHODOX CHRISTIAN CULTURE

In the French, Russian, and Chinese cases, revolutionary iconoclasts attacked religion, as it was associated with past forms of domination, with vengeance:

> The Hébertists were not only the party of social revolution, they were also the leaders of the anti-Christian movement which reached its height in the autumn of 1793. The Revolution was no longer satisfied with the liberal Catholicism of the Constitutional Church, it had come to regard Christianity itself as a counterrevolutionary force which must be destroyed in order to make way for the new religion of humanity. As early as 26 September Fouché had announced at Nevers that he thought it was his mission "to substitute the worship of the Republic and natural morality for the superstitious cults to which the people still unfortunately adhere," and in the following months at Lyons he staged an elaborate anti-Christian demonstration in which a donkey wearing a cape and mitre dragged a missal and the Gospels through the streets. During the autumn all the churches in Paris were closed, Notre Dame became the Temple of Reason, and the Constitutional Bishop of Paris, Gobel, with his leading clergy, made a public renunciation of their ministry at the bar of the Convention.[68]

As we have seen, something of the same kind of attack was made upon "pagan" religions of the south in 1975. But what of the Orthodox Christian Church at the center? In the context of the frenzy of the Somali invasion, Mengistu not only consolidated his role as dictator, he and the Derg began to appropriate Orthodox Christian culture. As long as the church bent to state purposes, there would be no attack on Orthodox Christian belief. When Patriarch Tewoflos, in office when the revolution began, failed to cooperate with the Derg, he was imprisoned in February 1976 (and later apparently murdered on direct orders of Mengistu).[69] But after the Derg had installed a more compliant patriarch, high officials of the Church began to be seen at state rituals—particularly during and after the Somali invasion. In January 1979, thirteen new bishops were consecrated (apparently on direct government instructions), by which point the Orthodox Church had become virtually an arm of the revolutionary state.[70]

> In the face of growing threat of secession in the north and east, the church was found to be a rallying ground for national survival. As a *quid pro quo,* the church gained important financial concessions which, to a certain degree, increased the church's subservience to the state. It received an annual subsidy of two million pounds as salary for its 1,729 patriarchate workers and a monthly allowance of eleven thousand pounds was to be paid by the Ministry

Figure 18. Ethiopian Orthodox Church leaders at a state function. Press photograph, Archives, Institute of Ethiopian Studies, Addis Ababa University.

of Finance to its higher officials, a figure roughly corresponding to the pre-revolutionary income that the church had gained from a variety of sources.[71]

One corollary of the Derg's appropriation of Orthodox Christian culture was the campaign against "foreign" religions and their Ethiopian converts that began in late 1978. As we have seen, the Orthodox Church had for centuries played a central role in the Ethiopian state and in defining Ethiopian nationhood. To convert to another religion was tantamount to rejecting Ethiopian nationality.

Ironically, the Derg's cadres took up the campaign of harassment against evangelical converts under the banner of the need for a "cultural revolution":

When the agitation started against the Christians in eastern Wallagga and Gamo Gofa in December 1978, the official propaganda in Addis Ababa was concerned with the need for a cultural revolution. At this stage the propaganda centered on what was called "the imported religion" as compared to "the inherited religion" of the Ethiopian Orthodox Church or Islam. In a number of cases the propaganda linked the Evangelical churches to imperialists and capitalists as they had relations with western countries. Sometimes the propaganda was a more general labelling of Evangelical Christianity as anti-revolutionary.[72]

Not only was Protestantism branded as a "foreign" religion, but all converts to it were increasingly dismissed as *pente,* "Pentecostals." Being branded as a "pente" was enough to imprison a person, sometimes even to torture or kill him or her:

> In Gamo Gofa administrative region a great deal of harassment took place simply because people were Evangelical Christians. In Arba Minch, for example, officials tried to force Mekane Yesus Church members to abstain from prayer meetings. In Gidole, a few miles further south, the reason given for closing the churches was that the Christians belonged to a foreign faith or were "Pentecostal." But there were no Pentecostal churches in the area. The people did not even know what the word meant.[73]

Why did government cadre identify all evangelical Christians as "pente"? The SIM as a missionary organization was, for example, hardly Pentecostal and had, in fact, discouraged and disapproved of ecstatic practices. There had, in actuality, been extremely few Pentecostal missionaries in Ethiopia at all.

Beginning in the 1960s, however, tiny but visible groups of young charismatics had developed within several churches in Addis Ababa—even the Orthodox, but also the SIM-associated Kale Heywet Church and the Lutheran-related Mekane Yesus. A major impetus for this movement came apparently from the exclusion of young educated people from leadership positions in the churches by rigid and often less-educated elders. By imitating the New Testament Church about which they read in the Bible, young people gained an identity otherwise denied them:

> *Speaking in tongues* became a distinguishing feature, albeit a temporary one, of the renewal movement. Some, but not all, preached that this sign, and this sign alone, proved possession of the Holy Spirit. . . . Singing and praying often became unnecessarily loud. One-line choruses were sung over and over scores of times accompanied by loud clapping, shouts of "Hallelujah, Amen" and ululating. A great deal of emphasis was placed on healing and prophecy. . . . Many within the renewal movement taught that *the baptism of the Spirit,* accompanied by tongue speaking, *imparted to the recipient a type of perfection.* This led to the teaching that such an individual was always right: being full of the Spirit how could he or she make any mistakes? they argued.[74]

This handful of self-confident young people—opposed and rejected by their own churches, particularly by the Orthodox—were almost fated to come into collision with the military. The Derg, after all, increasingly demanded its own kind of total commitment. During the Somali invasion, the government organized demonstrations in which all were commanded to raise their left hand and to curse their enemies. Many of the young enthusiasts refused to do so. Some even went so far as to preach that the invasion was God's judgment on a sinful nation.

These highly visible statements of "disloyalty" to the nation (which probably occurred only in Addis Ababa) were overlaid, then, on long-held ideas about the connection between Orthodoxy and nationhood in the first place and on more recent Marxist theories about the dangers of Western imperialism.[75] By 1979, all evangelical Christians had become "Pentecostals" in Derg discourse: pentes had rejected the nation and the revolution.

A Gedeo church elder: In 1983 the persecution began against the church. The first indication of this occurred when the church was doing some development work. The cadres began to spread rumors that this development was done through American dollars. They said, "The church people come and take pictures of naked children and send these kind of pictures out—so that they can get more money." They accused the church of trying to educate the young people against the revolution and against communist ideology. The local officials singled out the Kale Hiywet Church as the main perpetrators of this evil. The cadres began to teach this throughout all the peasant associations. Right after this they began to try and imprison believers. These prisoners were told that this new religion was passing away and were encouraged to deny both their faith and the church. . . . Then they started closing churches. . . . not all at one time but over a period of a year. By that time they had closed all three hundred churches in the Gedeo district. . . . At that time, many of us church elders tried to challenge the authority of the various peasant associations. . . . On Tir 3rd [in the Ethiopian calendar], I knew that they were looking for me and that I would be imprisoned. I decided not to flee. . . . In Wenago the peasant association had a room which they used as a prison. They kept us there in that room for two months. Their accusation was that we were enemies of the revolution. . . . We were given indoctrination classes by the cadres. They would give us endless lectures about the meaning of the revolution. They would tell how that religion had no place in the revolution. We were taught the philosophy of Marx and Lenin. At the end of these indoctrination classes we were given a statement to sign. . . . [I refused.]. . . . they separated me from the other elders and took me to the police station. There I was put into a horrible prison cell for seven months. . . . They pressed up to seventy people into this tiny room. At night we slept on top of each other for lack of room. The room would be so hot from the stuffy air, that we prisoners would remove all our clothes to try and get some coolness. Our breath would rise up onto the ceiling where it would condense forming droplets of sweat. These in turn would swell up in size until they dripped down on us like rain. . . . One night the General Secretary of the district

Ethiopian Workers' Party went to the place where the other believers were imprisoned and got them out of the prison. He lined them all up in a line. He had a revolver in his right hand and a club in his left. He told them "Renounce the Kale Heywet Church," and began beating the believers one by one. He would beat them on their head until they were bleeding and fainted one by one. There were twenty-six who were beaten in this way. . . . After some time, the official grew tired and had no more strength to beat them. He said, "If I killed each one of you and made a report that I had done so, there would be no one who could oppose me." But all the community took note of the cruelty of this official and began to feel sorry for the believers. Even the people's militia soldiers began to support the believers. Even unbelievers began bringing food to the believers because they felt sorry for them.[76]

As "foreign" religions were suppressed, Orthodox Christian Amhara cultural commitments, now secularized to a degree, were celebrated. Unlike the case of France, there was little iconoclastic destruction of old political symbols at the center of Ethiopian politics. Photographs of Haile Selassie were taken down, but new ones of Mengistu were soon put in their place, sometimes in the old frames. Public statues such as that of the imperial lion, a symbol of Ethiopian emperors, as well as Menelik upon his rearing horse, remained standing in Addis Ababa.[77] Mengistu's secularized version of highland Christian tradition emerged particularly on occasions of state ritual:

> In his rare public appearances in Addis Ababa, the Ethiopian leader sits on a kind of throne, a red velvet upholstered gold-lacquered chair emplaced above and in front of the less ornate seats provided for the other senior figures of the regime. In these and in other ways, Mengistu Haile Mariam can be looked upon as a monarch, an emperor, a successor to Haile Selassie and to Menelik.[78]

This emphasis upon monarchical dignity should not be misunderstood as only a dictator's penchant for pomp. Rather, what was being asserted on such occasions was a deeply held notion of Orthodox Amhara culture: that authority always has to be both personally and powerfully exerted from above and from a distance.[79] In the context of revolutionary rituals, then, Mengistu was a monarch who destroyed monarchy. When the head of state—widely identified as a descendant of slaves—sat upon a throne, he implicitly proclaimed the equality of all Ethiopians in the new order, as long as they recognized the legitimacy of the vanguard party.[80]

> In the time of the imperial regime, it was common to see pictures in which Father, Son and Holy Ghost, enthroned in the clouds, projected a beam of light onto the emperor (symbolically situated at mid-point between heaven

Figure 19. Mengistu Haile Mariam at a state function, c. early 1980s. Press photograph, Archives, Institute of Ethiopian Studies, Addis Ababa University.

and earth), who in turn diffused it to a waiting people. At the tenth anniversary celebrations [of Haile Selassie's deposition] along with the official decorations provided by the North Koreans, it was also possible to find homemade tributes in which the gift of grace, embodied in a celestial trinity of Marx, Engels, and Lenin, similarly descended to the grateful masses by way of Mengistu Haile Mariam.[81]

As Lefort remarks, it is altogether impossible to imagine Robespierre sitting upon a throne. But then French revolutionaries occupied a dif-

Figure 20. Vernacular Marxism. Mengistu speaking in a provincial setting, the homemade pictures of Marx and Engels surmounted by one of himself. Press photograph, Archives, Institute of Ethiopian Studies, Addis Ababa University.

ferent discursive space. Before the rise of the world metanarrative of modernity, French intellectuals, despite their admiration for England, were involved in no love-hate relationship with a more "advanced" nation; consequently, some Frenchmen could attempt to destroy their past, including the Church, with an almost unbounded enthusiasm. To Ethiopian revolutionaries two centuries later, many aspects of tradition had to be preserved; without them, the essence of Ethiopian identity, its distinctiveness vis-à-vis other nations, was impossible to define.

Compared to Ethiopia, revolutionary France also occupied a markedly different position within an international system of states. For France, no foreign power existed with a military technology vastly different from its own. Almost two centuries later, the Ethiopian revolution took place in a world in which the gap between the relatively powerful and the weak had dramatically expanded. The international context was now dominated by two world powers with massively superior military technology. The dénouement to the revolution in Ethiopia was conditioned by this fact. When one faction led by one leader was able to tap into the military resources of the international system, the cultural upheaval that might be expected to occur during a period of intense class struggle was contained and reversed.

In this context, Marxism, with its abstruse vocabulary and the attendant notion that those initiated in the mysterious laws of its science should occupy a special place, fitted with deeply ingrained Orthodox Christian notions. According to Christopher Clapham, both the Soviet Union and Ethiopia were heirs to Byzantium:

> The idea that a Leninist party state is particularly well adapted to the legacy of Coptic Orthodox Christianity is not to be dismissed out of hand. Both Orthodoxy and Leninism provide a model of absolute rule, sustained by an esoteric official ideology which the people are expected to accept, even if they cannot understand it, and which is sustained by a priesthood of the initiated.[82]

Given the elective affinity between Orthodoxy and Leninism, the revolution never created a new notion of the nation—one that genuinely escaped the presuppositions of the old overlay of traditional ethnic hierarchies and the metanarrative of modernity. The old symbols of nationality were centered on aspects of Amhara and Tigrean culture that had distinguished it as a "civilization," as "higher" than others: that is, writing, the Ethiopic script; monumental architecture like the rock churches of Lalibela; and the glory of Ethiopian emperors. The difficulty was that these symbols increasingly divided as much as they unified. The revolution itself had encouraged lower-status ethnic groups to see themselves as equal to all others. Yet, the revolution—now deterritorialized by the Cold War—did not produce the necessary new cultural definition of the nation in which different ethnic groups could truly take their places.

From one perspective, the Ethiopian revolution may represent the last great modernist revolution of the world, but from another, it resembles the first postmodern one. Modernity, as we have seen, was an obsession of revolutionary actors in Ethiopia; and yet, particularly after the late 1970s, there was a constant and disorienting slippage between symbol and referent. Culturally conservative movements were carried out under the name of a "cultural revolution." Profoundly irrational plans were forced upon peasants in the name of science and progress. And all the while, Mengistu began to look more and more like Haile Selassie.

CHAPTER 7

The Revolutionary State at the Grass Roots

Modernist Institutions in Maale during the 1980s

In their private life, members and candidates must distance themselves from every dangerous and bad addiction and habit (Article 3.5). . . . Members and candidates must choose their friends from the point of view of the [communist] goal to which they have committed themselves. One must not have friends simply for reasons of having grown up together or been educated together or worked together. . . . Members and candidates must make a choice of spouse in light of the political ideology they are advancing. They will have to verify in advance whether the prospective mate has the love of the revolution and for the partisans. . . . Members and candidates must not perform their marriages in religious ceremonies (Article 2.4). Members and candidates must not have more than one spouse at a time (Article 2.5). . . . Although it is said that marriage is a contract based on mutual love, it should not be broken whimsically. For this reason, the Party wishes its members to establish home life, to give regard to marriage conduct, and to live with respect for the family. In as much as communists stand as examples for others, they must show, with their stand, that marriage is a respectable thing. . . . Members and candidates should make it their daily function—on top of what is being done in the schools—to help, support and teach their children in a language that they can understand about patriotism, the revolution, international proletarianism, and to snuff out of them any anti-socialist inclination.

Workers' Party of Ethiopia,
"Clarification of the Guidelines for Conduct"
[translation from the Amharic]

If Cold War developments helped to stabilize the Marxist metanarrative at the center of Ethiopian politics in the decade after 1977, local developments in Maale would seem to have done the opposite. Elders slowly realized that the new government would not allow Maale to reinstate a kati—if only to operate as a religious figure. As the efficiency and volume of tax collection increased, as more and more Maale young men were forced into the Ethiopian military to fight (and sometimes die) in wars that few local people understood, and most particularly, as drought in the early 1980s brought home to Maale the inevitable consequences of *not* having a kati (after all, kings were thought to bring the rains), most non-Christian Maale turned to sullen opposition to the new government and to a renewed interest in "tradition."

On the side of evangelical Christians, revolutionaries in 1975, the direction of movement was similar, though their expression of political commitments differed. By the late 1970s, the government's campaign to suppress all evangelical Christian sects in the country had reached Maale. A number of Kale Heywet church buildings were confiscated and turned into government schools, some Maale Christians were thrown in jail for opposing these measures, and most evangelical Christians turned from enthusiastic participation in revolutionary institutions to a principled resistance: "We support the government. We pay our taxes. Why is the government persecuting us?"

These shifts pose a paradox, for the revolutionary state hardly weakened at the grass roots. Just the opposite: it grew stronger and more effective in most areas, including most regions of Maale until the late 1980s. Under Haile Selassie, the imperial state had floated above the heads of most peasants. After 1975, the revolutionary state began to penetrate deeper and deeper into local communities. Peasant associations—each with its own jail, as well as school and clinic—became much more efficient conveyer belts of state policy than the old Maale elite had been. When peasants like the Maale did not support such changes—when they sometimes even violently resisted them—how was the revolutionary state nonetheless able to expand its controls?

THE SOCIALIST VANGUARD IN MAALE

The first part of the answer to this question involves the formation of a small group of revolutionary "true believers" in Maale—probably not many more than eight to ten young men. In the early days, these young men worked, often selflessly, for the new order. As the Ethiopian Workers' Party was formed in the early 1980s, they became members and constituted the local communist cell. It was difficult to obtain complete information on this group (either during or after the revolutionary period), but as far as I am able to determine, all had attended SIM schools and were, at one time, Christians. By the time the revolution commenced, some had already left the church, while the rest would do so as the government's campaign of suppression began.

For this handful of young men, the Christian narrative of religious conversion and enlightenment was transformed into a Leninist narrative of social revolution and progress. After all, both of these stories grounded personal identity in a similar way (calling forth a vanguard vis-à-vis the surrounding populace), and both configured local-cum-global history in a comparable way (locating Maale as a "backward" or "unreached" area that would be redeemed and improved). According to both stories, the whole world was progressing in a certain direction, and the vanguard would provide a way for Maale to "catch up," to take its proper place in the future.

To motivate the transition from the first narrative to the second, Marxist teachers of these young men—most were sent to political school at some stage of their careers—identified foreign missionaries with the machinations of imperialism. And imperialism was one of the causes of Ethiopia's (and Maale's) backwardness: Imperialist agents like missionaries had deluded and divided the Ethiopian people, deflecting them from the true path of progress. (Of course, evangelical Christians could also reject Marxism as delusion; indeed, they interpreted persecution as a test foretold in the Bible—one that only made them stronger. It was as if narrators of Marxism-Leninism and evangelical Christianity were competing to occupy the same cultural space.)

How much the Maale vanguard actually absorbed of socialist philosophy is debatable. What most of them *did* believe in was the progressive nature of the revolution. If Ethiopia was "behind" in relation to other countries, Maale was "behind" compared to other areas of Ethiopia. Maale revolutionaries learned to explain this double backwardness not only as a consequence of imperialism (this was a minor theme locally) but as an outcome of the past system of local "exploitation." Let me follow these themes in the life and stories of the Maale revolutionary who rose highest in local administration, Ziso Mamo.

Ziso was a member of the large Christian lineage in Koibe headed by Sime (whose conversion narrative I recounted in Chapter 5). Ziso had begun his education in mission schools in Bako and had gone on to complete the seventh grade in Jinka by 1974. Fluent in Amharic and reasonably conversant in English (having lived with a missionary at one point), Ziso rose in the revolutionary order to become a member of the party and chairman of the regional peasant association based in Jinka.

Recounting his feelings two decades later (after Mengistu's state had fallen), Ziso described the beginning of the revolution in 1975:

> Really at that time, I don't think that anyone thought as much as me, that anyone was as happy as I was . . . at the time that the revolution started. If you ask me what made me so happy, when I was a child, I was herding cattle. When I was looking after the cattle, I had one female calf. When she slept during the day, I got in between her legs and slept. When I got sleepy, I slept that way. She was really like my blanket, that little calf. There was one landowner, an Amhara called Muluneh Mengesha, he came and made us sell the calf along with the mother cow who had just calved again. I was looking forward to drinking the milk. All these three he made us sell in order to pay rent. I was hoping and hoping that somehow God would destroy such things when the revolution came, and I was extremely happy. Because I was so happy, when people elected me, I was willing to work, even without payment, without anything. Saying this, I started the work [of the revolution].[1]

By that point, Ziso (and before him, his father) had already left the church, despite their long history of association. As far as Ziso was concerned—around twenty then, chafing under the authority of church elders who were much less educated than he—church discipline was simply too grating. Elders demanded that all Christian marriages first be approved by them. Young men who skirted this requirement were required to pay five birr in order to continue in the church.

> When I looked in the Bible for where it said to do things like that [control marriages], I couldn't find it anywhere. While I was angry and arguing with the church elders about this, my father's elder brother's daughter was sick, and we wanted to take her to Gidole to the hospital. I asked the church elders for a letter for the road [so that other Christians would help them]. They told me to ask in Bako. But when I wrote to Bako, they also wrote telling the church officials there not to give me the letter since I was always causing problems. When a friend of mine told me this, I became really angry. My relations with them became really bitter. . . . One day in church after we had argued, we were having communion, Christ's body and blood. We had communion once a month. While they gave communion to everyone around, they skipped me. I didn't say anything. Then they asked for anyone who hadn't been given bread and honey water to raise their hands. I raised my hand. "We meant to skip you," they said. "Now, let us pray." I objected, "No, I'm not going to pray. I want to know my sin that you have deliberately skipped me. God knows my mind. You don't." I stood up. They had placed the bread and honey water on the ground. They covered their eyes and said, "Let us pray

now." I went and put the bread in my mouth, and I drank the honey water. "This is not your body. It's a symbol of Christ's body. This is not your blood. It's a symbol of Christ's blood." Immediately, everyone looked up and began to whisper among themselves. . . . They told me that I would die, that it was written in the Bible that anyone who stole communion would die. . . . After awhile, they told me that I was "tied up" [couldn't participate in the church] until I asked for forgiveness. After a while I apologized, and they told me that I couldn't take communion for three months. . . . When I was freed, they were having an association [mahibir] meeting in Bule and they called me. I went. I got there in the evening and the elders were in their own house. What they were talking about I didn't know. We other people who came didn't have any-thing to do. We laid down. We stood up. We were completely bored. The elders meanwhile sat in a different place. People gave the elders the best food and coffee. Everything they gave to the elders. Even if we had good food, we didn't have anything to do. We waited and waited. The next morning they were still talking, we couldn't imagine about what. Nobody knew. We didn't have anything to do. It reached four o'clock, and I decided that I was going to leave this religion completely. I made my decision. I went back to Koibe, and I decided to ask for the money back I had paid the church when I apologized. On Sunday, after reading the Bible and praying, they were about to stand up. I raised my hand. "What is it?" they asked. "Will you permit me to tell you something that I have been thinking about?" I asked. Because I had earlier been a little respectful with them, they didn't expect that I would say anything bad. While they were expecting something good, I got up and said, "I have lived in this religion for a good while now. During that time, I have tried to make things right, but the bitterness of wrong things has overwhelmed me. Give me back the money I gave you. From now on, take red ink and cross out my name on the list of Christians." My father's younger brother, the one called Gebao, Assefa's father, he was a church elder, and he got up and said, "My child, think about your future income. Those two dollars you paid won't do anything for you." I replied, "Don't worry about my income. Just give me my money." They went to the trunk and opened it and took out the money and gave it to me. I said, "Stay well," and I left. I left just like that and that's the way I have stayed until this very day.[2]

In early 1978, Ziso was sent to Addis Ababa to the Yekatit 66 polit-ical school, along with about forty other students from the administra-tive region of Gamu-Gofa. After selling his own cow to get to Arba Minch, he was given 280 birr to support himself for two months (schooling in Addis Ababa continued for one month). The red versus white terror made the students suspicious of one another; about a month before, the library of the school had been bombed and a teacher from Gamu-Gofa had died.

They [the teachers] taught us that during Haile Selassie's time, everyone said that the country was beautiful, very beautiful, even the people were considered beautiful. But when educated people went and lived in other countries, they realized that even though the country was beautiful, Ethiopia's people remained poor and dirty. Some couldn't even clean themselves by shaving their heads. Some couldn't wash their hair. Some went around with lice. We were a country scratching morning to night. That was what caused the revolution to explode. That was what caused Haile Selassie to be pushed from his throne. It was because of the scratching, the troubles, the injuries of the people that he fell. In addition to that, the teachers described a few foreign countries, particularly the Soviet Union. They told us how people lived there, how they had developed and progressed. . . . But what was the main thing they taught us? The landowners, the big ones, the ones who made their wealth from the farmers—that way of life had to be destroyed. Everyone had to become equal. That was what we learned first. We really didn't learn much about socialism.[3]

When he returned in Maale, Ziso would have taught these lessons in the peasant associations, but because the state was rapidly expanding the number of schools in areas in which there had been none before, Ziso (with a seventh-grade education, one of the most educated Maale in all the country) was ordered to become the first-grade teacher in Bunati. He taught there for a year and then returned to farm in Koibe. Once in Koibe, he was elected chairman of the peasant association in early 1980. Political cadres came from Jinka for the election:

The cadres gathered the people together to elect a chairman who would do the work. There were a few people who wanted to take things back to the time of Haile Selassie. But there were others who liked the revolution that had come. Realizing this, the cadre taught the people about the revolution as compared to Haile Selassie's time. They said that there were people who wanted to take things backward, but that they [the cadre and by implication, the state] did not like them. Because of this, the people who didn't like the revolution simply sat quietly and didn't raise their hands. The people who liked the new way then started to nominate people and after that everyone raised their hands. The cadre asked who the people liked and the people chose.[4]

For almost two years, Ziso served as chairman in Koibe during a critical turning point in local history (about which I will have more to say below). Then, in early 1982, he was elected first to the chairmanship of the woreda peasant association (the next higher level above local associations) and then after only one week, to the chairmanship of the awraja peasant association (yet one step further in the hierarchy). These positions took him outside Maale to Jinka and, after he was elected to the control committee of the administrative region itself (an additional step up), to Arba Minch. Ziso's education, his fluency in Amharic, the language of towns and the nation, and his reputation among cadre as a staunch supporter of the revolution were key factors in his swift rise. By the end of the revolutionary period, the administrative region of Gamu-Gofa had been split into two, with Jinka the new capital of South Omo. When the revolutionary state fell, Ziso was an official in the peasant association for the administrative region of South Omo, with a monthly salary and the use of an old four-wheel-drive vehicle (that worked sometimes).

Any person who occupied Ziso's position was expected to join the party, and his own contact with party cadre began in 1982:

> While I was chairman of the awraja peasant association, they sent Hasen Ahimed from Arba Minch to organize the party. At that time there was a period of testing in which they studied the people. Who had really worked for the revolution? Who had truly worked for the people? Who would reject bribes? Who would tell the truth? Who wouldn't take other people's property? Who wouldn't do bad things to people? Who wouldn't get drunk and fall down? Those were the principles of the party set out in the handbook. That kind of person was chosen. It wasn't only me.[5]

Each party member was given an identification card and had to pay dues. There were two stages of membership. First, there was a temporary stage and then a permanent one. Ziso was a temporary member for three months, and then he was admitted to permanent membership. The party newspaper came to Jinka, and Ziso read it; books came, and Ziso bought them. As far as he was concerned, the party was good:

> For the party people, the ones who had become members, drunkenness was prohibited and that was very good as far as I was concerned. Taking bribes and telling lies, committing crimes on the people—these things weren't right. To speak the truth forthrightly and to stand boldly for the people—when they said that these were the things that were needed, we people below, we really entered into the work. But the people above us, whether they did likewise or whether they were crooked, I don't know. I worked this way until the day Mengistu Haile Mariam fled the country. Until then, I stayed a member of the party.[6]

In Maale itself, party members probably never numbered more than ten. Most peasant association chairs and secretaries were members, though not all. Locally, the party met once a month (more frequently if needed). They discussed local conditions, they passed information upward in the hierarchy, they considered new persons for membership, and they criticized each others' faults.

For Ziso, party discipline sometimes resembled church discipline.

Some party members interpreted the party handbook as narrowly as Christians did the Bible. When asked to explain this comparison, Ziso, embarrassed, replied:

> I'll tell you hiding part of the answer. When I was living in Arba Minch I was without my wife. I found a girlfriend. I was living in a compound like this [with different rooms]. We on the control committee of the regional peasant association all lived together in the same compound. Every once in awhile I would go out and sleep with my girlfriend. My work didn't suffer. I didn't do anything bad for the party. But they almost threw me out.[7]

In a party meeting, Ziso was accused by the secretary of the local cell (also an ex-Christian). The secretary pointed to the party handbook, where it said that members must love their wives and children and not run after other women. Everyone in the room (even though they were doing the same thing, according to Ziso) criticized him. It was only the secretary (who had his wife nearby) who did not have a girlfriend. Ziso was forced to write a letter of apology. He was placed on probation for a period of three months, and a letter describing his transgression was transmitted to the main party offices in Arba Minch and to Addis Ababa. But not before Ziso had reacted angrily:

> They treated me like a criminal. When I was a Christian, I got angry and left over just such a matter. I came close to leaving the party. They tried to make everyone's path very narrow. They looked only at the principles in the book. They didn't see my situation. I was far from my wife. At one point, I got so angry that I called them "the vagina control committee."[8]

But Ziso did not leave the party (even though he insisted that he could have without serious consequences). As party discipline slacked into the late 1980s, he kept his girlfriend—and his belief in progress and the ability of Mengistu Haile Mariam to lead Ethiopia to a new future. After it became capital of South Omo, Jinka was electrified for the first time. Telephone service was installed. Many new hotels were built with accouterments like espresso machines to accommodate the government workers who came. All these aspects of life in Jinka functioned as icons of progress, signs of what the revolution had accomplished in southern Ethiopia. Interviewed in 1995, Ziso recalled his thoughts about Mengistu as a leader:

> According to the way that I was thinking then, Mengistu Haile Mariam was very strong. Even tired people he made them fell stronger. He was the kind of person who said that as long as we have one bullet and one person we won't retreat. We thought he was a very strong person. We really believed in

him. Truly, I wasn't the only one who thought like this. Many people in Ethiopia believed in him. Unless death reached him, he wouldn't leave the country. We thought that he really loved the country. When they said that he had fled, we thought that there was no one left who loved the country, who stood for the nation. No one who loved the country. I realized that everyone was really only for himself, but when there were no problems, they appeared as if they loved their country and those with whom they worked.[9]

One ingredient of expanded state power in Maale was, then, a very small group of committed local supporters, a group organized in a peculiarly modern way: in cells whose purpose was to lead others not so enlightened, cells composed of a vanguard who constantly examined one another's behavior to detect the smallest deviance from party guidelines, who reported on local conditions to superiors. Even though this revolutionary group was extremely small, it had an impact on Maale out of proportion to its numbers. Acting as leaders of the peasant associations, these men drew up complete tax lists of household heads for the first time in local history, they conscripted the young and jailed those they suspected of anti-revolutionary commitments.

THE GROWTH OF THE
REVOLUTIONARY STATE FROM BELOW

The ability of the new state to penetrate local communities cannot, however, be explained only by the actions of a vanguard. The revolutionary state did not simply exercise power downward (though, as I shall show, dramatic displays of armed force were at times an essential ingredient in its success). State power also grew upward. Ironically, even though they came to hate the new order, many Maale participated in the very institutions that strengthened the state at the grass roots. This occurred particularly in local conflicts in Maale in which one side or the other appealed to the state to deal with its enemies.

Both these processes, the exertion of coercion from above and the pressure for state intervention from below, were patterned over social space. In relation to the first, the ability of the state to intervene coercively in local affairs decreased with distance from the administrative centers, where virtually all police and cadre were stationed. Immediately preceding the revolution (and continuing afterward), Maale territory had been split between two administrative centers, the northern half (regions 1 and 3) under the town of Saula, the southern half (regions 2 and 4) under Jinka. By the early 1980s, the pattern of roads from these administrative centers into Maale expanded as peasant associations themselves built tracks into areas where motor transport had never before reached. Local traditionalists were of two minds about this development since they were intensely aware that roads made it easier for the state not only to provide schools and clinics but also to bring in police and cadre.

The principal line of communication from Saula to the two peasant associations in region 1 remained, for the entire revolutionary period, the old Italian-built road from the 1930s (which followed the edge of 1). Compared to the two peasant associations in region 1, the other two in region 3 were considerably more inaccessible: they could be reached only by footpaths over a mountain range.

In the southern half of Maale territory, the lines of communication changed during the revolutionary era. Previously, the old Italian-built road from Jinka to region 1 had furnished the principal line of communication between Jinka and region 2 (reached by a footpath over a mountain pass from region 1). By the early 1980s, the revolutionary government had built a new road directly from Jinka to the edge of region 2, which brought peoples there in closer contact with the administration. Peasant-built tracks allowed motor transport to reach all three of the peasant associations in region 2 by the mid-1980s. Finally, the single peasant association in region 4 remained remote, accessible only by footpaths over mountain passes from region 2.

If the ability of the state to exercise coercive power from above was one factor shaping social space, the demand for state intervention from below was, as I have pointed out, another. The latter pressure typically followed the pattern just delineated: highest in regions 1 and 2, and lowest in 3 and 4. These contrasts stemmed from the fact that conversion to evangelical Christianity had undermined previous Maale methods of local conflict resolution, and conversion was, as I have already shown, concentrated in regions 1 and 2. As a result, people in those areas—without functioning modes for dealing with the tensions of everyday life—began to look to the state.

How had Christian conversion undermined previous Maale methods of conflict resolution? Understanding this development requires some appreciation of the social organization of local Maale communities before the missionaries arrived. The basic building block of local Maale society in the mid-twentieth century was not simply lineage or residence groups (though indirectly these factors played their part) but various kinds of communal work groups.[10] People who "worked together," *wola sofene,* constituted the most solidary social and political groups at the local level.

Social solidarity was maintained within work groups by any number of mechanisms designed to prevent friction from occurring in the first place and to dampen conflicts when they did erupt. During my fieldwork in Bala in region 2 during the year 1974–75, all local court cases took place between individuals from *different* work groups.[11]

Consider the effects of missionization on Maale work organization: No Maale Christian could drink beer (and remain a member of the local church). The growth of Christian churches in regions 1 and 2 during the 1960s meant, then, a fundamental reordering of the network of local solidarities, for virtually all forms of Maale "working together" required beer. As the number of Christians grew, they organized, with the help of Welaita evangelists, their own way of working together, called *maddo,* "helping," which was composed exclusively of Christians and was presided over by church elders themselves. The owner of the field provided coffee and food, and the group worked in rotation among its members like a Maale *mol'o* work group—except that the Christian groups tended to worked relatively longer hours.

No member of a Christian maddo group was allowed to work in other kinds of work parties that depended upon beer. If a Christian did so, then he or she was expelled from the maddo group. This meant that Christian communities in Maale became more and more encysted as they developed into relatively self-sufficient labor pools, cut off from their traditionalist neighbors. Christians not only worshipped together, they "worked together."

In this context, there were few cooperative ties between Maale Christians and traditionalists. Given the fact that Christians believed that traditional religion was not simply different from Christian belief but indeed the very source of evil and sin, conflicts were not long in coming. But when dissension did develop, it tended to fester and snowball out of control. Before, crosscutting ties between those who "worked together" (ties that traditionalists had self-consciously maintained) helped to dampen and contain local social frictions. But by the late 1960s, these mechanisms no longer operated across belief groups.

The revolution, with its attack on Maale kingship and chiefship and the seeming rise of evangelical Christians to power, greatly exacerbated tensions between traditionalists and Christians. In regions 1 and 2, this meant that a relatively strong demand developed—perhaps more so among Christians, though at times among traditionalists as well—for the revolutionary state to solve local conflicts. As state agents responded, they inevitably became more involved in local affairs, and the power of the revolutionary state grew, even though (with the exception of the Maale vanguard) it was no local person's intention that it should do so.[12]

In summary, the operation of two factors—the demand for the intervention of the state from below and the exercise of coercive power from above—meant that the degree to which the revolutionary state penetrated local Maale communities varied across social space.

In the Maale periphery, local society was hardly affected. For the entire revolutionary period, there was only one peasant association chairman in region 4. An extremely wealthy man of traditional prestige before the revolution (though technically not a chief), uneducated and never a Christian, this chairman managed to keep the revolutionary state at arm's length. When state agents arrived to conscript Maale to fight in the war with Somalia, for example, he bribed the men to leave empty handed. After the chairman had been successful in protecting local people in this way, there was no potential local opposition with interests in bringing this matter to the attention of higher authorities. There were few Christians in region 4 and never any member of the party (this pattern was similar for region 3, the northern periphery, though not as extreme).

Although one man served for almost twenty years in region 4, chairmen of peasant associations in regions 1 and 2 changed on average every two to three years. Often, a change occurred when political cadre in Jinka or Saula became dissatisfied with how their directives were being carried out, and new elections (of the type that Ziso described above) were held. In this environment, chairmen in the core areas of Maale had to mediate quite actively between the state and local peoples. Because local opposition figures (including other members of the party, with ties to Jinka and Saula) were always present, core leaders typically faced a precarious situation. They could not control the process of articulation with the state. They could not prevent state agents from obtaining local information, nor could they prevent local opposition figures from going over their heads.

THE ATTACK ON EVANGELICAL CHRISTIANITY

Let me follow out, in more detail now, relations between Maale Christians and traditionalists into the 1980s. Doing so will clarify the extent to which interaction among Maale regions was more complex than I have presented so far. As it happened, a turning point was reached in the early 1980s: the resulting truce between the state and local society held until the very end of the revolutionary period.

The suppression of "foreign" or "invasive" religions began slowly in the late 1970s and took its significance, as I have shown, from politics at the center. In many locales in the south, this kind of suppression made little political sense, for evangelical Christians there had furnished the vanguard of revolutionary support. However, as Ethiopia switched Cold War alliances from the United States to the Soviet Union, Ethiopian evangelical Christians everywhere were left standing alone, facing the wrong direction—their ties to Westerners increasingly visible. This switch in the narrative of progress at the center of Ethiopian politics furnishes, as I have shown in the previous chapter, the context for understanding how evangelical Christianity came to be seen as both un-Ethiopian and a threat to socialism.

Kale Heywet churches associated with the Sudan Interior Mission and Mekane Yesus churches affiliated with the World Lutheran Federation became particular targets in the south, and by 1980 their property had been confiscated and believers imprisoned. By the mid-1980s, this campaign reached its apogee when in some administrative regions such as Welaita all evangelical Christian religious services had been suppressed.

The situation never reached this endpoint in Maale. Koibe was the center of Christian activity in Maale by the late 1970s. There, Maale Christians had built a tin-roofed Bible school (one of the few tin-roofed buildings in the country at that point). As political cadres from Jinka began to agitate against evangelicals, a Christian, Isha Dussa, still served as chairman of the Koibe peasant association in 1978. About a year later, Isha received a letter from the Ministry of Education in Jinka ordering him to confiscate the Koibe Bible school and turn it into an ordinary school for local children. After Isha received the letter, he apparently showed it to local church elders, and together they decided to hide the letter and ignore it. What they had not counted upon was the arrival of new teachers assigned to the former Bible school. This brought the matter into the open and created tensions between Christians and others like Ziso who supported the revolution: "How could Christians hide something from us that was going to help everyone?"

Open resistance to the revolutionary government always invited a show of force, a kind of theater of power. At the beginning of the school year, September 1979, the woreda administrator in Jinka swept into Koibe with an armed escort, installed the new teachers' classes in the Bible school building, arrested those who attempted to resist, and took them to Jinka to jail. Significantly, this was the context in which, five or six months later, new elections were held in the Koibe peasant association—and Ziso replaced Isha as chairman, as I described above. When cadre came to organize the election, they pointed out that people in Koibe "had become tired" and the revolution had to be revived.

Despite the beginning of the campaign against evangelicals, some of the people elected to peasant association offices below Ziso were Kale Heywet Christians (although none had been arrested by the woreda governor). At first, Ziso and they worked well together, but about a year later, in early 1981, the stakes of the conflict between Christians and others were raised when the woreda administrator returned and, this time, ordered the church building itself, not just the Bible school, confiscated. The administrator announced that whatever local Christians called themselves, they were really pente: "Before they [the Christians] tried to prevent our taking the Bible school. Because they have become people who resist the government, they will be allowed only their own houses. Everything else—church fields and church buildings—will become the property of the peasant association."

This escalation of the attack on evangelical Christianity in Maale seems to have been related to the national campaign rather than to local conditions. (Up-and-coming administrators could always add to their revolutionary credentials by attacking and exposing anti-revolutionaries.) Ziso's reaction, as chairman of the association, was, "Well, if this is a government order, fine." Five or six prominent local Christians were once again arrested and taken to jail in Jinka for three months.

The closing of the church in Koibe immediately unified evangelical Christians across Maale. They wrote a letter to the government and, in the revolution's own rhetoric, protested: "How can you take away from us what we built with our own hands, with our own sweat?" In response, a larger group of well-armed cadre once again descended on Koibe and, in a meeting with Maale Christians, demanded to know who had written the letter (which had been unsigned but simply stamped with the church seal). One by one, they asked the people present: "Did you say this?" Thus confronted by armed agents of the state, many denied any knowledge of the letter. A few bravely stepped forward and were taken off to prison.

A few weeks later, when it seemed that the matter had been settled, the Koibe peasant association gave the church building to one of the schoolteachers for his house (confiscation being always an easier alternative for local association officials, who otherwise had to extract labor from local inhabitants increasingly reluctant to offer it).

Here is what happened next, in the words of the Koibe peasant association chairman, Ziso:

> After we had installed the teacher in the church building, one day, a day like this, on Sunday, when I didn't in the least expect it, the Christians came to the church with their guns. Where they had planned this I don't know. They threw the teacher and his things out, and they occupied the church and began to pray to God. The teacher ran to my house to tell me what was going on. If I had gone there, there would have been bloodshed. I decided to let the people above know what was going on. I didn't take this matter on myself. I thought that if people above didn't come and solve this problem, that either I would die or that I would have to kill someone. That day I wrote a letter to the woreda.[13]

By this time, many Christians in Koibe began to drag their feet in carrying out peasant association directives. Virtually every order that Ziso gave became a confrontation. In one such showdown, he had to fire his gun at one of his own relatives. Christians began to buy guns and take them to church. Ziso received an order to suppress all religious services in his district (there were two other churches besides the one in Koibe), but in view of the local opposition, he was afraid even to attempt to carry out the order. According to Ziso: "It wasn't a matter of religion at that point. It had become armed struggle. I didn't know how I would survive. I just didn't know. And then the elections for the leadership of the woreda peasant association came along [the next higher administrative level, to which he was elected chairman] and I got back my life a little."[14] After having proven himself loyal to the new order in a difficult situation, Ziso began his movement up the revolutionary hierarchy. How many other revolutionaries in Ethiopia rose after they had alienated themselves from their own communities? In any case, a few months later, the woreda administrator returned with police and once again took the church building in Koibe by force and installed the teacher. State agents believed that they could not afford to let such openly stated opposition succeed.

At that point, local Christians reluctantly bowed to political realities and let the old building go. Instead, they constructed a new church building, a thatched-roof house. But they continued to worship openly throughout the entire revolutionary era in Maale.

THE SUPPRESSION OF TRADITION

The early 1980s were also a turning point for those who were turning more and more toward Maale "tradition." An influential chief from region 4, Galshila, the chief of Irbo, led an armed uprising in April 1980: The vice-chairman of the peasant association in Bala was tied up and ridden around the marketplace like a donkey. After the chairman of the local peasant association, Taddesse, managed to escape to Jinka and bring back a force of police and machine-gun-carrying cadre, the uprising was put down, but not before thirty-eight Maale were arrested and imprisoned in Jinka, some of them, like the chief, for many months.

Irony of ironies, to traditionalists like the chief of Irbo, the new government was an *amana* government—a believers' government, an evangelical Christian government. That revolutionaries like Taddesse and Ziso had left the church five or six years before and, indeed, that the revolutionary state had begun a campaign against evangelical Christianity (the Bible school in Koibe had been confiscated but not yet the church) made little impression on traditionalists' views.

The immediate trigger for the counter-revolution was drought. In early 1980, the rains began as usual and crops sprouted, but then just when precipitation should have reached its maximum, the rains totally disappeared—leaving the sorghum and maize slowly to wither and die in the fields. To traditionalists, this calamity was the result of not having a king (it rained when the king, followed by the chiefs and lineage elders, prayed to their ancestors). And traditionalist anger was directed precisely at those local Maale who had been instrumental in opposing the kingship: evangelical Christians. The chief of Irbo's men attacked and looted the property of Christians in region 2, slaughtering and eating their cattle and goats, cutting down their coffee trees, and raping their wives.[15]

To put the uprising in context, let me return to the events of the revolution in Bala and follow the history of the chairmanship of the peasant association established there. Taddesse, chairman during the uprising in 1980, was the same Taddesse who five years earlier had guided the zemecha to the sacred grove that contained the king's bones. Elected as the first chairman of the local peasant association, Taddesse was a figure very much like Ziso. He had been to mission school in Bako and spoke Amharic fluently. More impetuous than Ziso (as a schoolboy at the station, he had received beating after beating for misbehaving), Taddesse was willing to attack Maale tradition in the most iconoclastic way.

Figure 21. Galshila, chief of Irbo, 1974. Photograph taken by the author.

After Taddesse and the zemecha students took the king's bones out of the sacred grove and buried them alongside a path, the tide turned against the zemecha students. As I pointed out in Chapter 2, the Derg asserted control of the local revolution by August 1975, and many zemecha were imprisoned for their "excesses." This change in atmosphere became apparent to Maale, and two of the Bala elders who traditionally helped to install Maale kings took the opportunity of traveling to Jinka to accuse Taddesse of desecrating a grave. (Aggrieved traditionalists, like evangelical Christians, thus sometimes took their matters to the revolutionary state—even though they hardly identified with the state's new rhetoric.) In the case at hand, the two elders won a temporary victory. Taddesse—even though he had been elected the first chairman of the new peasant association—was jailed for approximately four months. After his release, he was removed from the chairmanship, and the man originally elected as the vice-chairman, Maja, took over leadership.

Maja at first enjoyed the overwhelming support of local traditionalists, in part because he was *not* Taddesse. As time wore on, however, Maja was not able to keep that support, for he combined qualities not often found in Maale: Maja was what might be called a non-Christian modernist. Very much a Maale peasant, uneducated, able to speak Amharic only haltingly, and unable to read or write, Maja nonetheless believed in the revolution. What attracted him was principally the notion of progress—that Maale would have access to medicine, education, and the world opening about them.

It was Maja, in fact, who led the spurt of building that occurred in Bala immediately after the revolution. In 1976, the entire market village (previously situated next to the king's compound) was moved closer to permanent water, and a school was constructed there for the first time in local history. Organizing this work, Maja was soon at loggerheads with traditionalists, who did not see the point of all this work—which they themselves had to do. The chief of Irbo—an elderly and respected, even feared man from the old order—led the opposition to Maja. One market day in Bala, Maja ordered people of the peasant association to go to Bushkoro and carry back cement sacks for the new school building. According to Maja:

> The chief of Irbo stood up and opposed my orders. He said that the new government had not established peace with the Banna in the south. The Banna were killing and robbing Maale. Why should Maale carry cement for the new school? The chief of Irbo said that he would prevent "his" people in Irbo from participating in this work. I then ordered the chief arrested, but he resisted the association policemen, pulling out his knife. That night apparently the policemen beat up the chief for his bad behavior. I was not there and did not see what happened. The next day the chief wanted to go to the clinic in Bushkoro to get his wounds attended. After I had arranged for seven policemen from Bala and three from Koibe to accompany us, we left for Bushkoro. But the chief's sons were waiting for us along the way, and they rescued him. In the shooting, one of their bullets grazed my leg.[16]

After that, rumors had it that the chief's sons were waiting and watching for an opportunity to kill Maja. Various local people tried to patch up the quarrel but to no avail. Tensions came to a head when a group of armed men from Irbo humiliated Maja by taking away his association-issued gun. After he fled to Jinka to seek the help of cadre, Maja returned to Maale, but in the meetings that ensued, Taddesse was reinstated as chairman of the association (despite the opposition of the majority of local people).

Why did Maja fail to remain in office? It seems clear that the answer lies mainly with the reaction of the cadre, not local Maale. According to Maja himself, he was replaced because he could not read and speak Amharic. When any order came, he had to depend upon others to decipher it; without their mediation (Could he always trust the translation?), Maja was not able to function. Given the burden of communication, it was apparently difficult for Maja to gain the full confidence of town-raised cadre. But there was probably also a cultural component to cadres' evaluations. Unlike Taddesse, Maja was "uneducated." It was difficult for any educated Ethiopian to see an uneducated peasant as a true local leader, one who could enact the metanarrative of progress and enlightenment. Even though he himself believed in the revolution, Maja eventually lost support from both sides: from traditionalists like the chief of Irbo because he was too progressivist, and from cadre because he looked too traditional.

So Taddesse returned to revolutionary leadership in Bala, and he used his savvy in cultural translation to paint his local enemies as anti-revolutionaries. When the end of the Maale year approached (the last month of *tudji* was when kings were installed), there was inevitably talk of reinstalling a Maale kati. Communicated to outsiders in Amharic, this was described as the return of a *balabbat,* a "big man" or "landlord"—something that no revolutionary could ever approve. To traditionalists in Maale, in contrast, the role that the Maale king had occupied on the eve of the revolution—particularly his role in land ownership and in local administration for the imperial state—was hardly traditional, having been created by Haile Selassie's government. When traditionalists asked for a Maale king, what they had in mind was mainly the king's priestly function according to local cosmology— his role in ensuring fertility and well-being for all Maale.

Conveying the complexities of cultural translation was not in Taddesse's interests. Having taken a vanguard role during the zemecha period, he had every reason to oppose any rehabilitation of the kingship. Instead, he used his savvy with cadre to deal with old enemies. Not long in office again, he accused the two elders who had him imprisoned in late 1975. According to Taddesse, these two were guilty of "anti-revolutionary activities": they were attempting to bring back a Maale king. Such an accusation (given the fact that elders *did* want a new king and that it was virtually impossible for any revolutionary outsider to sympathize with their story once translated into Amharic) was enough to get the two men imprisoned for a number of months. Local association policemen were ordered to arrest the men in Maale and to take them to Jinka, where they were turned over to the state. In these maneuvers and others, Taddesse could depend upon the local peasant association to carry out his orders.

Waxing strong as the revolutionary state waxed strong (the red terror was defeated and the Somali invasion repulsed in the late 1970s),

Taddesse stayed in office for the next five years. But his impetuousness almost invited traditionalist opposition; indeed, in a way, Taddesse's very power depended upon a traditionalist opposition.

As I have already mentioned, it was the chief of Irbo who led the fated traditionalist uprising. As the drought of early 1980 grew more serious, the chief began consulting traditional figures about reinstalling Ottolo as kati (Ottolo was the Maale king earlier deposed by the machinations of Arbu; see Chapter 3).

It seems that the chief secretly approached Taddesse to sound him out on the response of the local peasant association. Many traditionalists believed that opposition to the Maale kingship was concentrated at the local level and that revolutionary officials above would not oppose their wishes for a kati. "Orthodox Christians have their priests. Why can't we have ours?" they asked.

What happened next is open to interpretation. According to Ziso, a revolutionary insider, Taddesse used a visit by a woreda administrator to intimidate traditionalists, to try to convince them that they had no chance of reinstalling another king. In something of a reenactment of the events of the original zemecha campaign, the administrator (at Taddesse's urging?) ordered peasant association police to reenter the sacred forest where the king's treasury was kept and confiscate two or three items for a museum display. He said that the spears, bells, and beads would be used to teach Ethiopians about their "feudal" past, a past superseded by the progress afforded by the revolution.

This confiscation was the last straw for traditionalists. To them, the king's sacred objects represented not a past made superfluous by progress but icons of a timeless standard against which the present would always be found wanting. In a matter of weeks, the chief of Irbo had mobilized supporters to attack Christians in Bala, to loot and rape, and to take over the peasant association.

Somehow, Taddesse managed to hide from the chief's men and escape to Ziso's house in Koibe (Ziso at that point was chairman of the peasant association in Koibe). Ziso relates what happened:

> The Irbo chief declared war on Bala. I don't know, maybe children who didn't yet have a mind remained behind. Maybe women weren't there. Everyone else was. When I saw them with my own eyes, there were so many that it was meaningless to try to count them. It frightened me. I was chairman of the Koibe peasant association then, and we heard that they had slaughtered all of Taddesse's cattle, raped his wife, cut down and threw away all his coffee trees. . . . Taddesse and a few others escaped into the bush, and

they came to my house in Koibe that night. They said, "What can we do? We don't have any money. How can we reach Jinka?" I fed them and loaned them money, and that night, they left for Jinka by the Boshkoro path. When they returned from Jinka, they brought a sizable force of police and cadre with them. When they came through Koibe, I thought I would go to Bala and see conditions for myself. We arrived at the schoolhouse in Bala. Before the people who had come to Bala were looking everywhere for Taddesse and the others. While they were still searching, the police force escorted Taddesse back and put him in the schoolhouse. The ones in the uprising were staying in Dufa. After we had settled Taddesse in the schoolhouse with the police and cadre, we heard something coming down from up there that sounded just like an airplane. The grass and the trees shook. When I saw them coming, I was shocked and very afraid. "What is this?" I said to myself. "No one can help me through this." "We're arrived," they said. Some carried poisoned arrows. Some had guns. And they were all spoiling to kill. "Go in and grab Taddesse and the others. Don't be afraid of the Amharas' guns. Have you ever seen them kill anybody before? Get in there and take them," they said. While they were about to shoot their weapons, a policeman stood up and began to swear in the name of the law. But no one was listening to him. The head of the police took off his cap and placed it on top of his gun and said, "Those of you who want Taddesse, you come and take this first. We are government people. If you think we are not government people, then come on. Take this. If you think we are not government people, come and get us." Then there was silence. The policeman asked, "Are you listening?"

They said, "Yes."

"Perhaps Taddesse has done something bad. Perhaps he has hurt you. But injured people cannot make things right by spilling blood. The law must be the one to punish. You now want to kill somebody. If you take him from our hands and kill him, then the government will hold us responsible. If you take him from us and kill him, then what can we tell the government? Taddesse and the others, we cannot give them to you. If you still want to take him, you are going to have to kill us first."

After he said this, they were taken aback somewhat. Before, there were many aiming rifles at the schoolhouse. There were many who were ready to throw rocks at the tin roof. They filled the school compound like ants. Slowly, the cadre went out among them and tricked them into cooling down. They told the people to chose elders to settle the matter between Taddesse and the people. They told the men that if they would talk, they [the cadre] would try to settle the matter. If not, they certainly could not give Taddesse to them.

After people started talking, the policeman gave me a note that said, "We're surrounded. We still have Taddesse and the others. But come and help us as soon as you can, even in the dark." At that point, it was about four in the afternoon. Getting out of there was a real problem for me. He rolled up the message tightly and gave it to me secretly. I acted like I was sick and started to go down the path slowly. The chief of Bala asked me where I was going. "My in-law [Ziso was married to a daughter of the chief of Bala],

I'm going home. They came and got me in Koibe. I really didn't want to come. My head is killing me. If I stay here, it's going to get the best of me. No, it's good if I go," I said, and I left.

Well, I crossed into my own district, and I put a bullet in my gun. "If anybody wants me here, I'll take care of them," I thought. I got home, and I left for Jinka at about one that night. I arrived by daybreak and told them that the policemen who were in Bala had been overcome. They called for reinforcements. I went back with a strong armed force from the awraja [the next higher administrative level].

In the meantime, the cadre who were already there had tricked the huge crowd that had surrounded them. "Go back to your houses. Let the elders you have chosen settle the matter," they said. At that point, the majority left for home. . . . When we got back, we arrested the Bala chief's son, the Bala chief's younger brother, the chief of Golo, the chief of Jato—all the chiefs, we tied them together like goats and took them to Jinka to prison. Taddesse and others had been seriously injured—all of his cattle finished, the coffee he had planted cut down and thrown away, his wife raped. . . . That is the complete story.[17]

DEMOBILIZATION AND THE DEMANDS OF ORDINARY LIFE

The memory of violent confrontations of the early 1980s served to inhibit opposition to the state in Maale for the rest of the revolutionary period. Once back on track, the demands of everyday life, the pressures of farming, the fact that all peasants in Maale needed, at times, a locally constituted authority to deal with their problems, such pressures from below encouraged peasant associations to become relatively effective centers of local administration. In regions 1 and 2 (but not in 3 and 4), each association had a communal field on which each household was required to contribute labor one morning a week. In some ways this represented a continuation from prerevolutionary times, when Maale were required to present labor tribute to the king and chiefs, as well as to some Amhara landlords. Crops from communal fields were stored in association-built granaries and then sold (often to local members of the association at below-market prices).

Each association was subdivided into smaller districts (Bala, for example, had been divided into thirteen by the mid-1980s), each with its own work captain.[18] Each of these districts reported to the station of the larger peasant association—with its flagpole and flag, meeting houses, police station and jail, clinic, and schools. Over the revolutionary period, schools in particular took root. For example, the one in Bala, established in the first years of the revolution, comprised six

Figure 22. The national flag at the Bala Peasant Association Station in the late 1980s. Peasant stations were, in some respects, vernacular copies of SIM mission stations. Photograph taken by the author.

grades by 1983: There were ninety boys and ten girls attending the first grade; thirty-six boys and three girls in the second; twenty-two boys and two girls in the third; seventeen boys and no girls in the fourth; seven boys and two girls in the fifth; and twelve boys and one girl in the sixth. In some ways, the local presence of educated teachers (none of whom were Maale) operated the same way as that of party members or, to a lesser extent, Christians; teachers at times could influence the operation of the peasant associations more than ordinary Maale (even though technically they were not members) because it was easy for them to go above the heads of local peasant association chairmen to officials in Jinka or Saula.

Given the dispersed settlements of Maale, peasant association stations tended to become the centers of local social and political life during the 1980s. Typically located next to clearings used for weekly markets (when association directives were communicated to the crowd), the station was the site for meetings of the youth association and the women's association. There, too, the committee of the main association heard court cases once a week. The following description from my field notes in Bala during April 1983 illustrates the banality of association power:

Figure 23. Schoolboys playing the new game of soccer, Bala, late 1980s.
Photograph taken by the author.

> There were a number of small cases yesterday. . . . Wono Joshi had a sick
> cow that he finally killed and sold the meat; the person in charge of collect-
> ing the money hadn't given him four birr. It was decided that the man would
> have to give the money in two weeks' time or be imprisoned [in the associa-
> tion jail]. Shifera Dore had taken three bundles of thatch from the associa-
> tion communal field; he did not deny the charge and was fined five birr. I
> think he finally paid four. Maja, the person in charge of protecting grazing
> lands, also accused Wogata Digga, a member of the committee, of taking
> thatch from the association field. Wogata also did not deny the charge but
> said that he did it because everyone else was doing the same. He also was
> fined. Takile Waci, a work captain for one of the thirteen districts of Bala,
> asked for clarification. He said that a household head, instead of coming to
> work on the association field himself, had sent a "child" in his place. Takile
> had sent the child back home and fined the man three birr for not working.
> The man refused to pay. The chairman of the association supported Takile's
> actions—the man would have to pay the fine.

A forced settlement of a past debt, a fine for cutting thatch, a decision
that a "child" could not substitute for an adult in work on communal
fields—these were some of the ways that Maale peasant associations
insinuated themselves into everyday life. In the end, it was these small,
mundane acts, in combination with the memory of dramatic shows of

force recounted above—the old chief arrested by machine-gun-carrying cadre, a Maale tin-roofed church turned into a new teacher's residence—that made revolutionary institutions in Maale effective. But by the mid-1980s virtually no Maale peasant "believed" in the new revolutionary order.

Afterword / Afterward

That which withers in the age of mechanical reproduction is the aura of the work of art. This is a symptomatic process whose significance points beyond the realm of art. One might generalize by saying: the technique of reproduction detaches the reproduced object from the domain of tradition. By making many reproductions it substitutes a plurality of copies for a unique existence. And in permitting the reproduction to meet the beholder or listener in his own particular situation, it reactivates the object reproduced. These two processes lead to a tremendous shattering of tradition

Walter Benjamin,
"The Work of Art in the Age
of Mechanical Reproduction"

The Ethiopian revolution, as it occurred in Maale and in the country as a whole, had everything to do with distinctly local concerns and parochial interests. At the same time, variously situated actors understood what they did and what happened about them in relation to a consciousness of a world far beyond. The resulting sedimentation of stories within stories has provided the framework for this book.

In an odd way, revolution in Ethiopia, as elsewhere, appeared to "need" its opposite, reaction. For it was precisely in the widening spiral of conflict that the cultural clothing of the old régime was rent: "[Revolution] appears to unchain a yearned-for future while the nature of this future robs the present of materiality and actuality, thus, while continually seeking to banish and destroy Reaction, it succeeds only in reproducing it: modern Revolution remains ever affected by its opposite, Reaction."[1]

At the center of Ethiopian politics, reaction came soon enough from the local intelligentsia, who resented the military's theft of what they regarded their own rightful place: leading the nation into a progressive future. In Maale, the forces of reaction took longer to develop. There, "traditionalists" initially were inclined to interpret the revolution as a return to, rather than a departure from, tradition. It took several years of increasing state penetration of local affairs, along with a drought in the early 1980s, to precipitate local reaction. By that time, rebellious peasants were no match for machine-gun-carrying cadre, and the memory of failed rebellion stabilized state-society relations in Maale for the rest of the decade.

If revolution, in some sense, "needed" reaction, it also had to have its local believers—not only those involved in the initial uprisings and upheavals but men who could be counted upon to extend and expand the struggle as the new state consolidated itself. In Maale, this role was played overwhelmingly by ex-Christians. By the 1970s foreign missionaries had produced what in the context of southern Ethiopia was an intensely modernist group of converts. When the revolution began to promise a new beginning, local Christians, particularly the educated young, entered into the work of attacking tradition as enthusiastically as Russian or Chinese revolutionaries. By the time the new state turned on evangelical Christianity, a handful of (then) ex-Christians were willing to follow and take up the work of the party.

The interaction between groups enacting different visions of the future finally produced an emergent reality, something different from the sum of its parts. In each of the contests that developed—and contests were required to ratchet the process to the next level—the roots of the new state grew deeper and deeper into local peasant societies: the revolutionary state conscripted soldiers on a scale unknown in Ethiopian history. It built roads, for the first time pushing beyond the network that the Italians had built in the 1930s. And it constructed schools and began to compel peasants to send their children to them.

Revolutionaries, once they had supplanted the *ancien régime*, looked to the newly won state as the scalpel with which to operate on Ethiopian history. From a detached point of view, the revolutionary project, given its enormity, was bound to fail at times. But from a revolutionary standpoint, failure—even more than success—was a spur for yet another round of state building. Reaction had to be combated, the future seized.

François Furet has drawn attention to this sort of dynamic in that founding event of modernism, the French revolution:

> That central notion for militant action, whose most systematic spokesman was perhaps Marat, was also the site of the power struggle among groups and individual leaders. Whoever controlled that site was in a dominant position so long as he could hold on to it. The power to govern legitimately was directly related to the ability to keep up the denunciation of the aristocrats' plot ["reaction"]: the constant raising of the ideological stakes was the rule of the game in the new system.[2]

A copy of a copy, the revolution eventually assumed a life of its own in Ethiopia, and what had begun as an attempt to apply reason to the future ended in profoundly irrational projects. In many areas of the south,[3] peasants were forced into new concentrated villages laid out on inflexible grid patterns—but typically without the state services that would make these new arrangements beneficial. One of my most vivid memories from the mid-1980s comes from flying in a small plane between Addis Ababa and Maale. Landscapes that had looked gently chaotic ten years before resembled nothing so much as the straight lines of a Mondrian painting. It seemed as if the revolutionary state had written its power on space itself.

I have attempted to explain these processes, but in the end, there is something ineffable about why things happened as they did. Modernist to the end, Trotsky threw up his hands: "It remains, of course, incomprehensible—at least with a rational approach to history—how and why a faction the least rich of all in ideas, and the most burdened with mistakes, should have gained the upper hand over all other groups, and concentrated an unlimited power in its hands."[4]

We recognize that a narrative cannot be summarized, or restated as an inventory of conclusions of "findings"; not that conclusions may not be drawn, but if one asks for reasons for accepting or rejecting them, the answer is not simply a recital of pieces of evidence (of the sort that would be advanced to support a generalization), but rather the repetition of the way in which the narrative has ordered the evidence. The situation is not unlike the apocryphal story told of many composers, for instance of Schubert: When asked what a sonata he had just played "meant," he responded only by sitting down and playing it again. The difference, of course, is that a historical narrative claims to be true, in a way that music does not.[5]

Modernity and modernism, or stated differently, postmodernity and postmodernism, are currently subjects of a sprawling, interdisciplinary conversation—one to which this book seeks to make some contribution. Postmodernism's problemization of modernity has been crucial. After all, not so long ago, anthropologists and others lived in a world in which notions of linear time, progress, and nations seemed merely natural; it was, after all, this world that made the modernization theories of the 1950s appear plausible.

But historical ethnography has not made the contribution to current debates that it could. Its potential, in particular, is to remind us that the question of modernity was not invented yesterday—or by high theorists. In actuality, a long, vernacular conversation has gone on for centuries among ordinary men and women the world over. What these men and women have thought and felt, at various times and places, may contain as much that is relevant to the end of the millennium as do the writings of the Western avant-garde. Vernacular modernisms, postmodernisms, anti-modernisms—along with their reactions, refusals, and rejections—help to frame contemporary questions in a much-needed, longer-term perspective.

In order to make these common voices available, anthropologists need to attend to ethnography and history in a new way. In this context, as J. D. Y. Peel has argued, narrative becomes a key issue:

> [Narrative] is a critical instrument of human agency, for it is the principal means by which agents integrate the temporal flow of their activities. Putting it another way, human beings produce sociocultural form through an arch of memories, actions, and intentions. Narrative is the way in which that arch may be expressed, rehearsed, shared, and communicated. It is this which gives human action its inherent historicity or lived-in-timeness and which requires an anthropology that, to be adequate to its subject matter, should be essentially historical.[6]

Not only is narrative key for understanding particular historical actors, but also the way that narratives interact and intertwine over time, are copied, changed, and passed across cultural space, is central to the task of constructing historical ethnographies. As Walter Benjamin pointed out some time ago, modern technologies of cultural reproduction have begun to augment and alter these latter forms of interaction. Instead of story, then, we have stories within stories within stories. I have sought to develop ways of analyzing the complexity of these connections by way of a particular arrangement of empirical materials—in other words, through narrative itself. A radical commitment to narrative, in this last sense, is required, I believe, if the potential of historical anthropology is to be realized.[7]

The century of the Enlightenment, of rationalist secularism, brought with it its own modern darkness. With the ebbing of religious belief, the suffering which belief in part composed did not disappear. Disintegration of paradise: nothing makes fatality more arbitrary. Absurdity of salvation: nothing makes another style of continuity more necessary. What then was required was a secular transformation of fatality into continuity, contingency into meaning . . . few things [are] better suited to this end than an idea of nation.[8]

I have taken the story of the Ethiopian revolution to the mid-1980s. By that point, the state related to local peasant communities dramatically differently from Haile Selassie's time. But if the revolutionary state had been modernized, it had also been made, paradoxically, more dependent upon the outside world—not just materially but also ideologically.[9]

As the Cold War came to a close at the end of the 1980s, the international order underwent a sea change, with the Soviet Union itself rejecting Marxism-Leninism and eventually disintegrating. Few people in the world anticipated this change—certainly not Ethiopians during most of the 1980s.

> In 1987 Mengistu's regime looked absolutely unassailable. . . . By 1981, he had organized the entire population into numerous kinds of local and national mass organizations. By 1984, he had personally and painstakingly organized the Workers' Party of Ethiopia and subsumed the mass organizations under it. By 1987, he had formalized the structure of the state through a constitution. . . . What is more, he had, with the aid and advice of the socialist countries, extended the state's security forces to an unprecedented level. . . . The army, which was well armed by the Soviet Union, was expanded to become the biggest military force in sub-Saharan Africa with almost half a million men under arms.[10]

Just as quickly as Ethiopians had taken up Marxism in 1975, they jettisoned it by the end of the 1980s. Mengistu himself distanced himself from Marxism-Leninism in March 1990. As Andargachew has argued, the regime died just as it had been conceived: in Ethiopians' imaginations of the world and the direction in which it was moving, and consequently in conceptions of how Ethiopia could take its place on the world stage:

> It is often claimed that Mengistu's regime collapsed because of a shortage of military supplies. . . . However, the military supplies from the Soviet Union had continued to trickle in almost to the last days of the regime. Also, there was no report of a shortage of weapons at all. Rather, the importance of the change in the international political scene appears to have been, not in starving the regime of weapons, but, rather, in disorientating it by creating a confidence crises among its erstwhile supporters (party functionaries, government officials and military officers).[11]

As military discipline in Mengistu's armies disintegrated, the principal organized forces in the country were a secessionist movement in Eritrea, the Eritrean Peoples Liberation Front (EPLF), and an insurgent

movement in neighboring Tigray province, the Tigray People's Liberation Front (TPLF), the latter led by Meles Zenawi. Meles became the
new Elvis of Ethiopian politics, taking up, just as suddenly as Mengistu
had Marxism, the banner of democracy and human rights. Since Mengistu had previously been apolitical as far as can be determined, the
switch for Meles was more striking: only a few years before, he had not
only subscribed to Marxism-Leninism but had held up Albania as the
model that Ethiopia should emulate.

With Meles now the defender of democracy, human rights, and economic development, the United States engineered a regime change in
Ethiopia in May 1991. At a peace conference in London, Assistant Secretary of State for African Affairs Herman Cohen publicly "recom-
mended" that a TPLF-dominated front occupy Addis Ababa.[12] Mengistu
was retired to a farm in Zimbabwe. The front, the Ethiopian People's
Revolutionary Democratic Front (EPRDF) took over the levers of power
in Ethiopia, and Eritrea, after a plebiscite, became independent.

As I have argued, Ethiopian political life had been dramatically deterritorialized after the late 1970s; it was as if the global had created a
vacuum that "raised" Ethiopian politics above local constraints. In
1990, this vacuum was suddenly punctured, and Ethiopian political
life dropped down, joltingly, into more localized contexts—though not
exactly to the same ruts. What were the effects of this transformation
in Maale?

Rather than analyze the complexities of postsocialist Maale (it may
be too early, in any case, to attempt to do so), I will briefly note the following. Peasant associations continued to operate into the mid-1990s,
maintaining law and order, settling court cases, and, all in all, presiding
over local communities. Quotidian life went on. Of course, the leadership of peasant associations in most places changed; but apparently the
associations themselves—local-level arms of the state with jails, schools,
and clinics—are destined to outlive the revolutionary period.

As old socialists in Maale like Ziso, now bitterly disillusioned, turned
to drink, evangelical churches took the place of the Workers' Party of
Ethiopia in purveying modernity to the Maale. Strengthened by persecution, Kale Heywet churches began to attract the young in increasing
numbers (many more of whom had gone to school by that point) with
new methods, one of the most striking being new forms of music accompanied by new instruments like guitars.

Not only did modernist churches undergo a revival at the beginning
of the postsocialist era, so did traditionalism. After more than a decade

and a half of rigid suppression, Maale were at last able to reinstall a kati. In the ritually appropriate last month of the Maale calendar, toward the end of 1994, an elaborate funeral was held to bury kati Arbu's bones (the same bones that had been buried briefly by the zemacha students in 1975 but then returned to the sacred grove). After so many struggles and so much conflict, Arbu was finally laid to rest on the top of the highest mountain in Maale, alongside the past kings of Maale. In the same rite, his son, Dulbo, was installed as the new kati.

Dulbo—who had lived outside Maale since 1975—married a young Maale girl, who would become the mother of the next king. Employed as a veterinary assistant in the next administrative region, Dulbo refused to move permanently to Maale. Instead, he became a sort of part-time king, with no official role in the government or in the peasant associations, who came periodically only to carry out essential rites—a role that, like so much else in postsocialist Ethiopia, rests upon yet another reinterpretation of tradition.

St. Petersburg, Russia, July 17, 1998—The Russians buried Czar Nicholas II today in true imperial fashion, beneath a ceiling of cherubim peeking from clouds, in a cathedral of mountainous oak and linden carvings sheathed in gold, among the white marble tombs of the czars who bestrode his empire for three centuries. And they buried him in a style of modern Russia, too: under imitation marble markers because there is no money for genuine stone; in a cathedral plundered by revolutionaries decades ago and half-restored today; at the center of enduring conflicts over whether the nation was venerating a monarch, a tyrant or even a fraud.[13]

In these ways, Maale traditionalism and modernist forms of evangelical Christianity quickly reasserted themselves. Exactly how struggles over the modern and the traditional will play out in postsocialist Maale is not clear. At this point, the encapsulating contexts of wider Ethiopia and the world system of states have been fundamentally altered. The end of the Cold War has brought with it an overwhelming Western triumphalism in which "development" and "democracy" have decisively replaced "revolution" in modernity's master-narrative.[14]

Have we seen, then, the end of revolution, in Ethiopia and elsewhere? Or will a new revolutionary narrative emerge once again to capitalize upon peoples' worst fears and catalyze their best hopes? Whatever happens, it seems likely that the structure of differences among stances toward "progress," for and against, for and against in both mixed and ambivalent ways, will continue—at least as long as we live in a modern world.

Notes

ORIENTATIONS

1. This is a phrase from Keith Michael Baker's analysis of that founding event of modernism, the French revolution. See his *Inventing the French Revolution* (Cambridge: Cambridge University Press, 1990). By "modernism," I mean a local, culturally encoded stance toward history, one that yearns to bring things "up to date." Modernity, on the other hand, refers to the wider cultural conversation in which modernists are typically a dominant part, but which includes others, from traditionalists to post-modernists.

2. The Maale, the people on which I shall focus this description, had an intense interest in and their own typology of the differences of power and wealth in the world. For elders in 1974, the principal actors on the world stage, besides the "Amhara" of northern Ethiopia (anyone from the north, even those from non-Amhara ethnic backgrounds like Oromo or Gurage, were identified by the Maale as "Amhara.") were the Italians and the British. The Amhara had conquered Maale and the surrounding area during the late nineteenth century—their grandfathers' time. Northern armies had been so overwhelming (and Maale fighters so weakened by a war with the neighboring Baaka) that the Maale had chosen to surrender. There was no question, then, that the Amhara were stronger than the Maale. Their ways and their language were associated with the prestige of the nation by the 1970s.

Beyond the Amhara were the Italians. Since most Maale had hardly identified with "Ethiopia" by the mid-1930s, they viewed the Italian invasion at that point as a liberation. The Italians flew in airplanes. They built roads (or rather, they forced Maale and other southerners to build roads). And, most of all, they abolished *gabbar* serfdom in the south (see Donham, "Old Abyssinia and the New Ethiopian Empire: Themes in Social History," *in* Donald Donham and Wendy James, eds. *The Southern Marches of Imperial Ethiopia: Essays in History and Social Anthropology* [Cambridge: Cambridge University Press, 1986], pp. 3–48). But the Italians did not prove strong enough to resist the British: The British, with Ethiopian patriots, kicked the Italians out of Ethiopia and restored Haile Selassie. Thus, *inglis aci,* England, was even more powerful than Italy.

America was a vaguer entity than any of these, one that elders had heard about mainly from Maale schoolboys (of whom there were few before the revolution). But even Maale elders tended to know that America was more powerful than England. This hierarchy was understood in distinctly local terms. More than anything else it was guns—old rifles made in Italy, Belgium, England, and the United States, often known in Maale by the country of origin—that furnished the principal icons of modernity, a modernity located, for the Maale, elsewhere. I was continually asked whether as an American I knew how to make guns. Amhara, Maale said, did not know how to make guns, but the Italians, the British, and the Americans did. If I was an American, why didn't I?

Thus, most Maale saw themselves as "poor" and "backward." One evangelical Maale convert in 1974 asked me, "Why in the world are you spending time learning Maale? This little language doesn't extend from that mountain to the next one [it was possible to see across the breadth of Maale territory, given the right altitude]. Here, we're only living in the dark."

3. The problem of how to describe local realities as they are conditioned by larger ones is hardly new within anthropology. Since the 1950s, anthropologists like Edmund Leach (*Political Systems of Highland Burma: A Study of Kachin Social Structure* [London: Athlone Press, 1954]), Eric Wolf (*Peasant Wars of the Twentieth Century* [New York: Harper & Row, 1969]), and Sidney Mintz (*Sweetness and Power: The Place of Sugar in Modern History* [New York: Viking, 1985]) have grappled with this problem.

Perhaps the most sophisticated methodological analyses to date have been presented by G. William Skinner and Carol A. Smith. See Skinner, "The Structure of Chinese History," *Journal of Asian Studies* 44 (1985): 271–292; and Smith, ed. *Regional Analysis,* 2 vols. (New York: Academic Press, 1976).

What is different about the present analysis is my attempt, like Arjun Appadurai's in *Modernity at Large* (Minneapolis: University of Minnesota Press, 1996), to address the problem of the local within the context of cultural flows defined by modernity. (See also Akhil Gupta and James Ferguson, eds. *Culture, Power, Place: Exploration in Critical Anthropology* [Durham: Duke University Press, 1997.]) Unlike Appadurai, however, I concentrate on aspects of "globalization" that are unrelated to international migration or to the electronic media. Appadurai argues for a kind of postmodern rupture that has, over the "past few decades," produced an emergent cultural reality. The processes I isolate for the Maale have a much longer history; for many places on the African continent, they predate colonialism.

4. C. L. R. James, *The Black Jacobins: Toussaint L'Ouverture and the San Domingo Revolution,* 2nd ed. (New York: Vintage, 1963), pp. 81–82.

5. By this point, there is a long list of anthropological statements on "his-

tory." In many ways, Eric Wolf initiated the recent conversation with his analysis of world capitalism, *Europe and the Peoples without History* (Berkeley: University of California Press, 1982). Marshall Sahlins reacted with a structuralist defense of local culture in *Islands of History* (Chicago: University of Chicago Press, 1985). Others have followed: William Roseberry, *Anthropologies and Histories: Essays in Culture, History, and Political Economy* (New Brunswick, NJ: Rutgers University Press, 1989); John L. and Jean Comaroff, *Ethnography and the Historical Imagination* (Boulder, CO: Westview Press, 1992); Michel-Rolph Trouillot, *Silencing the Past: Power and the Production of History* (Boston: Beacon Press, 1995); and finally, in an attempt to sum things up, Nicholas B. Dirks, Geoff Eley, and Sherry B. Ortner, eds., *Culture/ Power/ History: A Reader in Contemporary Social Theory* (Princeton: Princeton University Press, 1994).

Historical anthropology seems to me, particularly of late, to be in danger of losing contact with the richness of ethnographic practice. Exceptions certainly exist—one thinks of Anna Tsing, *In the Realm of the Diamond Queen: Marginality in an Out-of-the-way Place* (Princeton: Princeton University Press, 1993), and David William Cohen and E. S. Atieno Odhiambo, *Siaya: The Historical Anthropology of an African Landscape* (London: James Currey, 1989). But it is striking the degree to which recent anthropological discussions of history have been detached from the intensive analysis of fieldwork-derived materials.

6. Michael Walzer, *Radical Principles* (New York: Basic Books, 1980), pp. 201–223. For Walzer's "class," however, I have substituted the term "peasant" below. As will become clear, I do not believe that class position among peasants in Maale directly translated into political action during the revolution.

7. Tom Piazza, "Jazz Piano's Heavyweight Champ," *New York Times,* 28 July 1996, p. 30H.

8. David William Cohen and E. S. Atieno Odhiambo, *Siaya: The Historical Anthropology of an African Landscape* (London: James Currey, 1989), pp. 113–114.

9. The anthropological study of "modernity" is well developed at this point. It has taken some time, however, for analysts to realize that this concept—at first assumed to characterize a societal type or mode of thought—has to be submitted itself to ethnographic description—centered on local people's own ideas of the modern. Note the progression in the following list: Paul Rabinow, *French Modern: Norms and Forms of the Social Environment* (Cambridge: MIT Press, 1989); Nicholas B. Dirks, "History as a Sign of the Modern," *Public Culture* 2 (1990): 25–32; Allan Pred and Michael Watts, *Reworking Modernity: Capitalisms and Symbolic Discontent* (New Brunswick, NJ: Rutgers University Press, 1992); Jean Comaroff and John Comaroff, eds. *Modernity and its Malcontents: Ritual and Power in Postcolonial Africa* (Chicago: University of Chicago Press, 1993); Marilyn Ivy, *Discourses of the Vanishing: Modernity, Phantasm, Japan* (Chicago: University of Chicago Press, 1995); Akhil Gupta, *Postcolonial Developments: Agriculture in the Making of Modern India* (Durham: Duke University Press, 1997).

See also Bruno Latour, *We Have Never Been Modern,* Catherine Porter, trans. (Cambridge: Harvard University Press, 1993 [1991]).

10. In this context, it seems to me that some varieties of postmodernism resemble modernization theories of the 1950s. They assume what they should in fact take as problematic, namely, how people themselves have defined "modernism," as well as "anti-modernism" and "traditionalism," or "postmodernism" for that matter.

For a finely crafted ethnographic description of a sort of indigenous "postmodernism," see Tsing, *In the Realm of the Diamond Queen*. According to Tsing, the Meratus sensibility is "one that nips at the pretensions of cultural periodizations and refuses their hegemony. Perhaps this kind of mocking, and self-mocking, style has long existed in the cracks and accommodations of colonizing modes of knowledge" (p. 254). An example of this style occurred when a Javanese engineer came through Kalawan:

> He was entertained so conventionally by regional standards that I doubt if he saw anything other than a typical rural settlement. Here, parody became hard to differentiate from the expected rhetoric of acquiescence as Uma Adang and other Kalawan leaders told the engineer how pleased they were that the central government had signed away their lands to 2,000 Javanese settler families. They always benefited, they said, from the wisdom of the government. I believe the engineer got no hint of the anger and fear that had seized the community with the news of the transmigration agency's plans. (p. 19)

All ethnographers face a constant temptation to homogenize what are actually more diverse cultural commitments. Are there really no local "modernists" among the Meratus? Even if they exist, Tsing's description persuades us that they do not exert cultural dominance. In this light, it is interesting to compare the Meratus response with the dramatically direct actions—including murder of colonial officials and missionaries—of the Kwaio described by Roger M. Keesing in *Custom and Confrontation: The Kwaio Struggle for Cultural Autonomy* (Chicago: University of Chicago Press, 1992). That such different outcomes are possible suggests that, as Tsing argues, different social groups have, well before their encounter with modernist ideas and institutions, built up certain cultural strategies for dealing with "outsiders." These different cultural styles condition the creation and understanding of local modernities.

11. See Stuart Gilbert's translation: *The Old Régime and the French Revolution* (New York: Doubleday, 1955 [1856]). See also François Furet's *Interpreting the French Revolution*, Elborg Forster, trans. (Cambridge: Cambridge University Press 1981 [1978]).

12. Marshall Sahlins has called this kind of triangle a "structure of difference" in "Goodbye to *Tristes Tropes*: Ethnography in the Context of Modern World History," *Journal of Modern History* 65 (1993): 1–25.

13. Jean-François Lyotard, "Discussion Lyotard-Rorty," *Critique* (May 1986): 583, quoted in Susan Dunn, *The Deaths of Louis XVI: Regicide and the French Political Imagination* (Princeton: Princeton University Press, 1994), p. 165.

14. Katherine Verdery, *What Was Socialism, and What Comes Next?* (Princeton: Princeton University Press, 1996), p. 24. Verdery's model of production under socialism does not apply to Ethiopia, where, in fact, very little of production was brought under direct party control, but her analysis of surveillance is certainly relevant. The security forces in Mengistu's Ethiopia were advised by East Germans.

15. John K. Fairbank, "Introduction," in *The Missionary Enterprise in China and America,* John K. Fairbank, ed. (Cambridge: Harvard University Press, 1974), pp. 1–2.

INTRODUCTION

1. Hannah Arendt, *On Revolution* (New York: Viking, 1963), p. 21.

2. Karl Griewank, *Der neuzeitliche Revolutionsbegriff* (Frankfurt: Suhrkamp, 1969), p. 145. For a partial English translation, see "Emergence of the Concept of Revolution," in *Revolution: A Reader,* Bruce Mazlish, Arthur D. Kaledin, and David B. Ralston, eds. (New York: Macmillan, 1971), pp. 13–18.

3. *Inventing the French Revolution* (Cambridge: Cambridge University Press, 1990), p. 214.

4. Benedict Anderson, *Imagined Communities: Reflections on the Origin and Spread of Nationalism,* rev. ed. (London: Verso, 1983); Ernest Gellner, *Nations and Nationalism* (Ithaca: Cornell University Press, 1983); Partha Chatterjee, *Nationalist Thought and the Colonial World: A Derivative Discourse?* (London: Zed Books, 1986).

5. As John Plamenatz, "Two Types of Nationalism," in *Nationalism: The Nature and Evolution of an Idea,* Eugene Kamenka, ed. (Canberra: Australian National University Press, 1973), p. 24, pointed out, "Nationalism, as distinct from mere national consciousness, arises when peoples are aware, not only of cultural diversity, but of cultural change and share some idea of progress which moves them to compare their own achievements and capacities with those of others."

6. Karl Marx, "The Eighteenth Brumaire of Louis Bonaparte," in *Surveys from Exile: Political Writings Vol II,* David Fernbach, ed. (New York: Vintage, 1974), pp. 146–147.

7. I take this phrase from William Kelly, "Japanese No-Noh: The Crosstalk of Public Culture in a Rural Festivity," *Public Culture* 2 (1990): 65–81. I do not mean to suggest that "crosstalk" began with modernity, though it was certainly amplified by the modern pace of cultural interchange.

8. Joseph R. Levenson, *Revolution and Cosmopolitanism: the Western Stage and the Chinese Stages* (Berkeley: University of California Press, 1971), p. 26.

9. Anderson, *Imagined Communities,* p. 80.

10. Arjun Appadurai, "Disjuncture and Difference in the Global Cultural Economy," *Public Culture* 2 (1990): 2.

11. Susan Harding, "Imagining the Last Days: The Politics of Apocalyptic Language," in *Accounting for Fundamentalisms,* Martin E. Marty and R. Scott Appleby, eds. (Chicago: University of Chicago Press, 1994), pp. 62–63.

12. Ernest R. Sandeen, *The Roots of Fundamentalism: British and American Millenarianism 1800–1930* (Chicago: University of Chicago Press, 1970), pp. 5–7.

13. Timothy P. Weber, *Living in the Shadow of the Second Coming: American Premillennialism 1875–1925* (New York: Oxford University Press). p. 14.

14. Ibid., p. 40.

15. George M. Marsden, *Fundamentalism and American Culture: The Shaping of Twentieth-Century Evangelicalism: 1870–1925* (Oxford: Oxford University Press, 1980), pp. 62–63.

16. Weber, *Living in the Shadow,* p. 35.

17. Sandeen, *The Roots of Fundamentalism,* pp. xvi–xvii.

18. Ibid., p. 37.

19. Ibid., pp. 50–55.

20. Weber, *Living in the Shadow,* p. 16 (see p. 10 for a typology of millennial beliefs). On "dispensationalism" in particular, see also Harding, "Imagining the Last Days," pp. 57–78.

21. Sandeen, *The Roots of Fundamentalism,* p. 39.

22. Marsden, *Fundamentalism and American Culture,* p. 11.

23. Quoted in ibid., p. 3.

24. Several tendencies operated within so-called modernist Protestantism. According to Marsden, *Fundamentalism and American Culture,* these include: "First, the progress of the Kingdom of God is identified with the progress of civilization, especially in science and morality. Second, morality has become the essence of religion and is indeed virtually equated with it. Third, the supernatural is no longer clearly separated from the natural, but rather manifests itself only in the natural" (p. 24).

25. Not all fundamentalists were premillennialists. As Marsden, *Fundamentalism and American Culture,* emphasized, "Fundamentalism was a loose, diverse, and changing federation of co-belligerents united by their fierce opposition to modernist attempts to bring Christianity into line with modern thought" (p. 4).

26. Harding, "Imagining the Last Days," pp. 63–64.

27. Louis O. Mink, *Historical Understanding,* Brian Fay, Eugene O. Golob, and Richard T. Vann, eds. (Ithaca: Cornell University Press, 1987), p. 185.

28. Renato I. Rosaldo, *Ilongot Headhunting, 1883–1974* (Stanford: Stanford University Press, 1980), pp. 21–22.

29. Hayden White, *Metahistory* (Baltimore: Johns Hopkins University Press, 1973).

30. David Carr, *Time, Narrative, and History* (Bloomington: University of Indiana Press, 1986), pp. 27–28.

31. Ibid, p. 29.

32. Marshall Sahlins, *Islands of History* (Chicago: University of Chicago Press, 1985); Sherry Ortner, *High Religion: A Cultural and Political History of Sherpa Buddhism* (Princeton: Princeton University Press, 1989); J. D. Y. Peel, "For Who Hath Despised the Day of Small Things? Missionary Narratives and Historical Anthropology," *Comparative Studies in Society and History* 37 (1995): 581–607.

33. Maurice Hindus, *Red Bread* (New York: Jonathan Cape & Harrison Smith, 1931), p. 5.

34. As Koselleck emphasized, the European Christian vision of the future against which modernism developed also had this notion of speeding up—speeding up toward the End. Modernist and anti-modernist conceptions share certain features even while they define themselves against one another. See *Futures Past: The Semantics of Historical Time,* Keith Tribe, trans. (Cambridge: MIT Press, 1985 [1979]), pp. 6–7.

35. Here I concur with Norman's critique of the strong version of Carr's

thesis. See Andrew P. Norman, "Telling It Like It Was: Historical Narratives on Their Own Terms," *History and Theory* 30 (1991): 119–135.

CHAPTER 1. THE METANARRATIVE OF MODERNITY IN ETHIOPIA: 1974

1. The last phrase was technically not a part of the list of Haile Selassie's titles but was one that the Emperor did not discourage, particularly among journalists. The Book of Revelation uses the phrase to refer to Christ.

2. For an account of the arrest, possibly embellished, see Raúl Valdés Vivó, *Ethiopia's Revolution* (New York: International Publishers, 1978 [1977]). According to Vivó (p. 15), the Volkswagen was white. Ryszard Kapuściński, *The Emperor: Downfall of an Autocrat*, William R. Brand and Kartarzyna Mroczkowska-Brand, trans. (New York: Harcourt Brace Jovanovich, 1983 [1978]), p. 162, describes it as green. Finally, Marina and David Ottaway, *Ethiopia: Empire in Revolution* (New York: Africana, 1978), p.58, claim the Volkswagen was blue. Whatever the color, the symbolic inversion involved in Haile Selassie's transport to prison in a "peoples' car" has captured writers' imaginations.

3. David A. Korn, *Ethiopia, the United States, and the Soviet Union* (London: Croom Helm, 1986), p. 124.

4. See Donald C. Johanson and Maitland A. Edey, *Lucy: The Beginnings of Humankind* (New York: Simon & Schuster, 1981).

5. Northern Ethiopia had an indigenous Orthodox Christian Church since the fourth century.

6. *Ethiopian Herald,* 4 September 1984, p. 2.

7. For a comparison of the recent histories of Sudan, Ethiopia, and Somali, see John Markakis, *National and Class Conflict in the Horn of Africa* (Cambridge: Cambridge University Press, 1987).

8. Christopher Clapham, *Transformation and Continuity in Revolutionary Ethiopia* (Cambridge: Cambridge University Press, 1988), p. 42.

9. George S. Petee, *The Process of Revolution* (New York: Harper, 1938), pp. 100–101, quoted in Samuel P. Huntington, *Political Order in Changing Societies* (New Haven: Yale University Press, 1968), p. 268.

10. Marina and David Ottaway, *Ethiopia*, pp. 1–2. See also Haggai Erlich, "The Ethiopian Army and the 1974 Revolution," *Armed Forces and Society* 9 (1983): 455–481.

11. Ibid, p. 2.

12. René Lefort, *Ethiopia: An Heretical Revolution?*, A. M. Berrett, trans. (London: Zed Press, 1983 [1981]), p. 54.

13. Andargachew Tiruneh, *The Ethiopian Revolution 1974–1987: A Transformation from an Aristocratic to a Totalitarian Autocracy* (Cambridge: Cambridge University Press, 1993), p. 42. Andargachew (p. 41) speculates that Endalkachew Makonnen, prime minister to be, may have been involved with this military group, particularly with Colonel Alem Zewd, in arresting those associated with the old prime minister.

14. Ibid., p. 39.

15. Marina and David Ottaway, *Ethiopia*, p. 3.

16. Patrick Gilkes, *The Dying Lion: Feudalism and Modernization in Ethiopia* (London: Julian Friedmann, 1975), p. 169.

17. Marina and David Ottaway, *Ethiopia*, pp. 3–4.

18. According to Marina and David Ottaway, *Ethiopia*, p. 47, what prevented the military movement from collapsing after early March was, in fact, civilian anger: "After two pay increases in less than ten days, military salaries were higher than those of many industrial workers and government employees." The resulting anti-military sentiment among the urban populace encouraged the more radical soldiers to link succeeding demands to wider political issues—that affected everyone—rather than narrowly defined economic ones—that benefitted mainly the military. In doing so, the radicals eventually "pushed the entire military to the forefront of the struggle for political change" (p. 48).

19. Lefort, *Ethiopia*, p. 63. According to Marina and David Ottaway, *Ethiopia*, p. 4, the demonstration by Moslems took place on 20 April: "It was probably the largest demonstration ever held in Addis; some estimates put the number of participants as high as 100,000."

20. Lefort, *Ethiopia*, p. 61.

21. John Reed, *Ten Days That Shook the World* (New York: Bantam, 1987 [1919]), p. 11.

22. Andargachew, *The Ethiopian Revolution*, p. 45.

23. Ibid., p. 46.

24. Haggai Erlich, "The Ethiopian Army and the 1974 Revolution," *Armed Forces and Society* 9 (1983): 455–481.

25. Marina and David Ottaway, *Ethiopia*, p. 50. See also Lefort, *Ethiopia*, pp. 58–64. Labels such as "reformist" and "radical" are always potentially misleading; they have to be understood in relation to the particular issues that divided Ethiopians at the time. I take these labels from Pliny the Middle-Aged, "The PMAC: Origins and Structure. Part I" *Ethiopianist Notes* 3(1978): 1–18, and "Part II" *Northeast African Studies* 1 (1979): 1–20.

26. Andargachew, *The Ethiopian Revolution*, p. 44. See also Haggai Erlich's important article, "The Ethiopian Army and the 1974 Revolution." *Armed Forces and Society* 9 (1983): 455–481.

27. Clapham, *Transformation and Continuity*, pp. 39–40. The presence in everyone's mind of the lesson of the 1960 coup—that everyone would "lose" if the military split—may provide part of the explanation for Ethiopia's uniqueness.

28. Andargachew, *The Ethiopian Revolution*, pp. 65–66.

29. Ibid., p. 54.

30. Ibid.

31. Reed, *Ten Days*, p. 86.

32. "How opposition would have polarized within the ruling classes and very probably elsewhere if a group of young officers with no past or prestige—who were, moreover, non-Amhara—had officially come out and openly proclaimed their aims and objectives may be imagined. On the contrary, the hard wing of the Derg was not bound by any public commitment which would have condemned it to eat its words later. It could pursue its gradual advance, putting forward objectives and suggesting candidates, as its current tactical needs dictated." Lefort, *Ethiopia*, p. 79.

33. Marina and David Ottaway, *Ethiopia*, p. 54. For an interpretation that puts more stress on a "grand design" in events, see Lefort, *Ethiopia*, pp. 79–81.

34. Lefort, *Ethiopia*, p. 68. See Asmarom Legesse, "Post-Feudal Society, Capitalism, and Revolution: The Case of Ethiopia," *Symposium Leo Frobenius II* (Bonn: Deutsche UNESCO Kommission, 1980), pp. 220–221, for a discussion of the rhetoric—entirely "feudal" rather than Marxist—that was used during September 1974 to justify the removal of the Emperor.

35. Marina and David Ottaway, *Ethiopia*, p. 56.

36. Ibid, p. 58.

37. Yohannis Abate, "The Legacy of Imperial Rule: Military Intervention and the Struggle for Leadership in Ethiopia 1974–1978," *Middle Eastern Studies* 19 (1983): 28–42.

38. Ibid., p. 59.

39. Lefort, *Ethiopia*, pp. 73–74. The other story was that the full body of the Derg condemned Aman and likewise voted on the guilt of the 150 detainees. According to Marina and David Ottaway, *Ethiopia*, p. 61, the Derg probably approved the death of Aman but may not have supported the idea of executing the political prisoners. In any case, the preeminent role of Mengistu and Atnafu seems clear.

40. Marina and David Ottaway, *Ethiopia*, p. 61.

41. Ibid, p. 81.

42. Andargachew, *The Ethiopian Revolution*, pp. 55–56.

43. Marina and David Ottaway, *Ethiopia*, p. 10.

44. Edward Hallett Carr, *The Russian Revolution: From Lenin to Stalin* (New York: Free Press, 1979), p. 163.

45. Clapham, *Transformation and Continuity*, p. 34.

46. The university had been founded in 1950 as University College and initially staffed by Canadian Jesuits.

47. There was a U.S. military communications base in Asmara; the Ethiopian military had been trained and equipped by Americans; and from 1950 to 1976, more than half of U.S. military assistance to the whole African continent ($275 million) went to Ethiopia alone. See Lefort, *Ethiopia*, p. 182.

48. Maurice Meisner, *Mao's China: A History of the People's Republic* (New York: Free Press, 1977), p. 18.

49. See Olga Kapeliuk, "Marxist-Leninist Terminology in Amharic and in Tigrinya," *Northeast African Studies* 1 (1979): 23.

50. Hinton, *Fanshen*, p. vii.

51. Dassalegn Rahmato, "The Political Economy of Development in Ethiopia," in *Afro-Marxist Regimes*, Edmond J. Keller and Donald Rothchild, eds. (Boulder, CO: Lynne Rienner, 1987), p. 157.

52. Marina and David Ottaway, *Ethiopia*, p. 63.

53. Andargachew, *The Ethiopian Revolution*, p. 96.

54. "Proclamation No. 31 of 1975," *Basic Documents of the Ethiopian Revolution* (Addis Ababa: Provisional Office for Mass Organizational Affairs, 1977), p. 18.

55. Elsewhere, I have argued against the sociological cogency of the feudal comparison for Ethiopian society. See my "Old Abyssinia and the New Ethio-

pian Empire: Themes in Social History," in *The Southern Marches of Imperial Ethiopia*, Donald Donham and Wendy James, eds. (Cambridge: Cambridge University Press, 1986).

Unfortunately, the cultural history of the notion of Ethiopia as a copy of a (now superseded) European past has not been written. My intuition is that it begins with the long and complicated European impression of the country as exceptional in relation to the rest of Africa. First, there was the myth of Prester John—the black Christian king that the Portuguese would eventually find in Ethiopia. Then, there was the survival of Ethiopian independence in the twentieth century during an age when the rest of Africa was carved up by European powers. In this context, Ethiopia was never so unambiguously and successfully "othered" as the rest of Africa. Europeans identified with Ethiopians in some ways. If "backward," Ethiopians nonetheless seemed to be on the same historical track as Europe. Whether educated Ethiopians' own notion of their country's "feudalism" may be traced to these European narratives is unclear.

56. Allan Hoben, "Social Soundness of Agrarian Reform in Ethiopia," Report to the USAID Mission in Ethiopia, 1976.

57. Below, I shall have more to say about the unusual parallels between the structures of the new peasant cooperatives designed by officials in the Ministry of Land Reform and the organization of extant Protestant mission churches in southern Ethiopia.

58. Marina and David Ottaway, *Ethiopia*, p. 67.

59. Ibid., p. 81.

60. In Amharic, the campaign was entitled *Idget Behibret Yeuḳetina Yesera Zemecha*.

61. *Development through Co-operation Campaign's Summary Report 1967/1968 E.C.* (Addis Ababa: Provisional Military Government of Ethiopia, 1976), pp. 1–2.

62. Marina and David Ottaway, *Ethiopia*, pp. 70–71.

63. Lefort, *Ethiopia*, p. 99. See also Dawit Wolde Giorgis, *Red Tears: War, Famine and Revolution in Ethiopia* (Trenton, NJ: Red Sea Press, 1989), p. 23, for a somewhat confused description of the March days: "Throughout the entire two-hour parade, Mengistu, filled with the contagious exuberance of the students, responded to their cheers by shouting back to them and saluting with his fist in the air, his face beaming down at them as they passed. I remember being so gripped by the electricity of that moment that I shouted myself hoarse along with the spectators and the students: 'Viva Mengistu! Viva Mengistu!' I was so overcome with emotion that I almost cried."

64. Estimates vary. According to Marina and David Ottaway, *Ethiopia*, p. 69, "Beginning in early 1975, the PMAC dispatched more than 50,000 high school and university students to 437 locations in the countryside." Lefort, *Ethiopia*, p. 100, reports that an official accounting after the campaign showed that 48,000 students had been involved at 50 centers and 397 stations.

65. Lefort, *Ethiopia*, p. 108.

66. Marina and David Ottaway, *Ethiopia*, p. 64.

67. Clapham, *Transformation and Continuity*, p. 50.

68. Hoben, "Social Soundness," p. 83.

69. To the extent that northern peasants were hostile to the revolution, not just neutral, ethnicity was probably a key factor. Northern peasants, especially Amhara, identified with the empire; they occupied a dominant place within it vis-à-vis recently conquered peoples in the south like the Oromo. As I shall explain below, a significant portion of the Derg, including Mengistu Haile Mariam himself, were not proper northerners. Even though the Derg never had anything like a majority of Oromo, it was identified as such—and as Muslim—by many Orthodox Christian northerners.

70. See Marina and David Ottaway, *Ethiopia,* chapter 6 for an extended discussion of the reaction of the rural elite to land reform.

71. Clapham, *Transformation and Continuity,* p. 58.

72. Lefort, *Ethiopia,* p. 108.

73. Ibid., p. 113–114.

74. Marina and David Ottaway, *Ethiopia,* p. 12.

75. Hoben, "Social Soundness," pp. 92–93.

76. Marina and David Ottaway, *Ethiopia,* p. 74

77. Ibid., p. 75.

78. Lefort, *Ethiopia,* p. 117.

79. Theda Skocpol, *States and Social Revolutions: A Comparative Analysis of France, Russia, and China* (Cambridge: Cambridge University Press, 1979), pp. 4–5.

80. Clapham, *Transformation and Continuity,* p. 1.

CHAPTER 2. REVOLUTION WITHIN A REVOLUTION

1. Samuel P. Huntington, *Political Order in Changing Societies* (New Haven: Yale University Press, 1968), p. 291.

2. James C. Scott, "Revolution in the Revolution: Peasants and Commissars," *Theory and Society* 7 (1979): 109–110.

3. Eric R. Wolf, *Peasant Wars of the Twentieth Century* (New York: Harper & Row, 1969), p. xv.

4. This is a phrase that James C. Scott appropriated from Régis Debray and that I have appropriated from Scott.

5. In the Maale language, the root of the verb to go up, *od-,* is different from to go along level ground, *lo-,* which is different again from to go down, *wutt-.* No matter relative elevation, however, when Maale went to Bala they described themselves as going up.

6. For further description of the ideology and political economy of nineteenth-century Maale kingship, see Donald L. Donham, *History, Power, Ideology: Central Issues in Marxism and Anthropology* (Cambridge: Cambridge University Press, 1990), pp. 89–129.

7. Later, traditionalists from the south claimed that they had been duped into joining the accusation by Protestants. Given the wiliness of most political actors in Maale and the reluctance of most to sign their name to any written document, this seems unlikely.

8. The literal translation of "exploit" in Chinese was "peel and pare"—

William Hinton, *Fanshen: A Documentary of Revolution in a Chinese Village* (New York: Random House, 1966), p. 63.

9. Interview with Dura Artamu, 25 April 1975.

10. Translation of Amharic document dated 21 November 1974, addressed to the Geleb and Hamer Bako Awraja Governor and Records Office, Jinka.

11. Interview with Taddesse [pseud.], field notes, 14 April 1983.

12. Translation of an Amharic document dated 30 December 1974, addressed to the Geleb and Hamar Bako Awraja Governor and Records Office, Jinka, signed by Urge Jimari and Kama Dunkala on behalf of the accusers.

13. Translation of an Amharic document dated 20 January 1975, addressed to the Geleb and Hamar Bako Awraja Governor and Records Office, Jinka, signed "From Koibe and Irbo."

14. Translation of a speech by the new awraja governor in Bushkoro, Maale, 21 April 1975.

15. Ibid.

16. Hinton, *Fanshen*, p. 5.

17. Wolf, *Peasant Wars of the Twentieth Century*.

18. I am not arguing that economic considerations had no effect on Maale rebellion. As will become clear, it was precisely the economic underbelly of cultural categories (evangelical Christians as an exploited but up-and-coming group; Orthodox Christians as landowners; and Maale traditionalists as political-economic losers) that lent cultural categories much of their significance in the revolution. It was never naked economic categories in themselves that mattered, however, but the local cultural construction of those categories.

19. It was not, in fact, the goal of the students who came to Maale to fan ethnic resentments. (It was difficult to tell, but most appeared to identify as Amhara themselves.) Just the opposite, they explicitly warned the peasants against "misunderstanding" their situation in this way. Nonetheless, class and ethnicity were so intertwined in Maale by 1975, that when the students tried to politicize the peasants against the old system of landlordism, they inevitably let loose feelings of ethnic resentment.

20. The above conversation was recorded in my field notes of 1 August 1975, and recounted to me by Taddesse.

21. Field notes, 23 July 1975.

22. After the student campaigners had been imprisoned in Jinka, I received an order from the awraja governor to return the kati's treasury to the people who traditionally watched over it. Around September, I did so.

23. Unlike the execution of the French king, however, the Maale burial was reversible. After being buried by the zemecha students, the king's bones were exhumed and replaced above ground in Dufa, the sacred grove, by the end of 1975. As I shall explain at the end of this book, the king's bones were finally buried yet again in the 1990s after the revolutionary regime had fallen, this time in the ritually proper way on the highest mountain of Maale, as Dulbo was installed as kati.

24. Susan Dunn, *The Deaths of Louis XVI: Regicide and the French Political Imagination* (Princeton: Princeton University Press, 1994), pp. 3–4.

25. Field notes, 11 August 1975.

CHAPTER 3. REVOLUTION AS
A RETURN TO TRADITION IN MAALE

1. Even among evangelical Christian converts—the most ideologically estranged from Maale beliefs—this notion was not entirely absent. One elder in 1975, admittedly a man who had recently quit the church, allowed as how the rains would not come to Maale as long as there was no kati.

2. At this point, I am presenting the ideology of the system; there were also material processes that continuously favored the higher status members of the lineages. See Donald L. Donham, *History, Power, Ideology: Central Issues in Marxism and Anthropology* (Cambridge: Cambridge University Press, 1990), pp. 94–103.

3. See Donald L. Donham, *Work and Power in Maale, Ethiopia*, 2nd ed. (New York: Columbia University Press, 1994), pp. 22–23 for the origin myth of Maale.

4. After the revolution, some Maale insisted that *no* traditional ritual would be effective without a kati. Nonetheless, many traditionalists carried on with family rituals.

5. Like most garrisons in the south, Bako was strategically perched upon the top of a mountain. Sometime after Haile Selassie established air service to the south in late 1950s, government offices in Bako were moved down the hill to a new town on flatter land, Jinka.

6. In many ways, the chief of Makana was a symbolic inversion of the kati. The only one of the Maale chiefs who belonged to the *raggi* moiety, the Makana chief represented the autochthonous people resident in Maaleland before the arrival of the first kati.

7. Field notes, 30 November 1975.

8. See my "Old Abyssinia and the New Ethiopian Empire: Themes in Social History," in *The Southern Marches of Imperial Ethiopia*, Donald Donham and Wendy James, eds. (Cambridge: Cambridge University Press, 1986), pp. 1–48.

9. The governor at Bako, *dejazmach* Biru Haile Mariam, arranged for a *tabot* or ark to be brought to Maale from the monastery at Debre Libanos. The priest who brought the ark in about 1903 was *aleka* Wolde Mikail, a man from Fice. The journey took more than month, and tending the ark—never letting it touch the ground—was arduous. The establishment of a church was necessary for the settlement of northerners in Maale; priests circumcised and carried out funeral rituals.

10. Field notes, 5 July 1975

11. Interview with Arregude Sulunge; field notes, 24 February 1975.

12. Interview with Digga Eroka; field notes, 26 April 1975.

13. These are my words, a summary of Ottolo Irbano's; field notes, 14 April 1975.

14. The *ţsozo* was the quiver that contained the body parts of all of the past kati.

15. The *doddo* and *kabo basso* were parts of the entrance of the lion house, the Maale ritual center, and Yeberi and Galai were the sacred mountains on which all past kati had been buried.

16. Interview with Dore Sulunge, 3 March 1975.

17. Interview with Arregude Sulunge, 27 February 1975.

18. This is a continuation of the previous quote from Sulunge's son.

19. This was another example of how the ritual aspects of the kingship were falling away by the 1930s. Traditionally, the kati and his close family did not attend funerals; he, after all, was the embodiment of blessing and well-being and was to be separated from all ill fortune. Irbano advised Tonna not to go to the funeral, but Tonna persisted.

20. To kill an enemy is a great honor in Maale. It makes a man a *zia,* a "bull."

21. According to one of Tonna's sons, Sinke, "No one could stand before my father, not even Amhara. Because of this, the Amhara told the people to say that Tonna was the murderer." Afterward, the elders were to confess their false accusation to Ottolo when the latter was about to be made kati. Maale believe that transgressions, *gome,* affect the lives of those who perpetrate them until confessions are made. In addition, after Ottolo was made kati, the chief of Bala, on behalf of his brothers, sent the chief of Makana to Ottolo to beg forgiveness. This is perhaps the strongest evidence for who actually murdered Abegaz.

22. Irbano was, in effect, giving his last will and testament: Tonna should succeed.

23. This was reported to me by Baki, one of Tonna's servants who was arrested with him.

24. In 1975, one story had it that Tonna had gone to America and was living there. One of Tonna's sons asked me if I were bringing news of him.

25. Interview with Baki Lungare, 22 March 1975.

26. They had placed all Amhara in the area under detention (the northern soldiers stationed in Maale had fought against the invasion), and they abolished the gabbar system. Like the Amhara before them, however, the Italians had to rule through local chiefs. Indeed, one of their strategies in the south was to encourage local institutions and local feelings against the previous system of Orthodox Christian **domination.**

27. After contact with the Orthodox Christian Amhara, the Maale described the intestine oracle as their "holy book"—they read it for indications of how to conduct their lives.

28. Interview with the chief of Bala; field notes, 17 August 1974.

29. Interview with Baki Lungare, 22 March 1975.

30. In fact, it was common for first sons of later wives to inherit, after which the kinship terminology was rearranged. In 1975, the holders of the two most important chiefships in Bala and Makana both had brothers who were chronologically older, as did the Gojo.

31. That is, "You're courting danger." The thatch of Maale houses is highly inflammable, and the danger of housing catching fire is ever present.

32. This was an indirect way of saying that the Bala chief's brothers' deeds had in effect killed Tonna.

33. As was the custom, Irbano's body lay in a house in the sacred grove of Dufa until a successor was installed.

34. Interview with Ottolo Irbano, 26 September 1974.

35. This way of reconciling the competing demands on southern kings—of

separating the ritual from the political—occurred in several other southern ethnic groups. See Jacques Bureau, "Etude diachronique de deux titres gamo,"
Cahiers d'études africaines 18 (1978): 279–291.

36. In a context in which cadastral surveys were nonexistent, where the
courts were far removed from the area concerned, and where it was commonly
accepted that officials could be influenced by gifts, land ownership was a difficult issue for the central administration to supervise.

37. Interview with Danyi Dubala, Jinka; field notes, 22 November 1975. I
also interviewed Manakule and he confirmed what Danyi had said: "Who was
the one who conducted the court case? It is Danyi wasn't it, the person who
worked underneath?" After Tolba became kati, he reregistered land and recognized Danyi's claims.

38. Interview with the chief of Bala; field notes, 17 August 1974.

39. Interview with Ottolo Irbano, 26 September 1974.

40. Field notes, 19 November 1975.

41. Baha also had a particular tie with the chief of Bola, which gave him
special influence over the latter. Baha was a classificatory mother's brother to
the chief (and hence was thought to have the power to curse his sister's son).
Baha appears to have been, then, a central actor in Ottolo's replacement.

42. By the mid-1950s, Artamu had apparently struck a deal with Danyi, the
northerner who claimed much of southern Bunka. Because Danyi's claim to the
land was weak, Artamu threatened to go to court against him if he did not share
the proceeds. After apparently coming to an amicable agreement, Danyi and
Artamu divided the people between them, the northerner using his ties to the
court, the chief using his traditional position to extract as much as they could
from Maale commoners. The power to take taxes from "tenants" functioned as
a strong form of social control; those who openly opposed the chief and northerner were taxed more, sometimes up to 150 birr a year.

43. Interview with Dura Artamu, Silsa Dombe, and Arregude Sulunge, 15
July 1975.

44. Interview with Arregude Sulunge, 27 June 1975.

45. Ibid.

46. As evident in earlier quotes, Maale elders never broke their necklaces,
except on ritual occasions. During first-fruits rites, they broke and restrung
their necklaces with the assistance of their *geta*, or ritual helper. Not just the
king, but every elder who sacrificed to the ancestors wore a necklace—with
beads that had been passed down from previous generations.

CHAPTER 4. THE DIALECTIC OF MODERNITY
IN A NORTH AMERICAN CHRISTIAN MISSION

1. Deborah J. Baldwin, *Protestants and the Mexican Revolution: Missionaries, Ministers, and Social Change* (Urbana: University of Illinois Press, 1990), p. 4.

2. The following description of Bingham is based on Brian A. McKenzie,
"Fundamentalism, Christian Unity, and Pre-millennialism in the Thought of
Rowland Victor Bingham (1872–1942): A Study of Anti-Modernism in
Canada," Ph.D. Dissertation, Toronto School of Theology, 1985.

3. Bingham quoted in McKenzie, "Fundamentalism, Christian Unity," p. 43.

4. Rowland V. Bingham, *Seven Sevens of Years and a Jubilee: The Story of the Sudan Interior Mission* (Toronto: Evangelical, 1943) p. 11.

5. Ibid., p. 9.

6. Brian Leslie Fargher, "The Origins of the New Churches Movement in Southern Ethiopia, 1927–1944," Ph.D. Thesis, University of Aberdeen, 1988, pp. 236–237. A shortened version of this thesis was later published as *The Origins of the New Churches Movement in Southern Ethiopia, 1927–1944* (Leiden: E. J. Brill, 1996).

7. Malcolm Forsberg, *Land beyond the Nile* (New York: Harper, 1958), p. 29.

8. Joel A. Carpenter, "Fundamentalist Institutions and the Rise of Evangelical Protestantism, 1929–1942," *Church History* 49 (1980): 62–75.

9. McKenzie, "Fundamentalism, Christian Unity," p. 278.

10. Ibid., p. 317. Bingham himself came to question dispensationalism, but he adopted an inclusive position on eschatology.

11. Ibid., p. 51.

12. Bingham, *Seven Sevens,* p. 39.

13. Ibid., p 93.

14. Ibid., pp. 119–123.

15. Esmé Ritchie Rice, ed., *Eclipse in Ethiopia and Its Corona Glory* (London: Marshall, Morgan & Scott, n.d.), p. xii.

16. Unlike most of the rest of Africa at the time, Ethiopia was an independent empire. No colonial government provided a umbrella for foreign mission activities; far from it, highland Ethiopians, many of them, were already Christians. A state church, the Ethiopian Orthodox Church, connected to the Coptic Church of Egypt, had existed for a millennia and a half in northern Ethiopia, and after repeated and usually negative encounters with European missionaries of various sorts, most foreign religions were associated with threats upon the nation. For the nineteenth century, see Donald Crummey, *Priests and Politicians: Protestant and Catholic Missions in Orthodox Ethiopia, 1830–1868* (Oxford: Clarendon Press, 1972).

17. Charles Rey, "'Abyssinia Today," *Royal African Society Journal* 21 (1921–22): 279–290, quoted in Fargher, "Origins," p. 413.

18. On *ras* Teferi's relationship to the "young Ethiopians," Ethiopia's first generation of intellectuals, see Bahru Zewde, *A History of Modern Ethiopia 1855–1974* (London: James Currey, 1991), pp. 103–111, 128–137. In his autobiography, composed in exile in England in 1937 (and published in Amharic in Ethiopia in 1973), Haile Selassie mused, "We have set out to the best of Our ability to improve, gradually, internal administration by introducing into the country Western modes of civilization through which Our people may attain a higher level." Haile Sellassie I, *My Life and Ethiopia's Progress, 1892–1937,* Edward Ullendorff, trans (Oxford: Oxford University Press, 1976), p. 5.

19. Asfa Yilma, *Haile Selassie: Emperor of Ethiopia with a Brief Account of the History of Ethiopia, Including the Origins of the Present Struggle, and a Description of the Country and Its Peoples* (London: Sampson Low, Marston, n.d.), pp. 138–140.

20. Harold G. Marcus, *Haile Sellassie I: The Formative Years, 1892–1936* (Berkeley: University of California Press, 1987), pp. 57–58.

21. Besides SIM, Teferi supported other missions as well. By 1935, there were ten different Protestant missions operating in the country, but SIM was more than three times as large as any other. See Ingeborg Lass-Westphal, "Protestant Missions during and after the Italo-Ethiopian War, 1935–1937," *Journal of Ethiopian Studies* 10 (1972): 89–101.

22. Thomas Lambie, *Doctor without a Country* (New York: Revell, 1939), p. 138.

23. Ibid., p. 162.

24. Lambie, "Conquest by Healing in Ethiopia," Lambie Miscellaneous Writings, EA-1, SIM International Archives, Charlotte, North Carolina.

25. Bulki Medical Reports, 1931, EA-2, SIM International Archives.

26. Marcella Ohman to Lambie, 12 June 1932, Bulki Correspondence, 1931–1936, EA-2, SIM International Archives. In a letter dated 19 November 1932, she acknowledges the receipt of the stethoscope: "When the Dejasmatch found out we had a stethoscope he was delighted."

27. This is Robert W. Strayer's phrase in *The Making of Mission Communities in East Africa: Anglicans and Africans in Colonial Kenya, 1875–1935* (London: Heineman, 1978), p. 157, quoted in Fargher, "Origins," p. 117.

28. Lambie, *Doctor without a Country,* p. 158.

29. The Ford was paid for by "former associates in the Mercy Hospital, Pittsburgh"—Lambie, *Doctor without a Country,* p. 159. By 1927, there were approximately three hundred automobiles circulating in Addis Ababa (Marcus, *Haile Sellassie I: The Formative Years,* p. 80.)

30. T. A. Lambie, Business with Gamo Governor over Purchase of a Car for Governor, 1933–34, EA-1, SIM International Archives.

31. Forsberg to Cain, 8 August 1935, Bulki Correspondence, EA-1, SIM International Archives. Another of Haile Selassie's sons-in-law, this time the governor of Gofa, another site of the SIM, had Lambie order "a camera, complete with developing and printing outfit." W. A. Ohman to Lambie, 28 May 1933, Bulki Correspondence, 1931–36, EA-2, SIM International Archives.

32. Note the seeming reserve, for an evangelical, in Bingham's comments on Haile Selassie in 1943: "We came to know him as a God-fearing man, a lover of the Bible and one who was primarily interested in the uplift and the well-being of his people" (*Seven Sevens,* p. 103).

33. Thomas A. Lambie, *A Doctor Carries On* (New York: Revell, 1942), p. 32.

34. Fargher, "Origins," p. 996: "The southern people did not initially know that it [evangelical Christianity] was essentially the same as the religion of the colonialists [i.e. northern Ethiopians]. They thought of it as another, totally different, religion."

35. On the link between modernity and conversion to Christianity, see Peter van der Veer, ed., *Conversion to Modernity: The Globalization of Christianity* (New York: Routledge, 1996).

36. W. Harold Fuller, *Run While the Sun Is Hot* (New York: Sudan Interior Mission, n.d.), pp. 160–161.

37. See Donald N. Levine, *Wax and Gold: Tradition and Innovation in Ethiopian Culture* (Chicago: University of Chicago Press, 1965).

38. Lambie, *Doctor without a Country*, p. 170.

39. Christian Missionaries Appear before Church Council, EA-1, SIM International Archives.

40. SIM Manual, 1991 edition, section 6–3.

41. The statement of "Principles and Practice" drawn up by Lambie's Abyssinia Frontiers Mission before the latter was incorporated into the Sudan Interior Mission, said that the Field Executive Committee would "formulate a policy for the development of the Native Church on sound Scriptural lines" (quoted in Fargher, "Origins," p. 360).

42. Fargher, "Origins," p. 257. The Swedish Evangelical Mission preceded the SIM into Ethiopia. Their missionary Cederquist refrained from organizing congregations, not so much because he wished to work through the Orthodox Church (he was apparently disillusioned with that prospect by the end of the 1910s), but rather because he feared the consequences. See Olav Sæverås, *On Church-Mission Relations in Ethiopia 1944–1969*, Studia Missionalia Upsaliensai 27 (Oslo: Lunde, 1974), p. 22. Cederquist's successor, Olle Eriksson, performed the first Swedish baptisms in Addis Ababa in 1921. These efforts were eventually to produce the other major evangelical church in southern Ethiopia, the Lutheran-affiliated Mekane Yesus Church.

43. Lambie, *Doctor without a Country*, p. 171.

44. Lambie was apparently better than his lieutenant Rhoad in adapting to the world of Ethiopian politics: "Mr. Rhoad had been several times, as he thought, on the point of signing an agreement, but always the Abyssinians drew back. The reason was that they did not know him very well. It was arranged in a few weeks after our arrival."(ibid., p. 209).

45. When Lambie wanted land in Addis Ababa for a headquarters for the mission, he was required to build a leprosarium; see ibid., p. 209. According to Fargher, "Origins," the medical contribution of the mission was considerable by the late 1930s: "The SIM was able to place a doctor for a brief time at Hosanna and for a longer time it had doctors at Soddo and in Addis Ababa. Clinics were opened in Bulqi, Chencha, Tuttiti, Homacho, Yerga Alam, Lambuda, Durami and Jimma" (p. 480).

46. Fargher, "Origins," pp. 995–996.

47. This was also true of Yoruba converts in Nigeria, according to David Laitin: "Both Peel and I, in our different studies, elicited only the shallowest answers to the 'why' question of conversion: 'Everyone was joining, so I joined,' or 'I wanted to move with them.' The most interesting answer we both received, and this from a number of informants from Islam and Christianity, was 'Because of civilization'. . . . This concept is associated with progress, health, and development." See David Laitin, *Hegemony and Culture: Politics and Religious Change among the Yoruba* (Chicago: University of Chicago Press, 1986), p. 36.

48. Fargher, "Origins," p. 486.

49. In what follows I am dependent upon SIM missionary records, which, no doubt, tend to exaggerate the changes involved in the conversion process.

50. Fargher, "Origins," p. 993.

51. No author, 10 January 1936, Bulki Miscellaneous, EA-2, SIM International Archives. The emphasis on the rejection of alcohol meant in particular fundamental changes in the way that southern Ethiopians arranged peasant production. In most southern societies, cooperative work parties rewarded with beer drinking were a mainstay of the local economy (see Donald L. Donham, *Work and Power in Maale, Ethiopia,* 2nd ed. [New York: Columbia University Press, 1994]). When Christian converts rejected beer, they had to rearrange social ties in order to cooperate only with other Christians. For an example of this process in Welaita during the 1930s, see Raymond J. Davis, *Fire on the Mountains* (Charlotte, NC: SIM, 1980), pp. 65–66. By 1945, however, so many of the Welaita had converted that the tables had been turned: Nonbelievers were forced to work with Christian neighbors on the latter's terms: "In many sections the believers so outnumber the unbelievers that the latter are forced to work their fields along with the believers. What a contrast from the early days when no Walamo would help work another man's field unless plenty of beer was served" (Walter and Marcella Ohman Prayer Letter, 15 December 1945, EE-2, SIM International Archives).

52. Fargher, "Origins," p. 714.

53. Norm to Marion, undated, Soddu Correspondence, EA-3, SIM International Archives.

54. E. Ralph Hooper writing in a pamphlet, *Ethiopia* (New York: Sudan Interior Mission, 1933), p. 23, quoted in Fargher, "Origins," p. 366.

55. Fargher, "Origins," p. 516.

56. L. A. Davison, Notes on the Situation in Walamo, May 1945, EE-2, SIM International Archives. According to W. Harold Fuller, the numbers are slightly different: "When Walter Ohman left Soddo there were only 48 Wallamo baptized believers and only one church. When he returned after World War II, the believers had multiplied to 10,000 in 100 churches" (*Run While the Sun Is Hot,* p. 158). In a 15 December 1945 prayer letter, Walter and Marcella Ohman themselves reported that there were "around two hundred churches and somewhere between 25,000 and 27,000 believers"(Walter and Marcella Ohman, Prayer Letters 1941–1950, EE-2, SIM International Archives).

57. Lambie, *A Doctor Carries On,* pp. 171–172.

58. Fargher, "Origins," p. 643.

59. Ibid., p. 261.

60. *Moody Monthly,* August 1933, p. 541, quoted in Fargher, "Origins," pp. 266–267.

61. Fargher, "Origins," p. 274.

62. Ibid., p. 738.

63. Ibid., p. 816.

64. Ibid., p. 390.

65. Walter and Marcella Ohman Prayer Letter, 15 December 1945, EE-2, SIM International Archives.

66. Explosions of religious fervor in the absence of foreign missionaries were not unusual in African history. See Richard Gray, "Christianity," in *The Cambridge History of Africa,* A. D. Roberts, ed., vol. 7 (Cambridge: Cambridge University Press, 1986), p. 140.

67. This was true at least among the Welaita in the 1930s and among the Maale in the 1960s and 1970s. Whether it continues to be an accurate description is perhaps another question. According to Dessalegn Rahmato, by the 1980s Kale Heywet believers in Welaita openly practiced polygyny. See his *The Dynamics of Rural Poverty: Case Studies from a District in Southern Ethiopia* (Dakar, Senegal: CODESRIA Monograph 2/92, 1992), p. 66.

CHAPTER 5. THE CULTURAL CONSTRUCTION OF CONVERSION IN MAALE

1. Johnny Bakke, *Christian Ministry: Patterns and Functions within the Ethiopian Evangelical Church Mekane Yesus* (Oslo: Solum Forlag A.S.; and Atlantic Highlands, NJ: Humanities Press), p. 121.

2. Mikre-Sellassie Gabre Ammanuel, "Church and Missions in Ethiopia in Relation to the Italian War and Occupation and the Second World War," Ph.D. Thesis, University of Aberdeen, 1976, p. 339.

3. For a full text of the decree, see J. Spencer Trimingham, *The Christian Church and Missions in Ethiopia* (London: World Dominion Press, 1950), pp. 68–71.

4. Field Letter No. 4, by Glen H. Cain, 5 August 1949, EE-2, Directives to Missionaries, 1944–50, SIM International Archives, Charlotte, North Carolina.

5. John B. Cumbers, "The Christian Church and the Kings of Ethiopia," Thesis, American Bible College, 1980, p. 91. By the 1970s, the result of the government policy of concentrating evangelical missions in the south was manifest. Provinces of the near south such as Wellegga and Sidamo, where evangelicals had long worked, enjoyed respectively the second and third highest literacy rates in the whole country. See Bakke, *Christian Ministry*, p. 223, n.2.

6. Bako was approved as a prospective site in December 1948; Ethiopia Area Council Notes, ME-1, 1948–1954, SIM International Archives.

7. Research by Peter Cotterell, SR-36, SIM International Archives.

8. Letter from Mr. John Groeneweg to Mr. Glen Cain, 2 January 1954, SR-36, SR-37, Bako Correspondence, SIM International Archives. The amount of $4,600 is penciled on Mr. Groeneweg's airletter.

9. Monthly Praise and Prayer Bulletins, March 26, 1954, EG-2, SIM International Archives.

10. It was against mission policy to post single missionaries by themselves. Single women occasionally added to the expatriate complement at Bako, but the station was always presided over by a couple. At one point, two couples may have overlapped at Bako, but that appears to have been the maximum.

11. Donald and Christine Gray, "These Lost Shankilla Sheep," *Sudan Witness* (Australia) (August 1957): 3.

12. One measure of the social distance between the expatriate missionaries and the people they hoped to convert is the following: By the late 1950s, the missionaries still referred to the Aari people (the ethnic groups immediately surrounding the mission station and neighbors to the Maale) as "Shankilla," a derogatory term that meant "black" and "slave" (see ibid.). "Shankilla" was

probably also the name that northern settlers in the area and local government officials used to refer to the Aari.

13. Walter and Marcella Ohman, Prayer letter, 30 June 1952, EG-1, SIM International Archives.

14. Interview with Minote, Jinka, 25 June 1997.

15. Many Maale, in contrast to Aari, could understand the Welaita language, and Welaita evangelists were able to learn Maale quickly.

16. Brian Fargher, "Aari People of Central Gamo Gofa, Ethiopia," in *Unreached Peoples: Clarifying the Task*, Harley Schreck and David Barrett, eds. (Birmingham, AL: MARC; and Monrovia, CA: New Hope, 1987), p. 210.

17. Mr. and Mrs. A. J. Fellows, "Jubilant Day," *Sudan Witness* (Australia) (September–October 1962): 1–2.

18. *Sudan Witness* (Australia) (November–December 1962): 3.

19. The expatriate missionaries at Bako never learned the local languages and in fact were required to use Amharic, the national language. This condition was included in the post-occupation mission policy and was meant to contribute to national unity. The notion of "believing in Christ" was, then, always (even in the Maale language) expressed with the Amharic verb, the stem of which is *aman-*. In Maale, Christians were known as *amana*, "believers." It would have been difficult to find a simple Maale word that adequately conveyed the Christian idea of "believing"—the notion of internal faith in a set of propositions—since this idea was, as Sime's narrative makes clear, quite alien to Maale culture.

20. There was a complex series of rituals that men carried out in Maale religion. Circumcision was one of the last; only wealthy and influential elders accomplished this.

21. Necklaces of antique beads, sometimes worth as much as a cow, were considered family heirlooms and were passed down from father to eldest son. Only lineage elders who had been "made to go out," that is, who had become heads of minimal lineage segments and were able to present first fruits to the ancestors, wore necklaces. As it happened, breaking one's necklace was a part of yearly rites in which elders presented the new crops to their ancestors. The idea of throwing away one's necklace "like trash" must have seemed outrageous. Some converts reportedly kept their necklaces in secret. It is interesting that the expatriate missionaries, who knew so little about Maale culture, correctly chose this as a key symbol to attack.

22. The notion of prohibitions, "taboos," was a highly developed part of traditional Maale religion. Early believers would have had no difficulty in understanding these.

23. As was normally the case, church elders "disciplined" Sime for his remarriage (remarriage being justifiable only in the case of adultery) by refusing him participation in the church—without confession and repentance.

24. Interview with Sime Jajo, 26 February 1984.

25. Missionaries' identification of virtually all traditional rites as "Satan worship" must have contributed to what seems an extraordinary degree of religious self-confidence. It also seems to have protected them from actually in-

quiring into local religions. This outcome is ironic to the degree that conveying Christian tenets in another language inevitably requires some knowledge of local religious notions (since eventually some of those concepts will be used to express Christian ideas). For a sensitive account of such problems with regard to SIM missionaries in the Sudan, see Wendy James, *The Listening Ebony: Moral Knowledge, Religion, and Power among the Uduk of Sudan* (Oxford: Clarendon Press, 1988), chapter 4. The fact that missionaries were required to use Amharic after the occupation—a language that already had an ancient Christian tradition—and that the publication of the Bible in southern languages was prohibited beginning in the 1940s probably added to the Ethiopian missionaries' protective bubble.

26. Interview with "Mrs. Paulos," Addis Ababa, Ethiopia, 4 June 1984.

27. In 1970, the monthly allowance paid to Welaita evangelists by their home church was raised from 22 to 30 Ethiopian dollars (see Monthly Praise and Prayer Bulletins, Bako, 25 September 1970, EG-2, SIM International Archives). Given the shortage of land in Welaita and its relative abundance in Maale, this meant that some Welaita evangelists probably lived better in Maale than they could at home.

28. Fargher, "Aari People," p. 210.

29. For another analysis of how the meaning of Christian conversion is conditioned by local cultural assumptions, see Tod D. Swanson, "Refusing to Drink with the Mountains: Traditional Andean Meanings in Evangelical Practice," in *Accounting for Fundamentalisms*, Martin E. Marty and R. Scott Appleby, eds (Chicago: University of Chicago Press, 1994), pp. 79–98.

30. A traditional way of saying that someone had died in Maale was to say that they *geshkene*, literally, that they have been "cleansed," or that they *tsiloida aadene*, that they had gone to truth or morality. There were then a series of symbolic connections between life, suffering, and the transgressions of norms on the one hand, and death, peace, and purity on the other hand. But the Christian notion of a continuing existence after death was alien to Maale thought.

31. Since spiritual things could not be directly apprehended, there was a sense in which Maale religion was always experimental, willing to break taboos as long as no consequences appeared. There was, after all, never a perfect consensus on just what the correct customs and taboos should be.

32. Occasionally it was a woman who took the lead in converting. Aulo's mother was the first person to convert in Dilokaiyo. According to my field notes of 13 July 1984:

> She went to Koibe to get medicine from the foreign missionary, Mr. Paulos, and after she had taken the medicine, he asked her to believe. She refused but on the way back, she said to herself that she would believe if God make it rain before she arrived home. It in fact did rain and she believed. When she entered the house of her husband's younger brother, he also believed. And later her husband, the head of his lineage, believed, but as he said, he did so because the intestine oracle had become so horrible. The husband went on to become one of the important early elders of the church.

33. It is impossible to substantiate with survey data, but it was my strong impression in the 1970s that Christian Maale were indeed wealthier than the

average nonbeliever. This was also the view of Christians themselves. When asked to explain why this might have been the case, Christians said that they participated in trading more. For example, during a drought in Bunati when grain grew quite expensive, some Christians went to Aariland (where they had Christian contacts) to buy grain in order to sell it back in Bunati. In addition to trading, Christians also apparently produced more. Again according to the Christians themselves, this was because they did not drink and worked longer and harder in the collective work parties that they organized among themselves. This the Welaita evangelists had taught them to do: to begin work earlier than the surrounding Maale and not to take the many rest stops for smoking and drinking. "We like one another. We are one. We have learned how to work together from the Bible. It is better to work for others than for yourself. Poor and rich must work together and become one. The rich must help the poor. In this way, we have become clever."

34. When asked why they had converted, the most knowledgeable believers replied that the main reason was the promise of eternal life. "In Heaven I have a life . . . I know I shall enter the kingship [katumo] of Heaven." The traditional idea of Maale kingship—in which an occupant ate but did not work—was used to express existence in Heaven. "Believers will have a life. Nonbelievers will receive judgment." But it was my impression that the appeals of an afterlife were not very great for most Maale. Certainly, when nonbelievers discussed Christianity, the single aspect of the new religion that they found most difficult to credit was a sentient existence after death.

35. This was apparently also the case in western Ethiopia with conversion to the Lutheran-inspired Mekane Yesus Church. See Øyvind M. Eide, *Revolution and Religion in Ethiopia: A Study of Church and Politics with Special Reference to the Ethiopian Evangelical Church Mekane Yesus 1974–1985* (Stavanger: Misjonshøgskolens; and Uppsala: Uppsala Universitet, 1996), p. 91.

36. None of these, unfortunately, have been studied, but there are references to prophets in the Aari highlands and in Welaita during the early twentieth century. One of the missionaries in Welaita before the Italian occupation, Earl Lewis, emphasized the role of the prophet Asa in Welaita in preparing the way for Christianity:

> It was not long after we arrived at Soddu that we learned something about an individual who had caused quite a revolution in the matter of demon worship and Satan worship in Walamo country. This was one whom they called Asa, and it seems that he came to Walamo from Gamo and he had some kind of a revelation that he imparted to the people. . . . He challenged the matter of Satan worship and taught that the people should worship only one God, because He alone was worthy of worship. . . . The form of offering their prayers seemed rather strange and interesting because on Sunday morning, the head of the house would go out and dip his fingers in honey, and then flip the honey toward the heavens as he prayed, and he prayed to God instead of Satan. Then this man taught them a kind of ten commandments, which were almost identical to the ten commandments that we have in the Word of God. There was a lot of interest in his message, and soon he had a great following. As the crowds began to follow him, then it became a kind of practice to more or less force people to give up witchcraft, particularly witch doctors, and many of the witch doctors in Walamo during that period shaved their long hair, and if they practiced witchcraft, they did it in hiding. This man became quite a figure and his ministry reached all the way up to

Kambatta, we understand. But when he was about at the height of his power and had great followings, he became quite proud, and it looked as if a lot of the people were following him because they expected him to do something about restoring the old kingdom to Walamo. After awhile it became a political issue and this man was put in prison; in fact he was kept in prison for many years and died there. But even when he was in prison, the numbers that followed him grew and multiplied, and when we went to Walamo, there were traces of this type of worship all over Walamo (letter from Rev. Earl Lewis to Rev. R. J. Davis, 12 September 1961, EE-2, Source material for the book *Fire on the Mountain,* Research of R. J. Davis, SIM International Archives).

37. Field notes, 10 July 1984.

38. Correspondingly, opposition to evangelical Christianity was highly concentrated among northern landowners (who were already Orthodox Christian, at least in name) and the Maale chiefs and king (who occupied central roles in the old religion). None ever converted to evangelical Christianity. The new king Arbu took the lead in opposing mission communities. In Bala, he finally forbade anyone living on his land to attend the school that was briefly established there in the mid-1960s.

39. The connection between evangelical Christianity and opposition to landlords recurs in areas of southern Ethiopia outside Maale. Albert E. Brant, *In the Wake of Martyrs: A Modern Saga in Ancient Ethiopia* (Langley, BC: Omega, 1992), reported with reference to the Gedeo: "Oppression had been the lot of these country people for many years. Not too long after our arrival in their midst, noticing our friendly attitude, the leaders of the tribe sent a delegation to ask me if I would help them in their struggle for freedom from serfdom. At that time I made it very clear that as a mission we kept completely out of politics" (p. 122).

40. Monthly Praise and Prayer Bulletins, 29 May 1964, EG-2, SIM International Archives.

41. Field notes, 7 March 1984.

42. The SIM's choice of the Amharic word, mahabir, is noteworthy, particularly in light of the fact that the Derg would later appropriate the same word for the peasant associations created by the revolution. In early twentieth-century Ethiopia, a mahabir was a voluntary association among Orthodox Christians that met periodically for feasting and fellowship, often on saints' days. By the 1950s (when presumably the word was first used among SIM missionaries to denote structures in the newly organized Kale Heywet Church), the Ethiopian capital, Addis Ababa, was the site for a new kind of mahabir—again a voluntary associations but one aimed at the secular ideal of development for the rural communities from which urbanites had come. Gradually, then, a series of meanings was associated with the idea of a mahabir—notions of progress and development being layered on top of older religious, communal meanings.

43. Research by Peter Cotterell, Bako, SR-36, SIM International Archives.

44. Monthly Praise and Prayer Bulletins, 26 April 1968, Bako, EG-3, SIM International Archives.

45. Statistics of Stations 1971, Bako, Research by Peter Cotterell, EG-2, SIM International Archives.

46. Interview with "Mrs. Paulos," 4 June 1984.

47. Monthly Praise and Prayer Bulletins, Bako, October 1967, EG-3, SIM International Archives.

48. Monthly Praise and Prayer Bulletins, Bako, May 31, 1968, EG-3, SIM International Archives.

49. Robert W. Hefner, "World Building and the Rationality of Conversion," in R. W. Hefner, ed., *Conversion to Christianity: Historical and Anthropological Perspective on a Great Transformation* (Berkeley: University of California Press, 1993), p. 27.

50. Michael Walzer, *The Revolution of the Saints: A Study in the Origins of Radical Politics* (Cambridge: Harvard University Press, 1965), p. 3.

CHAPTER 6. MARXIST MODERNISM AT THE ETHIOPIAN CENTER

1. See, for example, Christopher Clapham, *Transformation and Continuity in Revolutionary Ethiopia* (Cambridge: Cambridge University Press, 1988), p. 10.

2. "U.S. development aid from 1951–1975 totalled $309 million, making Ethiopia the largest recipient of U.S. economic aid in Africa. The total consisted of $132 million in development loans, $112 million in technical assistance grants, $35 million in PL 480 food programs, and $30 million for the Peace Corps. U.S. aid concentrated on education and training and funded an agricultural college at Alemaya, a public health college in Gondar, programs at Haile Sellassie I University, and the support of Ethiopian students in the United States" (Terrence P. Lyons, "Reaction to Revolution: United States–Ethiopian Relations 1974–1977," Ph.D. Dissertation, Johns Hopkins University, 1991, p. 54).

3. Benedict Anderson, *Imagined Communities: Reflections on the Origin and Spread of Nationalism*, rev. ed. (London: Verso, 1991), pp. 156–157.

4. Joseph Levenson, *Revolution and Cosmopolitanism: The Western Stage and the Chinese Stages* (Berkeley: University of California Press, 1971), p. 23.

5. For an outline of the differences in outlook among Ethiopians during this period, see Addis Hiwet, *Ethiopia: From Autocracy to Revolution* (London: Review of African Political Economy, 1975), chapter 3.

6. Quoted in Richard Caulk, "Dependency, Gebre Heywet Baykedagn, and the Birth of Ethiopian Reformism," in *Proceedings of the Fifth International Conference on Ethiopian Studies,* Robert L. Hess, ed. (Chicago: University of Illinois at Chicago Circle Office of Publication Services, 1978), pp. 569–581. See also Addis Hiwet, *From Autocracy to Revolution,* pp. 68–77.

7. Girmame had been educated in the United States and had a master's degree in political science from Columbia University. For accounts of the attempted coup, see Richard Greenfield, *Ethiopia: A New Political History* (London: Pall Mall Press, 1965), chapters 17–19; and Harold G. Marcus, *Ethiopia, Great Britain, and the United States, 1941–1974* (Berkeley: University of California Press, 1983), chapter 5.

8. Randi Rønning Balsvik, *Haile Selassie's Students: The Intellectual and Social Background to Revolution, 1952–1977* (East Lansing: African Studies Center, Michigan State University, 1985), pp. 96–97.

9. Ibid., p. 94.

10. According to Marcus, *Ethiopia, Great Britain, and the United States,* p. 6, U.S. assistance did not alter the course of local events.

11. Donald N. Levine, *Wax and Gold: Tradition and Innovation in Ethiopian Culture* (Chicago: University of Chicago Press. 1965), p. 92. Levine noted that members of the Ethiopian military, having had more experience overseas and having been trained in a highly rationalized profession, tended to be more impatient to modernize Ethiopia than the rest of the new elite (pp.189–190). This observation was prophetic of later events.

12. This was a process that varied widely across Africa, and a number of factors appear to have been involved. One was probably the different ideologies of colonial rule. In French colonies, the educational system was theoretically geared toward producing Frenchmen (even if they were black), whereas in British colonies, the notion of local autonomy and indirect rule held out no such assimilationist possibilities. Indeed,. British policy may have encouraged new elites to invent connections with a traditional past. Whether white settlers were present and whether the struggle for liberation involved peasant mobilization were probably additional factors that affected how notions of tradition were mapped onto the cultural construction of new nations. See Ali A. Mazrui, "Francophone Nations and English-Speaking States: Imperial Ethnicity and African Political Formations," in. *State Versus Ethnic Claims: African Policy Dilemmas,* Donald Rothchild and Victor A. Olorunsola, eds. (Boulder. CO: Westview Press, 1983).

13. Terence O. Ranger, *Peasant Consciousness and Guerrilla War in Zimbabwe: A Comparative Study* (London: James Currey, 1985); David Lan, *Guns and Rain: Guerrillas and Spirit Mediums in Zimbabwe* (Berkeley: University of California Press, 1985).

14. The idea of *hibrettesebawinet,* a sort of indigenous Ethiopian communalism, distilled from local historical experience and Ethiopian religion parallels, in some ways, Tanzanian ideology. Promulgated by the Derg in December 1974, it remained ideologically unelaborated and was officially supplanted by the notion of scientific socialism by mid-1976. See Dessalegn Rahmato, "The Political Economy of Development in Ethiopia," in *Afro-Marxist Regimes: Ideology and Public Policy,* Edmond J. Keller and Donald Rothchild eds. (Boulder, CO: Lynne Rienner,, 1987), pp. 157–159.

15. Andargachew Tiruneh, *The Ethiopian Revolution 1974–1987: A Transformation from an Aristocratic to a Totalitarian Autocracy* (Cambridge: Cambridge University Press, 1993), p. 29.

16. Michael M. J. Fischer and Mehdi Abedi, *Debating Muslims: Cultural Dialogues in Postmodernity and Tradition* (Madison: University of Wisconsin Press, 1990), point out the similar role in the shaping of Muslim fundamentalism played by Middle Eastern students studying in the West.

17. Dawit Wolde Giorgis, *Red Tears: War, Famine and Revolution in Ethiopia* (Trenton, NJ: Red Sea Press, 1989), pp. 9–11. Dawit was in the Ethiopian military when he was a student at Columbia University in the mid-1970s and was, therefore, not accepted into student Marxist circles as were others. He nonetheless enthusiastically supported the revolution during its early years.

After serving as a high official in the party and heading the government's famine relief commission, Dawit defected and accepted asylum in the United States in December 1985. *Red Tears* attempts to justify its author's actions and to set out "what went wrong."

18. John Plamenatz, "Two Types of Nationalism," in *Nationalism: The Nature of Evolution of an Idea*, Eugene Kamenka, ed. (Canberra: Australian National University Press, 1973), p. 34.

19. Balsvik, *Haile Selassie's Students*, p. 294. Student leaders exhibited a "sense of historical mission, of being instruments in an inevitable process of change, of playing a role no other group was prepared to perform in Ethiopian society" (p. 295).

20. Ibid., p. xiii.

21. Robert H. Bates, "Modernization, Ethnic Competition, and the Rationality of Politics in Contemporary Africa," in *State Versus Ethnic Claims: African Policy Dilemmas*, Donald Rothchild and Victor A. Olorunsola, eds. (Boulder, CO: Westview Press, 1983).

22. It may be more accurate to say that Menelik was a "Shewan" emperor rather than an "Amhara" one. As Gerry Salole has argued in a provocative piece, Shewa, Menilek's base of power, had its own regional identity to some extent, one that reflected a long and complex interplay between ethnically different populations of Amhara and Oromo. See Salole's "Who Are the Shoans?" *Horn of Africa* 2 (1979): 20–29.

23. See my "Old Abyssinia and the New Ethiopian Empire: Themes in Social History," in *The Southern Marches of Imperial Ethiopia: Essays in History and Social Anthropology*, Donald Donham and Wendy James, eds. (Cambridge: Cambridge University Press, 1986), pp. 8–13.

24. On the effect of schooling on the formation of notions of modernity and nationalism, Donald N. Levine wrote, "The teachers also provide practical information of various sorts to assist the acculturation of their charges. They teach the etiquette of modernity. . . . Thus, besides promoting respect for impersonal standards and the sense of Ethiopian nationalism, the teachers fulfill a third extracurricular function of some importance: that of making the schools a vehicle for social mobility, a place to acquire the minimum of European habits which is essential for attaining high status in a modernizing society" (*Wax and Gold*, p. 115).

25. Quoted in Øyvind M. Eide, *Revolution and Religion in Ethiopia: A Study of Church and Politics with Special Reference to the Ethiopian Evangelical Church Mekane Yesus 1974–1985*, Studiea Missionalia Upsaliensia, no. 66 (Stavanger: Misjonshøgskolens; and Uppsala: Uppsala Universitet, 1996), p. 97.

26. Clapham, *Transformation and Continuity*, p. 196.

27. See David A. Korn, *Ethiopia, the United States and the Soviet Union* (London: Croom Helm, 1986), p. 107; Dawit Wolde Giorgis, *Red Tears*, p. 348; and Lefort, *Ethiopia*, pp. 275–280.

28. Lefort, *Ethiopia*, p. 278.

29. Revolutionary politics and ethnic notions interacted complexly in Ethiopia. At the beginning of the terror in 1977, many students were arrested. The *New York Times* of March 9 of that year reported, "Colonel Mengistu . . .

made a secret visit last week to a police station where hundreds of students were under arrest. His intent, informants say, was to free them after delivering a stern warning. But the students started chanting 'Baria,' a pejorative word that means slave, and he was unable to speak. The students were not released" (p. A12). These students were very likely influenced by, if not members of, the EPRP.

30. Dawit, *Red Tears*, pp. 30–31.

31. On Mengistu's prospects under the old order, David Korn observes: "The senior ranks of Haile Selassie's army were not closed to commoners, but Mengistu, with his low-class origin, his very dark skin, his inelegant Amharic, and his record of obstreperousness, was an unlikely candidate to move to the top" (*Ethiopia, the United States, and the Soviet Union*, p. 109). Dark skin would not have been so much a barrier as slave descent (though, ideologically, the two tended to be equated in imperial Ethiopia).

32. Marina and David Ottaway, *Ethiopia: Empire in Revolution* (New York: Africana, 1978), p. 99: "After the massive and continuous street demonstrations of February and March, the populace in Addis Ababa, unlike its counterpart in Paris during the French revolution or St. Petersburg during the Russian revolution, played a singularly unimportant role in immediately subsequent events."

33. Ibid., pp. 113–114.

34. One of the best discussions of the political groups formed is Andargachew, *The Ethiopian Revolution*, chapter 5.

35. Ibid., pp. 154–155.

36. Marina and David Ottaway, *Ethiopia*, pp. 119–120.

37. *Basic Documents of the Ethiopian Revolution* (Addis Ababa: Provisional Office for Mass Organizational Affairs, 1977), p. 17.

38. Lefort, *Ethiopia*, p. 175.

39. Marina and David Ottaway, *Ethiopia*, pp. 139–141; Lefort, *Ethiopia*, pp. 178–179. See also Robert G. Patman, *The Soviet Union in the Horn of Africa: The Diplomacy of Intervention and Disengagement* (Cambridge: Cambridge University Press, 1990), pp. 191–193.

40. Marina and David Ottaway, *Ethiopia*, p. 146.

41. Kapuściński, *The Emperor*, p. 5.

42. Clapham, *Transformation and Continuity*, p. 56.

43. Andargachew, *The Ethiopian Revolution*, p. 211.

44. Clapham, *Transformation and Continuity*, p. 57.

45. Ibid., p. 63.

46. Marina and David Ottaway, *Afrocommunism*, 2nd ed. (New York: Africana, 1986), p. 4.

47. Ibid., p. 7.

48. V. Sofinsky and A. Khazanov, "The Imperialist Design for the Horn of Africa," *New Times* 7 (1978): 4; quoted in Patman, *The Soviet Union*, p. 238.

49. Patman, *The Soviet Union*, p. 177. For a description of U.S. policy, see Korn, *Ethiopia, The United States and the Soviet Union*, pp. 12–18.

50. Patman, *The Soviet Union*, p. 114.

51. I. M. Lewis, *The Modern History of Somaliland: From Nation to State* (London: Weidenfeld & Nicolson, 1980), p. 14, quoted in John Markakis, *Na-*

tional and Class Conflict in the Horn of Africa (Cambridge: Cambridge University Press, 1987), p. 218.

52. Patman, *The Soviet Union,* p. 113.

53. See Ibid., chapter 4.

54. Ibid., p. 151.

55. Ibid., p. 165.

56. Ibid., p. 173.

57. One writer has raised the possibility that Moscow's secret services may have played a role in his successes. See Lefort, *Ethiopia,* p. 206.

58. In February 1975, as it stepped up its assault on Eritrea, the Derg had requested an emergency airlift of $30 million worth of small arms and ammunition. "After a considerable delay, the U.S. State Department informed the PMAC that it was only prepared to sell Ethiopia $7 million worth of ammunition. . . . The U.S. decision angered the PMAC" (Patman, *The Soviet Union,* p. 175). Again, in May 1976, the Americans warned the Derg that arms shipments would be affected if a planned attack by peasant militia on Eritrea was carried out. These and other incidents made it clear to Derg hardliners that the United States was a dubious ally.

59. Patman, *The Soviet Union,* p. 194.

60. Marina and David Ottaway, *Afrocommunism,* p. 175.

61. See Markakis, *National and Class Conflict,* pp. 224–230, for the events that led up to the Somali invasion of Ethiopia.

62. Ibid., p. 231.

63. Patman, *The Soviet Union,* p. 223.

64. According to Lefort, *Ethiopia,* p. 216, this mobilization around nationalism was more successful in the cities than in the countryside.

65. Ibid., p. 257.

66. In this narrative, I have perhaps not stressed enough the role of the Eritrean question in the politics of the Derg. Many of the shutouts involved the question of what to do in relation to Eritrean secessionists. Mengistu and his faction took an uncompromising line on national unity. So in 1978, with the Somali threat contained, Mengistu turned his attention to Eritrea.

Previously, the Soviet Union had supported the Marxist Eritrean Peoples Liberation Front (EPLF). Now, Moscow quickly reversed itself and provided arms and advisers to the Derg for an onslaught on Eritrea. As Lefort pointed out, the dynamic of the Cold War had won out against actual political interests: "Breaking its [the USSR's] word, reversing its alliances . . . : for many progressive forces all this looked more like the practice of a great imperial power than the behaviour they expected of the 'fatherland of socialism'; it provoked embarrassment even with the communist movement; and it raised so high the investment by the USSR and its allies in Ethiopia that their first aim must simply be not to lose it, then to show that it is well placed and can pay dividends. Moscow has gone too far in Ethiopia to let the revolution run its own free course" (p. 272).

67. Lefort, *Ethiopia,* p. 226.

68. Christopher Dawson, *The Gods of Revolution* (New York: New York University Press, 1972), p. 95.

69. Eide, *Revolution and Religion,* p. 140.

70. Ibid., p. 207.

71. Haile Larebo, "The Orthodox Church and the State in the Ethiopian Revolution, 1974–84," *Religion in Communist Lands* 14 (1986): 153.

72. Eide, *Revolution and Religion,* p. 249.

73. Ibid., p. 251.

74. Fargher, "The Charismatic Movement of Ethiopia, 1960–1980," *Evangelical Review of Theology* 12 (1988): 349–350.

75. As early as his statement of the "national democratic revolution" (April 1976), Mengistu had called attention to how imperialism sometimes used missionary activity as a "guise" with which to "infiltrate" a country.

76. Statement of a Gedeo elder taken by a SIM missionary in July 1990.

77. On the destruction of old political symbols in the French and Russian revolutions, see, respectively, Stanley Iderza, "Iconoclasm during the French Revolution," *American Historical Review* 60 (1954): 13–26; Richard Stites, "Iconoclastic Currents in the Russian Revolution," in *Bolshevik Culture: Experiment and Order in the Russian Revolution,* Abbott Gleason, Peter Kenez, and Richard Stites, eds. (Bloomington: Indiana University Press, 1985).

78. Korn, *Ethiopia, the United States and the Soviet Union,* p. 107.

79. See Donald N. Levine's statement of this theme in *Wax and Gold.*

80. On the public perception of Mengistu, see Lefort, *Ethiopia,* pp. 74, 278.

81. Clapham, *Transformation and Continuity,* p. 79.

82. Ibid., p. 96.

CHAPTER 7. THE REVOLUTIONARY STATE
AT THE GRASS ROOTS

1. Interviews with Ziso Mamo (a pseudonym) over five days, Addis Ababa, July 1995.

2. Ibid.

3. Ibid.

4. Ibid.

5. Ibid.

6. Ibid.

7. Ibid.

8. Ibid.

9. Ibid.

10. See Donald L. Donham, *Work and Power in Maale, Ethiopia,* 2nd ed. (New York: Columbia University Press, 1994).

11. See ibid., chapter 4.

12. Given the destabilization created by the revolution, it was striking to observe how traditional Maale rearranged work group organization in 1975. Some *mol'o* continued into the new era, but in those areas of Maale most affected by the revolution—regions 1 and 2—some people spontaneously began to organize a new kind of work group. Independent of any urging by government officials, these new groups were called mahabir (after the mahabir, the

peasant associations, created in mid-1975). See Donald L. Donham, "An Archaeology of Work in Maale, Ethiopia," *Man* 29 (1994): 147–159.

13. Interviews with Ziso Mamo.

14. Ibid.

15. A secondary target of traditionalists was Muslim traders who lived in the market village of Bala. One of them, after returning from service in the Ethiopian army, had served as a policeman for the association. One day, he had attempted to enforce national law and arrested a young Maale man from region 4 for carrying a gun. The peasant association in Bala subsequently confiscated the gun. But since every important man in region 4 owned a gun, any attempt by revolutionaries to control or confiscate guns immediately raised traditionalist ire in Maale. For all of its effectiveness, the revolutionary state was never able to confiscate guns across the board.

16. Interview with Maja, Bala, April 1984.

17. Interviews with Ziso Mamo.

18. A list of the household heads who cultivated in each district was drawn up, and it was illegal for anyone to move his residence without permission from the new peasant association. In 1983 in Bala, for example, a young man was fined sixty birr for simply moving to Bala without permission.

AFTERWORD / AFTERWARD

1. Reinhart Koselleck, *Futures Past: The Semantics of Historical Time,* Keith Tribe, trans. (Cambridge: MIT Press, 1985 [1979]), p. 18.

2. François Furet, *Interpreting the French Revolution,* Elborg Forster, trans. (Cambridge: Cambridge University Press, 1981 [1978]), p. 55.

3. Because of its distance from political centers, villagization had not occurred in Maale by the time the revolutionary state lost momentum at the end of the 1980s.

4. Leon Trotsky, *The Revolution Betrayed: What Is the Soviet Union and Where Is It Going?* (Detroit: Labor Publications, 1991 [1937]), p. 38.

5. Louis O. Mink, *Historical Understanding* (Ithaca: Cornell University Press, 1987), p. 198.

6. J. D. Y. Peel, "For Who Hath Despised the Day of Small Things? Missionary Narratives and Historical Anthropology," *Comparative Studies in Society and History* 37 (1995): 582–583.

7. In my view, historical ethnography has yet to make the contribution it could to anthropology. Ironically, part of the reason for this failure is the widespread commitment to "theory" within the profession—to the often (over)generalizing discourse through which anthropoloists still tend to make their careers. In doing so, the potential for history to reform anthropological practice is undermined. What narrative offers in contrast is a "method": a way of analyzing complex connections across time. Theoretical issues remain, of course, but they are embedded, in more complex ways, in the arrangement of empirical materials.

8. Benedict Anderson, *Imagined Communities: Reflection on the Origin and Spread of Nationalism* (London: Verso, 1991), p. 11.

9. Edmond Keller, *Revolutionary Ethiopia: From Empire to People's Republic* (Bloomington: Indiana University Press, 1988), pp. 164–271.

10. Andargachew Tiruneh, *The Ethiopian Revolution, 1974–1987: A Transformation from an Aristocratic to a Totalitarian Autocracy* (Cambridge: Cambridge University Press, 1993), p. 344.

11. Ibid., p. 365.

12. Terrence Lyons, "The Transition toward Democracy in Ethiopia: Observations on the Elections in Welega, June 1992," Testimony prepared for presentation to the House Foreign Relations Subcommittee on African Affairs, 17 September 1992, Washington, DC: Brookings Institution.

13. *The New York Times,* 18 July 1998, p. A1.

14. On "development," see James Ferguson, *The Anti-Politics Machine: "Development," Depoliticization, and Bureaucratic Power in Lesotho* (Minneapolis: University of Minnesota Press, 1990); Arturo Escobar, *Encountering Development: The Making and Unmaking of the Third World* (Princeton: Princeton University Press, 1995); and Akhil Gupta, *Postcolonial Developments: Agriculture in the Making of Modern India* (Durham: Duke University Press, 1997).

Bibliography

UNPUBLISHED SOURCES IN THE SIM INTERNATIONAL
ARCHIVES, CHARLOTTE, NORTH CAROLINA

Cain, Glen. "Field Letter No. 4," 5 August 1949, Directives to Missionaries, 1944–50, EE-2.
Cotterell, Peter, Research Notes, SR-36.
Cotterell, Peter, Statistics on Stations 1971, Bako, EG-2.
Davison, Laurie. "Notes on the Situation in Walamo," May 1945, EE-2.
Ethiopia Area Council Notes 1948–1954, December 1948, ME-1.
Forsberg, Malcolm. Letter to Glen Cain, 8 August 1935, Bulki Correspondence, EA-1.
Groeneweg, John. Letter to Glen Cain, 2 January 1954, Bako Correspondence, SR-36/37.
Lambie, Thomas. "Business with Gamo Governor over Purchase of a Car for Governor," 1933–34, EA-1.
Lambie, Thomas. "Christian Missionaries Appear before Church Council" [a description of events in January and February 1928], 14 April 1928, EA-1.
Lambie, Thomas. "Conquest by Healing in Ethiopia," 1935, Lambie Miscellaneous Writings, EA-1.
Lewis, Earl. Letter to R. J. Davis, 12 September 1961, source material for Davis's book, *Fire on the Mountain*, EE-2.
Monthly Praise and Prayer Bulletin, Bako, 25 September 1970, EG-3.
Monthly Praise and Prayer Bulletin, Bako, 26 April 1968, EG-3.
Monthly Praise and Prayer Bulletin, Bako, October 1967, EG-3.
Monthly Praise and Prayer Bulletin, Bako, 29 May 1964, EG-2.

Monthly Praise and Prayer Bulletin, Bako, 26 March 1954, EG-2.

"Norm." Letter to "Marion," undated, Soddu Correspondence, EA-3.

Ohman, Marcella. Letter to Thomas Lambie, 19 November 1932, Bulki Correspondence, 1931–1936, EA-2.

Ohman, Marcella. Letter to Thomas Lambie, 12 June 1932, Bulki Correspondence, 1931–1936, EA-2.

Ohman, Walter. Letter to Thomas Lambie, 28 May 1933, Bulki Correspondence, 1931–36, EA-2.

Ohman, Marcella. Report to Thomas Lambie, 1931, Bulki Medical Reports, EA-2.

Ohman, Walter and Marcella. 15 December 1945, Prayer Letters 1941–1950, EE-2.

Ohman, Walter and Marcella. Prayer letter, 30 June 1951, EG-1.

Unknown author. Letter, 10 January, 1936, Bulki Miscellaneous, EA-2.

ORAL EVIDENCE AND LOCAL DOCUMENTS IN THE AUTHOR'S POSSESSION

References to field notes (by date) are indicated in the notes above and are not referenced here. Collected below are mainly more extended taped and transcribed texts in Maale (unless otherwise indicated).

Arregude Sulunge. Interview, 27 February 1975. In his fifties, Arregude, and before him his father, had been closely associated with Maale kings. Arregude was one of the Bala elders who held the right to determine succession to the kingship.

Arregude Sulunge. Interview, 27 June 1975.

Awraja governor of Geleb and Hamar Bako. Speech [in Amharic, simultaneously translated into Maale] in Bushkoro, Maale, 21 April 1975.

Baki Lungare. Interview, 22 March 1975. Baki was an elderly man, a member of the mani caste of tanners and potters. He had served Maale kings and had been arrested with Tonna in the 1930s and subsequently lived outside Maale for some time.

Dore Sulunge. Interview, 3 March 1975. (See above, Arregude Sulunge, his elder brother.) Dore lived in Bala.

Dura Artamu, Silsa Dombe, and Arregude Sulunge. Interview, 15 July 1975. Dura lived in southern Bunka and was the son of the chief of Bunka. His half-brother, Gwiye, inherited the chiefship after Artamu died in the 1980s. Silsa was a servant of the past Maale king and lived in Bala. Arregude is described above.

Ottolo Irbano. Interview, 26 September 1974. Ottolo was king of Maale in the 1940s and 1950s. His deposition is described above. In the 1970s, he lived in Bio.

Maja. Interview, April 1984. Maja was the second chairman of the Bala peasant cooperative.

Minote. Interview, 25 June 1997. Minote was one of the original Welaita evangelists who worked and lived in Maale. Eventually Minote settled in Jinka, where I interviewed him.

Paulos, Mrs. Interview in English, Addis Ababa, 4 June 1984. She and her husband were the missionary couple at Bako who converted Sime Jajo.

Signed "From Koibe and Irbo." Letter [in Amharic] to the Geleb and Hamar Bako Awraja Governor and Records Office, Jinka.

Sime Jajo. Interview, 26 February 1984. Sime was head of the large and influential Kalati lineage in Koibe. He was the first to convert to Christianity in Maale.

Unsigned. Letter [in Amharic] to the Geleb and Hamar Bako Awraja Governor and Records Office, Jinka, 21 November 1974.

Urge Jimari and Kama Kunkala [from Koibe]. Letter [in Amharic] to the Geleb and Hamar Bako Awraja Governor and Records Office, Jinka, 30 December 1974.

Ziso Mamo [pseud.]. Interviews over five days, Addis Ababa, June 1995. Ziso was a member of the Workers' Party of Ethiopia and compared to other Maale had risen high in the revolutionary order.

PUBLISHED SOURCES

Abbink, Jon. "Transformations of Violence in Twenthieth-Century Ethiopia: Cultural Roots, Political Conjunctures." *Focall: Tijschrift voor Antropologie* 25 (1995): 57–77.

———. "Refractions of Revolution in Ethiopian 'Surmic' Societies: An Analysis of Cultural Response." In *New Trends in Ethiopian Studies*, Vol. 2. Edited by Harold G. Marcus. Lawrenceville, NJ: Red Sea Press, 1994

Addis Hiwet. *Ethiopia: From Autocracy to Revolution*. London: Review of African Political Economy, 1975.

Andargachew Tiruneh. *The Ethiopian Revolution 1974–1987: A Transformation from an Aristocratic to a Totalitarian Autocracy*. Cambridge: Cambridge University Press, 1993.

Anderson, Benedict. *Imagined Communities: Reflections on the Origin and Spread of Nationalism*. Revised Edition. London: Verso, 1991.

Appadurai, Arjun. *Modernity at Large*. Minneapolis: University of Minnesota Press, 1996.

———. "Disjuncture and Difference in the Global Cultural Economy." *Public Culture* 2 (1990): 1–24.

Arendt, Hannah. *On Revolution*. New York: Viking, 1963.

Asad, Talal. *Genealogies of Religion: Discipline and Reasons of Power in Christianity and Islam*. Baltimore: Johns Hopkins University Press, 1993.

Asfa Yilma. *Haile Sellassie I: Emperor of Ethiopia with a Brief Account of the History of Ethiopia, Including the Origins of the Peasant Struggle, and a Description of the Country and Its Peoples*. London: Sampson Low, Marston, n.d.

Asmarom Legesse. "Post-Feudal Society, Capitalism, and Revolution: The Case of Ethiopia." *Symposium Leo Frobenius II*. Bonn: Deutsche UNESCO Kommission, 1980.

Bahru Zewde. *A History of Modern Ethiopia 1855–1974*. London: James Currey, 1991.

Baker, Keith Michael. *Inventing the French Revolution*. Cambridge: Cambridge University Press, 1990.

Bakke, Johnny. *Christian Ministry: Patterns and Functions within the Ethiopian Evangelical Church Mekane Yesus.* Oslo: Solum Forlag A.S.; and Atlantic Highlands, NJ: Humanities Press.

Baldwin, Deborah J. *Protestants and the Mexican Revolution: Missionaries, Ministers, and Social Change.* Urbana: University of Illinois Press, 1990.

Balsvik, Randi Rønning. *Haile Selassie's Students: The Intellectual and Social Background to Revolution, 1952–1977.* East Lansing: African Studies Center, Michigan State University, 1985.

Bates, Robert H. "Modernization, Ethnic Competition, and the Rationality of Politics in Contemporary Africa." In *State Versus Ethnic Claims: African Policy Dilemmas.* Edited by Donald Rothchild and Victor A. Olorunsola. Boulder, CO: Westview Press, 1983.

Benjamin, Walter. "The Work of Art in the Age of Mechanical Reproduction." In *Illuminations.* Edited by Hannah Arendt and translated by Harry Zohn. New York: Schocken, 1968 [1955].

Berman, Marshall. *All That Is Solid Melts into Air: The Experience of Modernity.* New York: Penguin, 1982.

Bingham, Rowland V. *Seven Sevens of Years and a Jubilee: The Story of the Sudan Interior Mission.* Toronto: Evangelical,1943.

Brant, Albert E. *In the Wake of Martyrs: A Modern Saga in Ancient Ethiopia.* Langley, BC: Omega, 1992.

Bureau, Jacques. "Etude diachronique de deux titres gamo." *Cahiers d'études africaines* 18 (1978): 279–291.

"The Campaign to Root Out 'Alien' Religion in Ethiopia." *Christianity Today,* 7 September 1979.

Carpenter, Joel A. "Fundamentalist Institutions and the Rise of Evangelical Protestantism, 1929–1942." *Church History* 49 (1980): 62–75.

Carr, David. *Time, Narrative, and History.* Bloomington: Indiana University Press, 1986.

Carr, Edward Hallett. *The Russian Revolution: From Lenin to Stalin.* New York: Free Press, 1979.

Caulk, Richard. "Dependency, Gebre Heywet Baykedagn, and the Birth of Ethiopian Reformism." In *Proceedings of the Fifth International Conference on Ethiopian Studies.* Edited by Robert L. Hess. Chicago: University of Illinois at Chicago Circle Office of Publication Services, 1978.

Chatterjee, Partha. *Nationalist Thought and the Colonial World: A Derivative Discourse?* London: Zed Books, 1986.

Clapham, Christopher. *Transformation and Continuity in Revolutionary Ethiopia.* Cambridge: Cambridge University Press, 1988.

Cohen, David William, and E. S. Atieno Odhiambo. *Siaya: The Historical Anthropology of an African Landscape.* London: James Currey, 1989.

Comaroff, Jean, and John Comaroff, eds. *Modernity and Its Malcontents: Ritual and Power in Postcolonial Africa.* Chicago: University of Chicago Press, 1993.

———. *Of Revelation and Revolution: Christianity, Colonialism, and Consciousness in South Africa.* Vol. 1. Chicago: University of Chicago Press, 1992.

Comaroff, John L., and Jean Comaroff. *Of Revelation and Revolution: The Dialectics of Modernity on a South African Frontier.* Vol 2. Chicago: University of Chicago Press, 1997.

———. *Ethnography and the Historical Imagination.* Boulder, CO: Westview Press, 1992.

Cotterell, F. P. "Dr. T. A. Lambie: Some Biographical Notes." *Journal of Ethiopian Studies* 10 (1972): 43–53.

Crummey, Donald. *Priests and Politicians: Protestants and Catholic Missions in Orthodox Ethiopia, 1830–1868.* Oxford: Clarendon Press, 1972.

Cumbers, John B. "The Christian Church and the Kings of Ethiopia." Thesis, American Bible College, 1980.

Davis, Raymond J. *Fire on the Mountains.* Charlotte, NC: Sudan Interior Mission, 1980.

Dawit Wolde Giorgis. *Red Tears: War, Famine and Revolution in Ethiopia.* Trenton, NJ: Red Sea Press, 1989.

Dawson, Christopher. *The Gods of Revolution.* New York: New York University Press, 1972.

Dessalegn Rahmato. *The Dynamics of Rural Poverty: Case Studies from a District in Southern Ethiopia.* Dakar, Senegal: CODESRIA Monograph 2/92, 1992.

———. "The Political Economy of Development in Ethiopia." In *Afro-Marxist Regimes.* Edited by Edmond J. Keller and Donald Rothchild. Boulder, CO: Lynne Rienner, 1987.

de Tocqueville, Alexis, *The Old Régime and the French Revolution.* Translated by Gilbert Stuart. New York: Doubleday, 1955 [1856].

Dirks, Nicholas B. "History as a Sign of the Modern." *Public Culture* 2 (1990): 25–32.

Dirks, Nicholas B., Geoff Eley, and Sherry B. Ortner, eds. *Culture/ Power/ History: A Reader in Contemporary Social Theory.* Princeton: Princeton University Press, 1994.

Donham, Donald L. "The Increasing Penetration of the Revolutionary State in Maale Life, 1977–1987." In *Ethiopia in Broader Perspective.* Edited by Katsuyoshi Fukui, Eisei Kurimoto, and Masayoshi Shigeta. Papers of the 13th International Conference of Ethiopian Studies. Kyoto, Japan: Shokado Book Sellers, 1997.

———. "An Archaeology of Work in Maale, Ethiopia." *Man* 29 (1994): 147–159.

———. *Work and Power in Maale, Ethiopia.* 2nd ed. New York: Columbia University Press, 1994.

———. "A Note on Space in the Ethiopian Revolution." *Africa* 63 (1993): 583–590.

———. "Revolution and Modernity in Maale: Ethiopia from 1974 to 1987." *Comparative Studies in Society and History* 34 (1992): 28–57.

———. *History, Power, Ideology: Central Issues in Marxism and Anthropology.* Cambridge: Cambridge University Press, 1990.

———. "Old Abyssinia and the New Ethiopian Empire: Themes in Social History." In *The Southern Marches of Imperial Ethiopia: Essays in History and*

Social Anthropology. Edited by Donald Donham and Wendy James. Cambridge: Cambridge University Press, 1986.

Duff, Clarence W. *Cords of Love: A Testimony to God's Grace in Pre-Italian Ethiopia as Recorded in Memorabilia of One of the Sudan Interior Mission's 'C.O.D.' Boys.* Phillipsburg, NJ: Presbyterian and Reformed, 1980.

Dunn, Susan. *The Deaths of Louis XVI: Regicide and the French Political Imagination.* Princeton: Princeton University Press, 1994.

Eide, Øyvind M. *Revolution and Religion in Ethiopia: A Study of Church and Politics with Special Reference to the Ethiopian Evangelical Church Mekane Yesus 1974–1985.* Studiea Missionalia Upsaliensia, no. 66. Stavanger: Misjonshøgskolens forlag; and Uppsala: Uppsala Universitet, 1996.

Erlich, Haggai. "The Ethiopian Army and the 1974 Revolution." *Armed Forces and Society* 9 (1983): 455–481.

Escobar, Arturo. *Encountering Development: The Making and Unmaking of the Third World.* Princeton: Princeton University Press, 1995.

Fairbank, John K., ed. *The Missionary Enterprise in China and America.* Cambridge: Harvard University Press, 1974.

Fargher, Brian Leslie. *The Origins of the New Churches Movement in South Ethiopia, 1927–1944.* Leiden: Brill, 1996.

———. "The Charismatic Movement of Ethiopia, 1960–1980." *Evangelical Review of Theology* 12 (1988): 349–350.

———. "The Origins of the New Churches Movement in Southern Ethiopia, 1927–1944." Ph.D. Thesis., University of Aberdeen, 1988.

———. "Aari People of Central Gamo Gofa, Ethiopia." In *Unreached Peoples: Clarifying the Task.* Edited by Harley Schreck and David Barrett. Birmingham, AL: MARC; and Monrovia, CA:: New Hope, 1987.

Fellows, Mr. and Mrs. A. J. "Real Warfare at Bako." *Sudan Witness* [Australia], March 1965.

———. "God Mightily at Work at Bako." *Sudan Witness* [Australia], November–December 1962, p. 3.

———. "Jubilant Day." *Sudan Witness.* [Australia], September–October 1962, pp. 1–2.

Ferguson, James. *The Anti-Politics Machine: "Development," Depoliticization, and Bureaucratic Power in Lesotho.* Minneapolis: University of Minnesota Press, 1990.

Fischer, Michael M. J., and Mehdi Abedi. *Debating Muslims: Cultural Dialogues in Postmodernity and Tradition.* Madison: University of Wisconsin Press, 1990.

Forsberg, Malcolm. *Land beyond the Nile.* New York: Harper, 1958.

Fuller, W. Harold. *Run While the Sun Is Hot.* New York: Sudan Interior Mission, n.d.

Furet, François. *Interpreting the French Revolution.* Translated by Elborg Forster. Cambridge: Cambridge University Press, 1981 [1978].

Gellner, Ernest. *Nations and Nationalism.* Ithaca: Cornell University Press, 1983.

Gilkes, Patrick. *The Dying Lion: Feudalism and Modernization in Ethiopia.* London: Julian Friedmann, 1975.

Goldman, Albert. *Elvis.* London: Penguin, 1982.

Gray, Donald and Christine. "These Lost Shankilla Sheep." *Sudan Witness* [Australia], August 1957, p. 3.

———. "Opening Bako Station, Ethiopia." *Sudan Witness* [Australia], December 1954, p. 6.

Gray, Richard. "Christianity." *The Cambridge History of Africa,* Vol. 7. Edited by A. D. Roberts. Cambridge: Cambridge University Press, 1986.

Greenfield, Richard. *Ethiopia: A New Political History.* London: Pall Mall Press, 1965.

Griewank, Karl. *Der neuzeitliche Revolutionsbegriff.* Frankfurt: Suhrkamp, 1969.

Gupta, Akhil. *Postcolonial Developments: Agriculture in the Making of Modern India.* Durham: Duke University Press, 1997.

Gupta, Akhil, and James Ferguson, eds. *Culture, Power, Place: Exploration in Critical Anthropology.* Durham: Duke University Press, 1997.

Haile Larebo. "The Orthodox Church and the State in the Ethiopian Revolution 1974–1984." *Religion in Communist Lands* 14 (1986): 148–159.

Haile Sellassie I. *My Life and Ethiopia's Progress, 1892–1937.* Translated by Edward Ullendorff. Oxford: Oxford University Press, 1976.

Hamer, John. "Practice and Change: An Episode of Structural Disjunction and Conjunction among the Sadama of Ethiopia." *Anthropological Quarterly* 58 (1985): 63–74.

Harding, Susan. "Imagining the Last Days: The Politics of Apocalyptic Language." In *Accounting for Fundamentalisms.* Edited by Martin E. Marty and R. Scott Appleby. Chicago: University of Chicago Press, 1994.

Hebdige, Dick. *Cut 'n' Mix: Culture, Identity, and Caribbean Music.* London: Comedia, 1987.

Hefner, Robert W., ed. *Conversion to Christianity: Historical and Anthropological Perspectives on a Great Transformation.* Berkeley: University of California Press, 1993.

Hindus, Maurice. *Red Bread.* New York: Jonathan Cape & Harrison Smith, 1931.

Hinton, William. *Fanshen: A Documentary of Revolution in a Chinese Village.* New York: Random House, 1966.

Hoben, Allan. "Social Soundness of Agrarian Reform in Ethiopia." Report to the USAID Mission in Ethiopia, 1976.

Hooper, E. Ralph. *Ethiopia.* New York: Sudan Interior Mission, 1933.

Horton, Robin. "On the Rationality of Conversion." *Africa* 45 (1975): 219–235, 373–399.

———. "African Conversion." *Africa* 41 (1971): 85–108.

Hunt, Lynn. *Politics, Culture, and Class in the French Revolution.* Berkeley: University of California Press, 1984.

Huntington, Samuel P. *Political Order in Changing Societies.* New Haven: Yale University Press, 1968.

Iderza, Stanley. "Iconoclasm during the French Revolution." *American Historical Review* 60 (1954): 13–26.

Ivy, Marilyn. *Discourses of the Vanishing: Modernity, Phantasm, Japan.* Chicago: University of Chicago Press, 1995.

James, C. L. R. *The Black Jacobins: Toussaint L'Ouverture and the San Domingo Revolution.* 2nd ed. New York: Vintage, 1963.

James, Wendy. *The Listening Ebony: Moral Knowledge, Religion, and Power among the Uduk of Sudan.* Oxford: Clarendon Press, 1988.

Johanson, Donald C., and Maitland A. Edey. *Lucy: The Beginnings of Humankind.* New York: Simon and Schuster, 1981.

Kapeliuk, Olga. "Marxist-Leninist Terminology in Amharic and Tigrinya." *Northeast African Studies* 1 (1979): 23–30.

Kapuściński, Ryszard. *The Emperor: Downfall of an Autocrat.* Translated by William R. Brand and Kartarzyna Mroczkowska-Brand. New York: Harcourt Brace Jovanovich, 1983 [1978].

Keesing, Roger M. *Custom and Confrontation: The Kwaio Struggle for Cultural Autonomy.* Chicago: University of Chicago Press, 1992.

Keller, Edmond. *Revolutionary Ethiopia: From Empire to People's Republic.* Bloomington: Indiana University Press, 1988.

Kelly, William. "Japanese No-Noh: The Crosstalk of Public Culture in a Rural Festivity." *Public Culture* 2 (1990): 65–81.

Korn, David A. *Ethiopia, the United States, and the Soviet Union.* London: Croom Helm, 1986.

Koselleck, Reinhart. *Futures Past: The Semantics of Historical Time.* Translated by Keith Tribe. Cambridge: MIT Press, 1985 [1979].

Kriger, Norma J. *Zimbabwe's Guerrilla War: Peasant Voices.* Cambridge: Cambridge University Press, 1992.

Laitin, David. *Hegemony and Culture: Politics and Religious Change among the Yoruba.* Chicago: University of Chicago Press, 1986.

Lambie, T. A. *A Doctor Carries On.* New York: Fleming H. Revell, 1942.

———. *A Doctor without a Country.* New York: Revell, 1939.

Lan, David. *Guns and Rain: Guerrillas and Spirit Mediums in Zimbabwe.* Berkeley: University of California Press, 1985.

Lass-Westphal, Ingeborg. "Protestant Missions during and after the Italo-Ethiopian War, 1935–1937." *Journal of Ethiopian Studies* 10 (1972): 89–101.

Latour, Bruno. *We Have Never Been Modern.* Translated by Catherine Porter. Cambridge: Harvard University Press, 1993 [1991].

Leach, Edmund. *Political Systems of Highland Burma: A Study of Kachin Social Structure.* London: Athlone Press, 1954.

Lefort, René. *Ethiopia: An Heretical Revolution?* Translated by A. M. Berrett. London: Zed Press, 1983 [1981].

Levenson, Joseph R. *Revolution and Cosmopolitanism: The Western Stage and the Chinese Stages.* Berkeley: University of California Press, 1971.

Levine, Donald N. *Wax and Gold: Tradition and Innovation in Ethiopian Culture.* Chicago: University of Chicago Press, 1965.

Lewis, I. M. *The Modern History of Somaliland: From Nation to State.* London: Weidenfeld & Nicolson, 1980.

Lincoln, Bruce. "Notes toward a Theory of Religion and Revolution." In *Religion, Rebellion, Revolution: An Interdisciplinary and Cross-Cultural Collection of Essays.* Edited by Bruce Lincoln. London: Macmillan, 1985.

Lyons, Terrence P. "The Transition toward Democracy in Ethiopia: Observa-

tions on the Elections in Welega, June 1992." Testimony to the House Foreign Relations Subcommittee on African Affairs, 17 September 1992. Washington, DC: Brookings Institution.

———. "Reaction to Revolution: United States–Ethiopian Relations 1974–1977."
Ph.D. Dissertation, Johns Hopkins University, 1991.

Marcus, Harold G. *Haile Sellassie: The Formative Years, 1892–1936.* Berkeley:
University of California Press, 1987.

———. *Ethiopia, Great Britain, and the United States, 1941–1974.* Berkeley:
University of California Press, 1983.

Markakis, John. *National and Class Conflict in the Horn of Africa.* Cambridge:
Cambridge University Press, 1987.

Marsden, George M. *Fundamentalism and American Culture: The Shaping of
Twentieth-Century Evangelicalism: 1870–1925.* Oxford: Oxford University
Press, 1980.

Marx, Karl. "The Eighteenth Brumaire of Louis Bonaparte." In *Surveys from
Exile: Political Writings Vol. II.* Edited by David Fernbach. New York:
Vintage, 1974.

Mazlish, Bruce, Arthur D. Kaledin, and David B. Ralston, eds. *Revolution: A
Reader.* New York: Macmillan, 1971.

Mazrui, Ali A. "Francophone Nations and English-Speaking States: Imperial
Ethnicity and African Political Formations." In *State Versus Ethnic Claims:
African Policy Dilemmas.* Edited by Donald Rothchild and Victor A. Olo-
runsola. Boulder, CO: Westview Press, 1983.

McKenzie, Brian A. "Fundamentalism, Christian Unity, and Pre-millennialism
in the Thought of Rowland Victor Bingham (1872–1942): A Study of Anti-
Modernism in Canada." Ph.D. Dissertation, Toronto School of Theology, 1985.

McLellan, Dick and Vida. "Having No Hope." *Sudan Witness* [Australia],
April 1958, p. 2.

Meisner, Maurice. *Mao's China: A History of the People's Republic.* New York:
Free Press, 1977.

Mikre-Sellassie Gabre Ammanuel. "Church and Mission in Ethiopia in Relation
to the Italian War and Occupation and the Second World War." Ph.D. Thesis, University of Aberdeen, 1976.

Mink, Louis O. *Historical Understanding.* Edited by Brian Fay, Eugene O.
Golob, and Richard T. Vann. Ithaca: Cornell University Press, 1987.

Mintz, Sidney. *Sweetness and Power: The Place of Sugar in Modern History.*
New York: Viking, 1985.

Moore, Barrington, Jr. *Social Origins of Dictatorship and Democracy: Lord and
Peasant in the Making of the Modern World.* Boston: Beacon Press, 1966.

Norman, Andrew P. "Telling It Like It Was: Historical Narratives on Their Own
Terms." *History and Theory* 30 (1991): 119–135.

Ortner, Sherry. "Resistance and the Problem of Ethnographic Refusal." *Comparative Studies in Society and History* 37 (1995): 173–193.

———. *High Religion: A Cultural and Political History of Sherpa Buddhism.*
Princeton: Princeton University Press, 1989.

Ottaway, Marina and David. *Afrocommunism.* 2nd ed. New York: Africana,
1986.

————. *Ethiopia: Empire in Revolution*. New York: Africana, 1978.

Patman, Robert G. *The Soviet Union in the Horn of Africa: The Diplomacy of Intervention and Disengagement*. Cambridge: Cambridge University Press, 1990.

Peel, J. D. Y. "For Who Hath Despised the Day of Small Things? Missionary Narratives and Historical Anthropology." *Comparative Studies in Society and History* 37 (1995): 581–607.

————. "Conversion and Tradition in Two African Societies." *Past and Present* 77 (1977): 108–141.

Piazza, Tom. "Jazz Piano's Heavyweight Champ." *New York Times*, 28 July 1996, p. 30H.

Plamenatz, John. "Two Types of Nationalism." In *Nationalism: The Nature and Evolution of an Idea*. Edited by Eugene Kamenka. Canberra: Australian National University Press, 1973.

Pliny the Middle-Aged [pseud.]. "The PMAC: Origins and Structure: Part II." *Northeast African Studies* 1 (1979): 1–20.

————. "The PMAC: Origins and Structure. Part I." *Ethiopianist Notes* 3 (1978): 1–18.

Pred, Allan, and Michael Watts. *Reworking Modernity: Capitalisms and Symbolic Discontent*. New Brunswick, NJ: Rutgers University Press, 1992.

Price, Richard. *Alabi's World*. Baltimore: Johns Hopkins University Press, 1990.

Provisional Military Government of Ethiopia. *Development through Co-operation Campaign's Summary Report 1967/1968 Ethiopian Calendar*. Addis Ababa: Provisional Military Government of Ethiopia, 1976.

Provisional Office for Mass Organizational Affairs. "Proclamation No. 31 of 1975." In *Basic Documents of the Ethiopian Revolution*. Addis Ababa: Provisional Office for Mass Organization Affairs, 1977.

Rabinow, Paul. *French Modern: Norms and Forms of the Social Environment*. Cambridge: MIT Press, 1989.

Ranger, Terence O. *Peasant Consciousness and Guerrilla War in Zimbabwe: A Comparative Study*. London: James Currey, 1985.

Reed, John. *Ten Days That Shook the World*. New York: Bantam, 1987 [1919].

Rey, Charles. "Abyssinia Today." *Royal African Society Journal* 21 (1921–22): 279–290.

Rice, Esmé Ritchie, ed. *Eclipse in Ethiopia and Its Corona Glory*. London: Marshall, Morgan & Scott, n.d.

Rønne, Finn Aasebø. "Christianity in the Dynamics of South Ethiopian Societies and Culture: Kambbaata-Hadiiyya." In *Ethiopia in Broader Perspective*, Vol. 3. Edited by Katsuyoshi Fukui, Eisei Kurimoto, and Masayoshi Shigeta. Papers of the 13th International Conference of Ethiopian Studies. Kyoto: Shokado Book Sellers.

Rosaldo, Renato. *Ilongot Headhunting 1883–1974*. Stanford: Stanford University Press, 1980.

Roseberry, William. *Anthropologies and Histories: Essays in Culture, History, and Political Economy*. New Brunswick, NJ: Rutgers University Press, 1989.

Sahlins, Marshall. "Goodbye to *Tristes Tropes*: Ethnography in the Context of Modern World History." *Journal of Modern History* 65 (1993): 1–25.

————. *Islands of History.* Chicago: University of Chicago Press, 1985.

Salole, Gerry. "Who Are the Shoans?" *Horn of Africa* 2 (1979): 20–29.

Sandeen, Ernest R. *The Roots of Fundamentalism: British and American Millenarianism 1800–1930.* Chicago: University of Chicago Press, 1970.

Sæverås, Olav. *On Church-Mission Relations in Ethiopia 1944–1969.* Studia Missionalia Upsaliensai 27. Oslo: Lunde, 1974.

Scott, James C. "Revolution in the Revolution: Peasants and Commissars." *Theory and Society* 7 (1979): 97–134.

Skinner, G. William. "The Structure of Chinese History." *Journal of Asian Studies* 44 (1985): 271–292.

Skocpol, Theda. *Social Revolution in the Modern World.* Cambridge: Cambridge University Press, 1994.

————. *States and Social Revolutions: A Comparative Analysis of France, Russia, and China.* Cambridge: Cambridge University Press, 1979.

Smith, Carol A., ed. *Regional Analysis.* 2 vols. New York: Academic Press, 1976.

Stites, Richard. "Iconoclastic Currents in the Russian Revolution." In *Bolshevik Culture: Experiment and Order in the Russian Revolution.* Edited by Abbott Gleason, Peter Kenez, and Richard Stites. Bloomington: Indiana University Press, 1985.

Strayer, Robert W. *The Making of Mission Communities in East Africa: Anglicans and Africans in Colonial Kenya, 1875–1935.* London: Heineman, 1978.

Swanson, Tod D. "Refusing to Drink with the Mountains: Traditional Andean Meanings in Evangelical Practice." In *Accounting for Fundamentalisms.* Edited by Martin E. Marty and R. Scott Appleby. Chicago: University of Chicago Press, 1994.

Trimingham, J. Spencer. *The Christian Church and Missions in Ethiopia.* London: World Dominion Press, 1950.

Trotsky, Leon. *The Revolution Betrayed: What Is the Soviet Union and Where Is It Going?* Detroit: Labor Publications, 1991 [1937].

Trouillot, Michel-Rolph. *Silencing the Past: Power and the Production of History.* Boston: Beacon Press, 1995.

Tsing, Anna. *In the Realm of the Diamond Queen: Marginality in an Out-of-the-way Place.* Princeton: Princeton University Press, 1993.

van der Veer, Peter, ed. *Conversion to Modernity: The Globalization of Christianity.* New York: Routledge, 1996.

Verdery, Katherine. *What Was Socialism, and What Comes Next?* Princeton: Princeton University Press, 1996.

Vivó, Raúl Valdés. *Ethiopia's Revolution.* New York: International, 1978 [1977].

Walzer, Michael. *Radical Principles.* New York: Basic Books, 1980.

————. *The Revolution of the Saints: A Study in the Origins of Radical Politics.* Cambridge: Harvard University Press, 1965.

Weber, Timothy P. *Living in the Shadow of the Second Coming: American Premillennialism 1875–1925.* New York: Oxford University Press, 1979.

White, Hayden. *Metahistory.* Baltimore: Johns Hopkins University Press, 1973.

Wolf, Eric. *Europe and the Peoples without History.* Berkeley: University of California Press, 1982.

————. *Peasant Wars of the Twentieth Century.* New York: Harper & Row, 1969.

Woman, John, Jr. *Zapata and the Mexican Revolution.* New York: Vintage. 1968.

Workers Party of Ethiopia. "Clarification of the Guidelines for Conduct." Addis Ababa: Workers Party of Ethiopia, n.d.

Yohannis Abate, "The Legacy of Imperial Rule: Military Intervention and the Struggle for Leadership in Ethiopia 1974–1978." *Middle Eastern Studies* 19 (1983): 28–42.

Index

Page numbers in italics refer to illustrations.